TOWARD MUTUAL GROUND

For Ita Ward with gratitude and appreciation
Gareth

With love to John Mc Donagh
Patricia

Gareth Byrne and Patricia Kieran eds

Toward Mutual Ground

Pluralism, Religious Education and Diversity
in Irish Schools

the columba press

First published in 2013 by
the columba press
55A Spruce Avenue, Stillorgan Industrial Park,
Blackrock, Co. Dublin

Cover by Bill Bolger
Cover images courtesy of Gareth Byrne
Josephine Keane has kindly granted the use of her
portrait image on the cover

Origination by The Columba Press
Printed in Ireland by SPRINT-print Ltd.

ISBN 978 1 78218 053 1

I t is with great sadness that the editors, Gareth Byrne and Patricia Kieran, and all at The Columba Press draw your attention to this book's cover, as it was Bill Bolger's final design before he passed away suddenly on 18 April 2013. The cover was completed the night before Bill departed. It is indicative of his magnificent work which has illuminated so many publications throughout the years. It was a privilege to have Bill as a work colleague and an honour to have him as a friend. He was a wonderful man and he will be dearly missed.

Acknowledgements

Both Gareth and Patricia would like to acknowledge the support, encourage-ment and expertise of participants at the *Toward Mutual Ground* Conferences held in October 2010 at Mater Dei Institute of Education (MDI), Dublin City University, and in March 2011 at Mary Immaculate College of Education and the Liberal Arts (MIC), University of Limerick. We are most grateful to our keynote speakers and workshop presenters and to all who contributed chapters to this book. We also wish to express our deep gratitude to conferences attendees who contributed to vibrant, insightful debates which have given impetus to this publication, and in a special way to the Minister for Education and Skills, Mr Ruairi Quinn TD, who launched this discussion at the Mater Dei Institute conference.

We are indebted to all those who helped to organise and host the *Toward Mutual Ground* conferences particularly to Dr Bradford Anderson, Research and Development Officer of the Irish Centre for Religious Education (ICRE), for his unstinting support in preparation of the two conferences and generous contribution during the editing of this book. We relied on the contribution of professional skills from many colleagues associated with the Irish Centre for Religious Education and its Advisory Board, from the Schools of Education, Theology and Humanities at MDI, as well as the Faculty of Education and the Department of Learning, Society and Religious Education at MIC.

In particular we would like to acknowledge and thank Dr Andrew McGrady, Director MDI, Dr Dermot Lane, former President MDI, Professor Michael Hayes, President of MIC, Professor Teresa O'Doherty, Dean of the Faculty of Education MIC, and Professor Claire Lyons, Head of the Department of Learning, Society and Religious Education at MIC. Each provided continuing support, advice and inspiration.

Many thanks are also due to colleagues in the Department of Learning, Society and Religious Education at Mary Immaculate College, especially Daniel O'Connell, Maurice Harmon and Thomas Grenham, as well as colleagues in Theology and Religious Studies and Professor Michael Healy, Director of Research at MIC. The ongoing support of the team of colleagues in the MDI School of Education is much appreciated: PJ Sexton, Sandra Cullen, Kevin Williams, Elaine McDonald, Enda Donlon, Sabrina Fitzsimons and Mary Coffey. Thanks also to Ethna Regan, Eoin Cassidy and Paula Kiernan and her team for their help at the MDI conference and to Sheila Kent, Perry Meskell, Sheila Callaghan, Paula Tracey, Holly Cowman and Brian Kirby and his team, whose expert work made the Limerick conference such a success.

Special thanks are due to all of those who provided invaluable financial support for the *Toward Mutual Ground* conferences especially Mater Dei Education and Research Trust and the MIC Faculty of Education. The Limerick conference was organised in partnership with the Professional Development Service for Teachers and we are thankful for their support.

Finally we would like to thank our editor and all of the staff at The Columba Press for their comments, suggestions and advice.

CONTENTS

Section iii: Pluralism and Religious Education in Irish Schools

Section iv: Religious Pluralism and Diversity: Critical Perspectives

Concluding Reflection

LIST OF ABBREVIATIONS

AI	Atheist Ireland
BEd.	Bachelor of Education Degree
CCC	Catechism of the Catholic Church
CCEA	Council for Curriculum, Examinations and Assessment
CEIST	Catholic Education an Irish Schools' Trust
CICE	Church of Ireland College of Education, Rathmines
CoGREE	Co-ordinating Group for Religion in Education in Europe
CND	Campaign for Nuclear Disarmament
CSO	Central Statistics Office
DEIS	Delivering Equality of Opportunity in Schools
DES	Department of Education and Skills
ENRECA	European Network for Religious Education through Contextual Approaches
ESAI	Education Studies Association of Ireland
ERB	Education about Religion and Beliefs
EU	European Union
EuFRES	European Forum for Religious Education in Schools
EWC	European Wergeland Centre
Forum	The Forum on Patronage and Pluralism in the Primary Sector
GCD	General Catechetical Directory
HEA	Higher Education Authority
ICCPR	International Covenant on Civil and Political Rights
ICE	Intercultural Education
ICRE	Irish Centre for Religious Education
IHRC	Irish Human Rights Commission
INTO	Irish National Teachers' Organisation
IPPN	Irish Primary Principals' Network
ISREV	International Seminar on Religious Education and Values
ITE	Initial Teacher Education
MDI	Mater Dei Institute of Education
MIC	Mary Immaculate College of Education and the Liberal Arts

NCCA	National Council for Curriculum and Assessment
ODIHR	Office for Democratic Institutions and Human Rights
OSCE	Organisation for Security and Cooperation in Europe
PDST	Professional Development Service for Teachers
PSC	Primary School Curriculum (1999)
	Primary School Curriculum (1971)
RE	Religious Education
REDCo	Religion, Education, Dialogue, Conflict
REMC	Religious Education in a Multicultural Society
RI	Religious Instruction
RME	Religious and Moral Education
RTAI	Religion Teachers' Association of Ireland
SEN	Special Educational Needs
SGN	*Share the Good News: National Directory for Catechesis in Ireland* (2010)
TMG	Toward Mutual Ground
Toledo	*Toledo Guiding Principles on Teaching about Religions and Beliefs* (2007)
TRES	Teaching Religion in a Multicultural European Society
UK	United Kingdom
VEC	Vocational Education Committee

CONTRIBUTORS

GARETH BYRNE is Head of Religious Education at Mater Dei Institute of Education, Dublin City University, and co-ordinates the Religious Education Pathway of the Professional Doctorate Programme, taught jointly by the School of Education Studies, DCU, and staff of MDI. Dr Byrne is co-ordinator of the Irish Centre for Religious Education. He was the writer for the Irish Catholic Bishops' Conference of the National Directory for Catechesis in Ireland, *Share the Good News*. As well as providing a variety of articles on religious education, he is author of *Religious Education Renewed: An Overview of Developments in Post-Primary Religious Education* (Dublin: Veritas, 2005) and co-editor with Raymond Topley of *Nurturing Children's Religious Imagination: Primary Religious Education Today* (Dublin: Veritas, 2004). His most recent contribution is 'Communicating Faith in Ireland: From Commitment, through Questioning to New Beginnings', in *Communicating Faith*, ed. by John Sullivan (Washington, DC: Catholic University of America Press, 2011). He is a priest of Dublin Diocese.

NIALL COLL is Senior Lecturer in the Department of Religious Studies, St Mary's University College, Queen's University, Belfast. He is author of *Christ in Eternity and Time: Modern Anglican Perspectives* (Dublin: Four Courts Press, 2001), and co-editor (with Paschal Scallon) of *A Church with a Future: Challenges to Irish Catholicism Today* (Dublin: Columba Press, 2005). He is Managing Editor of 'Le Chéile', a journal published twice yearly, under the auspices of the St Mary's University College's Religious Studies Department, to articulate and promote the vision of Catholic education locally. He is a member of the CCEA Religious Education Advisory Group; The Irish-Inter Church Committee and The Irish-Inter Church Meeting Theology Forum.

GAVIN D'COSTA was born in Kenya, East Africa. He came to England in 1968 and completed a first degree in English and Theology at Birmingham University. He studied at the University of Cambridge for his doctorate and then taught in London. His doctoral work on John Hick's theology of religions led him into work with the Church of England and Roman Catholic Committees on Other Faiths, advising these communities on theological issues. He also advises the Pontifical Council for Other Faiths, Vatican City. In 1998 he was visiting Professor at the Gregorian University, Rome. He started teaching in the University of Bristol in 1993 where he is Professor in Catholic Theology. Among his works are *Theology and Religious Pluralism* (1986), *Sexing the Trinity* (2000), *Theology in the Public Square* (2005), *Disputed Questions in the Theology of Religions* (2009), and he has edited a two-volume work on *Theology and the Intellectual Disciplines* (2010, 2012). He is married with two children and has a dog.

SUZANNE DILLON is an Assistant Chief Inspector with the Department of Education and Skills. She taught Religious Education and English in a voluntary secondary school before joining the Inspectorate in 2002. In that capacity, she represented the Department on the National Council for Curriculum and Assessment (NCCA) Religious Education syllabus committee. She was instrumental in introducing inspection of the preparation of students for Junior Certificate examinations in Religious Education, following study of the Religious Education syllabus prepared by the NCCA.

JANE DONNELLY is education policy officer of Atheist Ireland, an advocacy group for atheism, reason and ethical secularism. She has authored Atheist Ireland submissions for the Forum on Patronage and Pluralism, and for various international UN, EU and Council of Europe human rights regulatory bodies. She has spoken at the OSCE human rights meeting in Warsaw, and she is chairing an international conference in Dublin in 2013 on empowering women through secularism.

MICHAEL HAYES is President of Mary Immaculate College. He is also a qualified psychotherapist and studied at the London Institute of Psychosynthesis. He is the editor of the international journal, *The Pastoral Review*. He has worked in pastoral ministry in the Archdiocese of Southwark and has taught in the Department of Theology and Religious Studies at Roehampton University. Prior to his appointment as President of Mary Immaculate College he was Vice-Principal and Professor of Catholic Pastoral Studies at St Mary's University College, Strawberry Hill in Twickenham, London. He was Head of the Department of Theology and Religious Studies, and the founding Head of the School of Theology, Philosophy, and History, at St Mary's University College where he is currently a visiting professor.

ANNE HESSION is a lecturer in religious education at St Patrick's College, Dublin, a College of Dublin City University. Her fields of academic research are in the religious education of children and the spirituality of children. She is co-author with Patricia Kieran of *Children, Catholicism and Religious Education* (Dublin: Veritas, 2005) and co-editor of *Exploring Theology: Making Sense of the Catholic Tradition* (Dublin: Veritas, 2007) and *Exploring Religious Education: Catholic Religious Education in an intercultural Europe* (Dublin: Veritas, 2008). She is currently working on the New Primary Religious Education Curriculum for Catholic Primary Schools in Ireland.

JONES IRWIN is Lecturer in Philosophy at St Patrick's College, Dublin, a College of Dublin City University. He is Co-director of the MA in Human Development. He has published and lectured widely. He was Visiting Fellow, Centre for Philosophy, Literature and the Arts, University of Warwick, 2008-10 and Visiting Fellow to Linköping TEMA Institute, Sweden, in 2012. His recent work has focused on philosophy of education and especially multi-denominationalism and different approaches to ethical education. His books include: *Derrida and the Writing of the Body* (Ashgate, 2010) and *War and Virtual War: The Challenges to Communities*, ed. (Rodopi, 2004); *Paulo Freire's Philosophy of Education: Origins, Developments, Impacts and Legacies* (Continuum, 2012).

ROBERT JACKSON is a leading figure in international debates about religions and education in Europe and beyond. He is Research Consultant at the University of Warwick and is also Professor of Religious Diversity and Education at the European Wergeland Centre, a Council of Europe related centre based in Oslo, specialising in intercultural, citizenship and human rights education. Professor Jackson was a member of the drafting team of the Council of Europe Ministerial policy recommendation on teaching about religions and beliefs and of the Organisation for Security and Co-operation in Europe's *Toledo Guiding Principles on Teaching about Religions and Beliefs*. He also contributes to the United Nations Alliance of Civilizations programme on Education about Religions and Beliefs. He is widely published and is currently contributing to various Council of Europe projects, in particular, on the dissemination of the Council of Europe Ministerial Recommendation on the religious dimension of intercultural education.

PATRICIA KIERAN is a British Foreign and Commonwealth Chevening Scholar, who teaches Religious Education at Mary Immaculate College, University of Limerick. With Anne Hession she is co-author of *Children, Catholicism and Religious Education* (Dublin: Veritas, 2005) and co-editor of *Exploring Theology: Making Sense of the Catholic Tradition* (Dublin: Veritas, 2007) and *Exploring Religious Education: Catholic Religious Education in an intercultural Europe* (Dublin: Veritas, 2008). She has published chapters and articles on the subject of Catholic Education, Roman Catholic Modernism, gender and inter-religious education. She has edited, with Thomas Grenham *New Educational Horizons in Contemporary Ireland: Trends and Challenges* (Peter Lang, 2012).

DERMOT A. LANE is the recently retired President of Mater Dei Institute of Education, Dublin City University and a priest of the Dublin diocese serving in Balally Parish. He is the author of numerous works including *The Experience of God: An Invitation to Do Theology, Revised and Expanded* (Veritas/Paulist Press, 2003), and editor with Brendan Leahy of *Vatican II: Historical and Theological Perspectives* (Dublin: Veritas, 2006). In recent times his research has focused on inter-religious education, his most recent volume contributing strongly to this theme on the 50th anniversary of the beginning of Vatican II: *Stepping Stones to Other Religions: A Christian Theology of Inter-religious Dialogue* (Dublin: Veritas, 2011).

ANNE LOONEY is Chief Executive of the National Council for Curriculum and Assessment, Dublin. A former post-primary teacher of Religious Education and English, she joined the full-time staff of the NCCA in 1997 and was appointed CEO in 2001. She was reappointed to the post in 2011. Anne holds a Doctorate in Education from the Institute of Education of the University of London. She has published on curriculum and assessment policy, school culture and ethos, and religious and civic education, and has presented papers in Ireland, north and south, in the US, Canada, Australia and China on a range of curriculum and assessment themes and on issues of school reform. As a teacher Anne led the development of Religious Education syllabuses for post-primary schools and examinations in Ireland in the 1990s. She is a member of the editorial board of *Irish Educational Studies*, and of the governing bodies of Mary Immaculate College, University of Limerick, and Mater Dei Institute of Education, Dublin City University.

ANDREW MCGRADY is the Director of Mater Dei Institute of Education, Dublin City University. He is a member of the International Seminar on Religious Education and Values (ISREV) and, for 2012–2016, is a member of the Teaching Council (of Ireland). He has participated in a number of projects at a national and European level relating to the Catholic School and the religious dimension of education. He is co-editor of the *International Handbook on the Religious, Spiritual and Moral Dimensions of Education* (Dordrecht: Springer 2007) and author of 'The Religious Dimension of Education at the Start of the Third Millennium', in *From Present to Future*, edited by E. Woulfe and J. Cassin (Dublin: Veritas, 2006).

TERRENCE MERRIGAN is Professor of Systematic Theology at the Faculty of Theology and Religious Studies, KU Leuven. His research focuses on the theology of inter-religious dialogue, Christology and Trinitarian theology, the origins and development of the Christian doctrinal tradition, and the thought of John Henry Newman. Professor Merrigan is co-ordinator of the Systematic Theology research unit and of the Christian Self-Understanding and Inter-religious Dialogue research group, which bring together researchers investigating these and related themes. He is also editor of *Louvain Studies* and *Louvain Theological and Pastoral Monographs*.

MICHAEL NUGENT is chairperson of Atheist Ireland, an advocacy group for atheism, reason and ethical secularism. He is a writer and activist. He has written or co-written five books and the comedy musical *I Keano*. He was chairperson of New Consensus, a peace group that campaigned against paramilitary terrorism in Northern Ireland. As chairperson of Atheist Ireland, he has spoken at conferences and meetings in Ireland, London, Copenhagen, Cologne, Brussels and Warsaw.

ELŻBIETA OSEWSKA is Associate Professor of Theology in the field of Pastoral Theology and Catechetics. She earned a PhD in Theology in Pastoral Theology at the Catholic University in Lublin, and a habilitation in Catechetics at Cardinal Stefan Wyszynski University in Warsaw. From 1990 to 1993 she lectured in catechetical centers in Belarus, Lithuania and Latvia. Subsequently she was Head of the Department of Family Affairs in the Chancellery of the Prime Minister in Warsaw. She is also a Religious Education consultant in the Provincial In-service Centre in Łomża. She is a member of the Society for European Catechesis, of the European Forum for Religious Education in Schools (EuFRES) Polish Section of Catechetical Lecturers, and the Polish Familiology Society. She has organized and presented at many conferences, symposiums and congresses in Poland and abroad. She is co-author and editor of many Religious Education textbooks. Her research interests include catechetics, family studies, pedagogy, Religious Education, Catholic education, practical theology, family policy, didactics, communication and ICT. She has published a number of articles and books on related topics.

MARIE PARKER-JENKINS is Professor of Education in the Department of Education and Professional Studies, University of Limerick, researching issues of social justice with particular reference to 'race' and ethnicity. Before having an academic career in the UK, she lectured in Bermuda, Canada and Australia where she obtained practical knowledge of children from culturally diverse backgrounds. She is the author of over 100 publications including books, reports, and conference and journal articles. Her research has included study of the expansion of religious schools, particularly those based on an Islamic ethos; and in her consultancy capacity, she has provided workshops on such subjects as citizenship, community and social identity. She has taught in five universities before coming to the University of Limerick, and her current research is concerned with responding to diversity within the Irish context. Recent books include *Aiming High: Raising the Attainment of Pupils from Culturally Diverse Backgrounds* (Hewitt, Brownhill & Sanders, 2007), and *In Good Faith: Schools, Religion and Public Funding* (Hartas & Irving, 2005).

RIK VAN NIEUWENHOVE is a Senior Lecturer in Theology and Religious Studies, at Mary Immaculate College. He studied Moral Sciences, Philosophy and Medieval History in the Universities of Ghent and Leuven. After obtaining his PhD he became a Lecturer in Theology in the School of Theology and Religions, Trinity College Dublin. His research interests focus on medieval theology (including Thomas Aquinas and Bonaventure); medieval spirituality (with specific attention to the spirituality of the Low Countries, including Jan van Ruusbroec); theology of the Trinity; theories of salvation and the relation between theology and art. Apart from many articles in international journals Dr Van Nieuwenhove has published a number of books, including *Jan van Ruusbroec: Mystical Theologian of the Trinity* (Indiana: University of Notre Dame Press, 2003). He has co-edited with J. Wawrykow, *The Theology of Thomas Aquinas* (Indiana: University of Notre Dame Press, 2005). He has also co-edited a volume in the Classics of Western Spirituality Series entitled, *Late Medieval Mysticism of the Low Countries* (NJ: Paulist Press, 2008). His most recent books are *An Introduction to the Theology of the Trinity*, with Declan Marmion (Cambridge: Cambridge University Press, 2011) and *An Introduction to Medieval Theology* (Cambridge: Cambridge University Press, 2012).

FOREWORD

Dermot A. Lane

On 21 October 2011, the Irish Centre for Religious Education hosted an international conference on the theme 'Toward Mutual Ground: Religious Education, Education and Diversity'. The conference was held in Mater Dei Institute of Education, a College of Dublin City University. A follow-up conference 'Toward Mutual Ground: Religious Pluralism in Educational Practice in Irish Schools', again in conjunction with the Irish Centre for Religious Education, took place in Mary Immaculate College of Education and the Liberal Arts, Limerick, on 23 March 2012. Both conferences sought to embrace diversity among the speakers and content. The proceedings of these two conferences follow in the pages of this publication: *Toward Mutual Ground: Pluralism, Religious Education and Diversity in Irish Schools*.

Comments by Ruairi Quinn TD

At the event in Mater Dei Institute, Mr Ruairi Quinn, Minister for Education and Skills, gave a brief but significant address. He shared with the participants of the conference how he had received the Medal for Christian doctrine as a Leaving Certificate student in Blackrock College and, subsequently, lost his faith while a student in University College Dublin. He described himself as 'a practising atheist' who had 'an abiding interest in religion for all of my adult life'. He noted that religious faith in modern Ireland is often treated with 'a level of derision and contempt it does not deserve'. He pointed out that 'religious education will have an important place in the future of education in Ireland'. He also said that 'religious education was part of a vital set of tools that people need if they are to be active citizens and they are to make informed choices about issues'. There was a striking honesty and realism running through the Minister's remarks as well as an indication of some of the challenges facing religious education in Irish schools.

Context of 'Toward Mutual Ground'

The themes addressed at the two conferences and presented here in this single volume were chosen for a variety of reasons:

- To take account of the changing landscape of education in Ireland;
- To engage the emerging reality of a culturally-diverse society;
- To address the existence of social and religious pluralism in Irish schools;
- To recognise some of the challenges implicit in the Minister's decision in March 2011 to establish a Forum on Patronage and Pluralism in the Primary Sector.

In April 2012 the *Report on the Forum on Patronage and Pluralism in the Primary Sector*, chaired by Professor John Coolahan, was published. This Report was significant for many reasons: for its magisterial overview of the history of primary education in Ireland, for the way it highlighted the necessity for plurality of provision in primary schools, for the importance it placed on widening parental choice, for the recognition it gave to the place of Religious Education in the curriculum, for its inclusive approach to education, and its acknowledgement of the goodwill among the education partners for change.

The Irish bishops since 2007, led by comments from Archbishop Diarmuid Martin, had called for greater diversity of provision and signalled their willingness to divest their patronage of some primary schools if and when it facilitates the educational wishes of parents and widens their choice of school-type.

The advent of pluralism, secularisation, multi-culturalism and the Forum Report are seen by some as a threat to the Church's involvement in education. Others see these developments as representing a unique opportunity for Catholic education to find its true identity in a pluralist society.

The 50th Anniversary of Vatican II
The question is: Can the Catholic Church rise to the challenges that have been gathering momentum since the beginning of the new millennium contained in this changing landscape? These challenges coincide with the 50th anniversary of the opening of the Second Vatican Council. There are principles enunciated at that Council that have a direct bearing on Catholic education and schooling. Many of these principles are still awaiting implementation. The principles include a clear commitment by the Catholic Church to religious freedom, to ecumenism, and to engagement with other religions.

More particularly, the Catholic Church at Vatican II made a conscious decision to enter into dialogue with the modern world. It spelt out this commitment to dialogue through the adoption of a new principle of mutuality between the Church and the world.

For example in Chapter Four of the *Pastoral Constitution on the Church in the Modern World* (1965) the Council devoted five separate sections (40–44) to the development of the principle of mutuality, applying it to the relationship between the Church and the world, the Church and other cultures, Catholicism and other churches, Christianity and other religions. Dialogue and mutuality between the Church and the world was discerned by the Council as the way forward for the Church in the twentieth century. What is distinctive about this new teaching at Vatican II is the recognition that the Church offers something to the world and at the same time also receives something from the world. The Church teaches the world but it also learns from the world. In effect, the Church at Vatican II formally seeks to move from being a Church that simply teaches to being a Church that both teaches and learns at the same time. Here was the Church emerging from a fortress mentality reaching out to others in a way that values difference, respects diversity, and appreciates otherness.

The Church's commitment to dialogue is well known, but what is not so well known is its commitment to dialogue *and* mutuality. This development at Vatican II has been described as a paradigm change in the self-understanding of Catholicism.[1]

One way of summing up what is taking place in Irish education at this time is that education, all of education including religious education, is about Teaching *and* Learning. The new emphasis in education is on learning, on the introduction of students to learning and how to learn, opening the way to a process of life-long learning. Education is for life and not just for points in the Leaving Certificate examination or a ticket for entry into a third-level Institution; instead, education is about opening windows of wonder and ensuring that they will remain open long after schooling.

The vision of Vatican II about the role of the Church in the modern world and the relationship between the Church and the world in terms of dialogue *and* mutuality is a vision awaiting implementation in theory and in practice. This vision of Vatican II is of particular significance for the Church's involvement in education, and in particular in the area of religious education.

If the Church is to remain in education, it will not be by simply divesting the number of schools by 50 per cent or 10 per cent under its patronage and simply continuing to do what it has done in the past. Instead, the Church's involvement in schools will only succeed by improving the distinctive quality of what it offers in teaching and learning, and the application of that process of teaching and learning to the area of religious education. The seeds of this new vision of Catholic education were sown at the Second Vatican Council. It is now time to allow those seeds to grow and flourish in the twenty-first century.

Debates in Europe
It would be unfortunate if the current debate in Ireland about Religion and Education were to take place in isolation from recent debates in Europe. There are at least two particular debates that are worth noting in the context of this publication.

First of all religious education has become a hot topic not just in Ireland but also in Europe and the UK. The Council of Europe, one of the oldest institutions, has spearheaded a number of conferences and publications on the relationship between Religion and Education. These initiatives have emphasised the importance of intercultural education, of teaching about religions and non-religious convictions, and of fostering respect for religious differences.

Within this debate, a second development in Europe has been the publication of the 'Toledo Guidelines on Teaching about Religions and Beliefs in Public Schools'. A third development has been the support of a three year EU-funded research programme on 'Religion, Education, Dialogue, and Conflict', known as the REDCo project, 2006–2009. A further development that should be mentioned has been the publication of the final Report and Recommendations of the Cambridge Primary Review, entitled *Children, Their World, and Their Education*, 2010, edited by Robin Alexander. This study concludes:

> On the question of religious education we take the view that religion is so fundamental to this country's history, culture and language, as well as to the daily lives of many of its inhabitants, that it must remain within the curriculum.[2]

These developments in Europe have implications for Ireland in relation to the teaching of religion in the school curriculum and likewise the debate in Ireland has implications for what is going on in Europe. The debate in Europe highlights the importance of education about religion and belief. This particular emphasis, however, begs a number of questions: can you have education *about* religion and beliefs without education *in* religion. Is it possible to teach about religion without some teaching in religion? Does teaching about religion without teaching in religion foster real learning and does it bring about inter-religious learning in support of mutual respect, and tolerance and appreciation?

Much of this debate in Europe in relation to teaching about religion and beliefs is premised on an Enlightenment paradigm of knowledge and understanding to the neglect of the importance of the personal, the aesthetic, the interpretative and transcendent dimensions of knowing and understanding.

On the other hand the debate in Ireland in the past may have been too focused on education in religion to the neglect of education about religion. Is it possible to go beyond these two approaches toward a higher synthesis of education about religion *and* education in religion? Can we not bring together a critical and creative engagement of both information about religion *and* formation in religion?

The second debate in Europe of significance for Ireland is a discussion about the relationship between Religion and Society, which is often referred to as a debate about the role of religion in the public square. It has been the view of the Enlightenment that religion has no role to play in modern society, that the advances of modernity and the accompanying secularization make religion redundant, and that therefore religion should be sidelined and privatised. This particular view of religion has changed in the last few decades under pressure from a variety of sources.

There is first of all the stinging critique of modernity by late modernity or what some call postmodernity. Secondly sociologists, like José Casanova and Grace Davie, note that the modern theory of secularisation has not succeeded in sidelining religion. Thirdly, the calm but critical refection on the events of 9/11, especially the 10th anniversary of 9/11, have brought to the fore some of the negative consequences of isolating religion from education and society.

The Narrowing of Modern Reason

At the centre of this debate about the relationship between Religion and Society is a concern about the narrowing of modern reason, a narrowing caused by the rise of technocratic and instrumental reason.

It is pointed out that this restriction of reason is no longer able to support the foundations of democracy, or promote the integration and cohesion of society, or deal with the new pathologies of modern society, not to mention the declining capacity of modern reason to address the excesses of market-driven capitalism and globalization.[3]

Further, this narrowing of reason is causing, according to President Michael D. Higgins, 'an intellectual crisis that is far more serious than the economic one which … dominates the programmes in our media'.[4]

The French philosopher, Jean Luc Marion, describes this narrowing of reason as 'the most profound crisis of our era' because it is unable 'to clarify questions that go beyond the mere management and production of objects' and therefore has little to 'say about the human condition'.[5]

The only way to overcome this intellectual impasse is to transform the disjunctions that have been allowed to develop in the modern era. This means recovering the unity between ethics and economics, between poetry and physics, between religion and society. The peculiarly modern disjunction between religion and society does not serve well the interests of society or of religion. This European debate about the relationship between Religion and Society has implications and lessons for the debate in Ireland around the relationship between Religion and Education in schools.

It is hoped the publication of the proceedings of these two conferences will stimulate debate among all of the Patrons, including the Catholic Church, so that all can respond imaginatively and courageously to the challenges currently facing education and religious education in Ireland at this defining moment.

Dermot A. Lane   *March 2013*

NOTES

1. John D. Dadosky, 'Towards a Fundamental Re-interpretation of Vatican II', *Heythrop Journal*, 49/Sept. (2008), pp. 742–763.

2. Robin Alexander, ed., *Children, Their World, and Their Education: Final Report and Recommendations of the Cambridge Primary Review* (Abington/New York: Routledge, 2010), p. 268.

3. Jürgen Habermas et al., *An Awareness of What is Missing: Faith and Reason in a Post-secular Age*, trans. Ciaran Cronin (Cambridge/Malden, MA: Polity Press, 2010).

4. Michael D. Higgins, London School of Economics and Political Science, 21 Feb. 2012.

5. Jean Luc Marion, *Le Monde*, 11 Sept. 2008.

INTRODUCTION

TAKING DIVERSITY OF BELIEF SERIOUSLY IN CONTEMPORARY IRELAND: THE CHALLENGE FOR RELIGIOUS EDUCATION IN IRISH SCHOOLS

Patricia Kieran

Belief is a complex subject. As a term it is difficult to pin down. In its broadest sense, belief can be understood as a firmly held conviction or acceptance that something is true. When it is applied to religious belief it includes both familiar and long-established well-known religions as well as more recent or unfamiliar religious traditions. However the term belief is multifaceted as it refers to non-religious traditions which include beliefs such as atheism, agnosticism, humanism and secularism among others.[1] While diverse beliefs provide different perspectives on reality, it would be incorrect to suggest that belief systems are reducible to a series of abstract cognitive statements, summing up what an individual holds to be true. Although beliefs have a cognitive dimension they consist of so much more than this and they impact on the ethical, ritual, affective, physical and spiritual dimensions of life. Neither can it be stated that beliefs are exclusively individual or personal. They are often culturally and communally manifested as they form a core part of a group's sense of identity and relationship to self, others and the world. When it comes to religious belief, belief usually engages the believer in self-transcending relationship with a deity or deities. In chapter two of this book Terrence Merrigan states that religion is 'comprehensive, incapable of abandonment and of central importance' for the life of the religious believer. It is evident that beliefs may have different personal, local, regional and national variations as well as historical and contemporary manifestations. Being Agnostic, Catholic, Church of Ireland, Jewish or Muslim in contemporary Ireland does not mean the same thing to all believers and so this book opens with a note of caution: we must take diversity of belief seriously for distinctive traditions cannot be treated in a monolithic fashion.

It is obvious that belief has the potential to unite or divide people as no one belief system is universally accepted as the exclusive source of truth by the planet's seven billion inhabitants. Indeed in the first chapter of this book Robert

Jackson states that 'if freedom of religion or beliefs is a given for society, then society inevitably will be plural'. Recent European policy and developments in research have led to an awareness of the importance of educating European citizens about the plurality of beliefs.[2] When it comes to religious belief the assumption that European countries are increasingly secularised and that religion has disappeared from the public space is not substantiated by research.

> In most European countries we have long assumed that increasing secularisation would lead to a gradual retreat of religion from the public space. This tendency has reversed itself in the course of the past decade as religion returned to public discourse. Regardless of the wide variety of conditions prevailing in different European countries it appears more and more important to study the increasingly influential factor of 'religion and religiosity' and its ambivalent potential for both dialogue and social conflict and tension.[3]

Policy documents from organisations such as the Council of Europe, OSCE and ODHIR have manifested a growing appreciation of the diversity and complexity of different interpretations of reality as well as the importance of educating students appropriately about religious and secular beliefs in European schools. The sheer variety and complexity of different interpretations of reality and often their radically distinct nature can overwhelm, repulse or confuse people. Sometimes unfamiliar belief systems appear so dissonant and disconnected from what is familiar that people shy away from encounter with them or misconceive, stereotype, or even despise them. In extreme circumstances negative stereotyping and misunderstanding can lead to conflict and violence. Herein lies one of the key arguments for acknowledging the place of Religious Education in the curriculum of schools in contemporary Ireland. A society that acknowledges a plurality of beliefs must ensure that citizens have an open, informed, respectful, critical and tolerant attitude toward those whose beliefs are different to theirs. Religious Education is one curricular area where children can learn about and from those whose beliefs are different to theirs while simultaneously developing their own belief perspective.

The history of the island of Ireland bears evidence of the perils of ignoring the need to educate children about diversity of belief. The consequences of such a deficit result in bigotry and religious intolerance as well as an intolerance of religion.[4] Much has been written about the savage potential of religious beliefs to motivate believers to commit unprecedented acts of violence and horrendous evil. However at European policy level, post-9/11, there has been a discernible shift from seeing religious belief in problematic terms as a potential source of conflict, to the beginnings of a much greater appreciation of religion as a potential, powerful, social, cultural and indeed political force for good. In 2002 the Council of Europe focused on the religious dimension of Intercultural Education (ICE) and posited that inter-religious education might help to contribute a solution to intercultural problems. In 2003 European Education

Ministers made ICE, including its religious dimension, a priority for further work. At a conference of the Co-ordinating Group for Religion in Education in Europe (CoGREE) in November 2005, the EU Commissioner for Education, Culture and Multilingualism, Jan Figel, spoke of the 'close relationship between education and religious and moral values' as being crucial for the future of Europe. In 2007, the Council of Europe published a reference book for teachers on religious diversity in Europe.[5] Furthermore, in a historic move, the European Commission supported research into religion in education.[6] This emphasis on religion and education at a European level has resulted in an increased number of conferences, publications, networks and research activities focusing on the area of Religious Education. Significant networks such as Teaching Religion in a Multicultural European Society (TRES), the European Community project on Religious Education, Dialogue and Conflict, The European Network for Religious Education through Contextual Approaches (ENRECA), and the European Wergeland Centre (EWC) in Oslo have initiated large-scale research into documenting and improving the teaching of beliefs and religion across Europe.[7]

All of the above initiatives suggest that taking diversity of belief seriously, including inter-faith co-operation and inter-religious dialogue, is vital as they have enormous potential to contribute to conflict resolution within Europe. Religious traditions, with their emphasis on shared values, social justice and responsibility, as well as the common good, have something very positive to offer Europe. Indeed chapter two of this book discusses Madeline Albright's views on politicians taking religion seriously at both a European and a global level. In 2008 Tony Blair suggested that:

> In an era of globalisation, there is nothing more important than getting people of different faiths and cultures to understand each other better and live in peace and mutual respect, and to give faith itself its proper place in the future.[8]

Furthermore shared conversation between non-religious and religious groups can lead to open-mindedness, fairness and respect. For secular and non-religious belief systems contribute to a broad vision of human rights, education and equity for all citizens. Crucially in Ireland, where the Catholic religious tradition is the belief of the overwhelming majority,[9] there is a need for a greater appreciation of the perspectives and rights of all citizens, including diverse minority religious groups as well as humanist, secular, atheist and other non-religious people.

The Toward Mutual Ground Conferences

It was with a view to furthering greater understanding of the challenges posed by pluralism and Religious Education in contemporary Ireland that two important national *Toward Mutual Ground* conferences were organised by the

Irish Centre for Religious Education in Mater Dei Institute of Education in November 2011, and Mary Immaculate College, in March 2012. The *Toward Mutual Ground* conferences offered participants from diverse educational and belief contexts an opportunity to explore questions of religious and belief identity and their implications for Religious Education in schools in Ireland.[10] The conferences included presentations from international academics, teachers, students, policymakers and school managers as they explored questions such as: 'How do we recognise and respond to religious pluralism in schools in Ireland?' 'How do we accommodate diversity of belief, both religious and secular, in educational practice in Ireland?' Speakers outlined key principles for understanding religious pluralism and reflected upon international research, as well as policy and contemporary educational practice in Ireland. In the second conference a series of thematically grouped workshops, led by key national and international personnel, served to highlight emerging issues on policy and practice, visions for the future, international dimensions as well as the current situation regarding religious pluralism and Religious Education in primary, post-primary and other educational contexts in Ireland.

The conferences were unique in the manner in which they brought together a cross section of people with a range of attitudes toward belief, pluralism and Religious Education in the search for mutual ground. Practicing teachers and students from Catholic, Protestant, Jewish, Muslim and Multi-denominational schools came together to speak about their experiences of religious pluralism in their own educational settings, while listening to diverse voices from academics and policymakers. Those with an interest in religion, education and Religious Education come to the conferences to hear what others were saying and to contribute to a debate which explored whether, in a cacophony of diverse voices, it is possible to conceive of or move toward mutual ground. The conferences contributed to a rich and dynamic debate. The voices of people coming from faith-based schools were heard alongside those who would like to see a secular or non-denominational educational system in Ireland. An international dimension focused on educational practices in Belgium, Central and Eastern Europe, the United Kingdom and Northern Ireland. Furthermore the conferences brought together practicing teachers and students to speak about their experiences of religious pluralism, Religious Education and educational engagement and dialogue in their own school settings. Participants heard a range of diverse voices address issues surrounding rights and responsibilities, good practice and emerging issues in the area of identity, ethos, Religious Education and diversity.

The Toward Mutual Ground Title
The conferences acknowledged the distinct integrity of diverse perspectives while encouraging people of a variety of beliefs, religious and secular, to focus

on the search for 'mutual ground'. In essence they engaged in dialogue about what constitutes good education and good Religious Education in a pluralist context which culminated in the publication of this book. This book is one end product of an ongoing process initiated by the Irish Centre for Religious Education, leading to the generation of a series of position papers at conferences focusing on religious pluralism, diversity and Religious Education in Ireland.

Each word in the *Toward Mutual Ground* title of the conferences and book has been carefully selected. The word '*Toward*' suggests a tentative movement in a particular direction which is not quite an assured point of arrival. Neither the conferences nor the book were under the misapprehension that for people of diverse belief, finding a mutually agreeable territory is a foregone conclusion or an easy and inevitable prospect. Diversity of belief means that understandings and convictions about truth are plural and are often contested.

The word '*Mutual*' represents a deliberate attempt to move beyond binary oppositions (e.g. religious and secular, Catholic and Protestant, Muslim and Jew) which can polarise and stereotype the perceived 'other' as inherently negative and lacking while affirming the intrinsic superiority and worth of those who hold beliefs identical to one's own.[11] In Ireland there has been a tendency to engage in a bipolar debate about religion in society and Religious Education in schools without appreciating the full complexity and nuance of the issues. Commentators have tended to construct the 'other' in unflattering terms. People are often labelled as being 'pro' or 'anti' faith in schools. Those of secular belief are sometimes portrayed as being inherently intolerant of religious belief or anti-religious. Atheists are not uncommonly seen by religious believers as people with little or no capacity for or interest in spirituality. Religious believers are sometimes construed as being indifferent to the human rights and concerns of humanists. Christians are caricatured as being hostile and resistant to members of other faiths. This book attempts to acknowledge and respect the radically different theological and ideological distinctions between people of diverse belief. However, it also acknowledges that to live in a modern Irish democracy people must move beyond a society where citizens are hermetically sealed into their own belief system for fear of being contaminated by other beliefs, either religious or secular. Mutuality necessitates a joint process involving one's encounter, acknowledgement, dialogue and collaboration with the other. At the heart of any process of mutuality is a desire to establish a reciprocated relationship of trust and respect as well as a willingness to listen to and learn from the other. This book identifies Religious Education as a potentially powerful subject area in Irish schools which can facilitate a relationship of openness, tolerance, respect and trust between people of different belief. Religious Education is located at the heart of the TMG conferences and book title and content because of its capacity to facilitate mutuality in the form of a shared activity or reciprocal relationship. However it is important to stress that mutual ground is not identical to neutral ground. If the term 'neutral ground' carries connotations of a value free no-man's land purged of individual identity, 'mutual ground' suggests a common area where the individual identities of different participants are acknowledged and belong.

The word '*Ground*' reinforces this notion of a broad general terrain or some common agreement or position, where people of different belief can legitimately feel that their distinct perspectives and traditions belong. This book provides an opportunity for participants to acknowledge the particularity and plurality of beliefs in educational contexts in contemporary Ireland. As part of the process of listening to the distinct voices of people from diverse beliefs and educational perspectives it is crucial that one begins to articulate one's own particular voice and to acknowledge one's own beliefs. The TMG conferences and book challenge people to explore whether it is possible to move beyond holding their beliefs in fractured isolation and to move toward some type of mutual ground with people of diverse belief. Of course the search for mutual ground is based on a respect for difference, an appreciation of the complex diversity and particularity of religion and belief and a desire to find areas of common concern, meaning and best practice in Religious Education in Irish schools. This book addresses the question: How can schools and Religious Education in particular, best respond to the diverse religious, spiritual and moral education needs of young people, supporting them toward becoming fully responsible and respectful citizens? The chapters of this book offer readers a unique opportunity to hear from policymakers, educationalists, theologians, religious educators, commentators and teachers as they respond to the question of how diversity of belief, both religious and secular, can be accommodated in educational practice in Ireland's schools. It opens the way for a renewed vision of Religious Education which can help young people honour and appreciate their own beliefs while coming to understand and respect the beliefs of others. The various chapters of this book present diverse perspectives on belief and education. While some individual authors acknowledge a key role for Religious Education in schools, others disagree with this opinion. Of course it is important to stress that the editors' views are not to be confused with those of any of the individual authors.

Taking Diversity of Belief Seriously in Schools

Schools are key locations where citizens are educated about diversity of belief and religious pluralism. The influential *Toledo Guiding Principles* are founded on two core principles: 'that there is positive value in teaching that emphasises respect for *everyone's* right to freedom of religion and belief, and second, that teaching *about* religions and beliefs can reduce harmful misunderstandings and stereotypes'.[12] This process is not easy or predictable. Misunderstanding and ambiguity are a constant risk. Premature attempts to blur boundaries or to homogenise people of different belief, by simplistically reducing their otherness to sameness, are unhelpful. Language is hugely significant in this process. The linguist Ferdinand de Saussure[13] reminds us that there is no inherent link between language and meaning. For all language is a system whose meaning is created by an ever shifting process of interpretation. Words such as 'belief' 'God', 'religion' or 'atheism' are some of the most symbolically loaded words in the English language and each individual interpreting them brings their own personal history, ethnicity, gender, prejudices, politics, etc. to the act of interpretation. Terms such as 'Religious Education', 'Catechesis', 'Religious Instruction', or 'Faith Formation' can be interpreted with radically different meanings, in different contexts, by dialogue participants. Therefore the selection, usage and clarification of appropriate terminology for education about beliefs in diverse contexts are key preoccupations for many writers in this collection of essays. In Ireland there is an urgent need to contextualise, clarify and critically evaluate the terminology that is used in discourse on belief and Religious Education. This book is part of the development of a dialogue which hopes to promote inclusive educational practices, especially in the area of Religious Education.

Robust conversation about beliefs and about what distinguishes one group of believers from others is a starting point for thinking about one's own beliefs as well as taking different beliefs seriously. It is only by being reflective and honest about differences, open and comfortable in talking about what is distinctive in one's own beliefs, while listening intently and respectfully to others when they speak of their beliefs, that we can seriously begin to think and talk about how and where we might share areas of commonality.

Religious Pluralism in Ireland
One of the reasons why diversity of belief has become a major issue within the school system in Ireland is because the school system is a microcosm of an increasingly diverse Irish society. Many commentators argue that while Ireland has been culturally and ethnically diverse for millennia this diversity has only recently been recognised.[14] It is important to stress that in the past religious diversity was not always acknowledged or accompanied by a peaceful and respectful recognition of the rights of the religious or non-religious other. Ireland's long history of cultural and religious diversity is also a story of invasions, settlements, and religiously fuelled conflict.[15] From the time of the expansion of Mesolithic farmers into the north of Ireland from 6,000 BCE onwards, through to its relatively sophisticated Stone Age farming society in 3,000 BCE,[16] up to more recent times, a cycle of invasion and assimilation has given Ireland a complex, diverse, and often contradictory, cultural, religious

and social history. This makes even generic statements concerning identity all the more difficult.[17]

An analysis of the religious affiliation of the Irish population in the twenty-first century underscores its diversity.[18] The 2011 census shows that the non-nationals living in Ireland represent 199 different nations and their numbers have increased over 143 per cent since 2002.[19] While the 2011 census revealed that Ireland is overwhelmingly Catholic (over 84 per cent),[20] it is important to note that Ireland's population embraces a variety of religious and secular perspectives. In 2011, 17 per cent of the population was born outside Ireland and while 51 per cent of non-Irish in Ireland are Catholics, non-Irish are three times as likely as Irish to say they have no religion (15 per cent versus 4.4 per cent). One of the most dramatic findings of the 2011 census is that the percentage of people ticking the 'No Religion' box has increased by 45 per cent since 2006, representing 5.9 per cent of the total population.[21] Non-religious people now represent the fastest growing category in the 2011 census data on religion. Inevitably policymakers are already asking what changes are necessary in the educational system to respond to their needs.

Education in Contemporary Ireland
In contemporary Ireland the State has an integrated approach to funding private and public schools so that faith schools are publically funded. A recent report states that Ireland's education system is unique among developed countries because, at primary level '96 per cent of primary schools in Ireland are under denominational patronage'.[22] Indeed while in some European countries only majority-faith schools receive public funding,[23] in Ireland public funding is allocated to minority and majority faith as well as inter-denominational and multi-denominational primary schools. In twenty-first-century Ireland there are numerous types of schools including: Catholic; Church of Ireland; Community National Schools; Educate Together; Inter-denominational; Jewish; Methodist; Multi-denominational; Muslim; Presbyterian; Quaker and Others.[24] In multi-denominational schools a plurality of religions and beliefs are taught without endorsing any one world view in particular.[25]

The Catholic Church is Patron to almost 92 per cent of all schools at primary level and exercises a vast influence on the Irish educational system. Catholicism's influence on education is by no means limited to the primary sector and many post-primary schools are managed by Catholic patronal bodies. Indeed the influence of faith communities in the Irish educational system extends to tertiary level. Of the five publically funded Colleges of Education preparing teachers to teach in primary schools, four are Catholic and one is Church of Ireland.[26]

In a recent study, Smyth, Darmody, McGinnity and Byrne explored ethnic diversity in Irish schools and estimate that ethnic minority students made up approximately 10 per cent of the primary school-going population. They note 'while there were no ethnic minority students in a significant number of primary schools, in others (mainly located in cities), these students made up more than a fifth of the total cohort. Importantly, these ethnic minority children represent a wide variety of cultures, linguistic groups and faith systems.'[27] Ethnicity and religious affiliation are closely intertwined and Smyth et al. suggest that while recent studies of minority ethnic groups have focused on linguistic and cultural issues, relatively little attention has been paid to religious diversity. Both TMG Conferences and this book represent an attempt to address this dearth of research documenting religious pluralism in Irish schools. Indeed to date research has been largely silent on the experience of non-religious or minority faith groups in schools in Ireland. An Irish Primary Principals' Network (IPPN) survey, administered to 450 primary school principals, found that 80 per cent of Irish primary schools cater for children from at least two religious backgrounds, 63 per cent of primary schools have classes containing between two and five different religions while over 16 per cent cater for children of six different faiths or more.[28] These findings illustrate the presence of a religiously diverse school population yet give no qualitative indication of the number of children from secular traditions, as well as children's overall experience within the system of schooling.

The Irish educational system is not immune from change. In the last two decades there has been a greater diversification of the educational sectors at all levels yet many suggest that this diversification is not reflective of Ireland's ethnically, religiously and linguistically diverse population. Ireland's population is highly educated[29] and a recent Independent International report on initial teacher education provision in Ireland stated that 'academic standard of applicants (to the teaching profession) is amongst the highest, if not the highest, in the world' and that in Ireland teaching is 'increasingly viewed as a high-status profession similar to the work of lawyers, doctors and engineers'.[30] This bodes well for education about beliefs in Irish schools. At post-primary level a state syllabus for Religious Education was introduced into the Junior Certificate cycle in 2000 (first examined in 2003) and the Leaving Certificate Cycle in 2003 (first examined in 2005), which has at its core, learning about and from diverse belief groups. A significant recent development has emerged from the National Council for Curriculum and Assessment (NCCA) *Towards a Framework for Junior Cycle* (2012) discussion document. This contains a radical plan to reform the Junior Cycle. Its implications for students' learning, progress and assessment in Junior Cycle Religious Education are uncertain.

At primary level as a consequence of the extraordinary level of public interest in the issue of faith schools, and the growing number of critical voices calling for a change to the existing system, the Government established a Forum on Patronage and Pluralism in the Primary Sector. The establishment of the

Forum was a key commitment in the programme for Government in 2011 and its aim was to ensure 'fairness in our schools'.[31] The Forum grew out of the realisation that there was 'a mis-match between the inherited pattern of denominational school patronage and the rights of citizens in a much more culturally and religiously diverse contemporary Irish society'.[32]

The recently published findings of the *Report of the Advisory Group on the Forum on Patronage and Pluralism in the Primary Sector* (April 2012) have been greeted with caution[33] or alarm by some as well as welcomed with applause by others. The Government's resolve to address the inadequacy of the Irish Educational system, particularly at primary level, to cater for diversity of belief and to offer greater choice to all stakeholders, has been subject to multiple interpretations.[34] The report recommends divesting a number of schools from Catholic to alternative types of patronage. Many religious leaders have welcomed the report. Archbishop Diarmuid Martin stated:

> These are challenging times. They are, however, great times to be involved in education. For the first time in generations there is real ferment in Irish educational reflection as we take a fundamental new look at our entire educational system. There is a sense of common search for a new and integrated educational policy which responds to the needs of today and tomorrow.

In April 2012, at the launch of the report Minister Ruairi Quinn stated:

> This report outlines the history and evolution of patronage in Irish society. It also shows the need for the primary school system to now adapt to the needs of a more diverse society.

The divesting of patronage and the transfer of ethos are complex matters. Within this mix there is also an increasing awareness of the rights of the child and the passing of a referendum to strengthen children's rights in the Constitution (2012) provides further evidence of the importance of listening to the voice of children in matters of belief.

This book documents many other important developments in Religious Education. In 2011 a National Directory for Catechesis in Ireland, *Share the Good News*, was launched containing a renewed vision of catechesis and Religious Education in the Catholic Church. In the same year the Irish Centre for Religious Education was founded and one of its key aims is the organization of conferences and the generation and co-ordination of scholarly research into Religious Education and education about beliefs in Ireland. In 2013 a new Primary Curriculum for Catholic Schools is nearing completion. A host of national conferences, most notably the Irish Human Rights Commission (IHRC) *Religion and Education* conference, as well as a host of publications on the issue of Religious Education and human rights in Ireland[35] have contributed significantly to the discussion. Whatever differences in emphases may be observed among participants in these debates, it is clear that for many Religious

Education has an even more important role to play in a time where diversity of belief is an increasingly evident aspect of a modern democratic Irish society.

Organisation of Content

The book is divided into four sections. Each section is grouped around a major theme in the discourse concerning religious pluralism and educational practice. The first four chapters in Section I of the book bring together the keynote addresses from the first TMG conference held in Mater Dei in November 2011. Chapter One traces recent European policy developments and research concerning Religious Education. Robert Jackson, a leading international figure in the world of education about beliefs, provides an overview of policy and practical developments in teaching about religions and non-religious beliefs across the huge geographical region of Europe. He explores the complexity of terminology and the variety of methodologies used in different countries, most notably in the United Kingdom. In Chapter Two Terence Merrigan emphasises the communitarian and public dimension of religion which is understood as a comprehensive form of life, constituted by doctrines, spirituality, ritual and normative practices which are of central importance to the ordering of the lives of believers. He argues that secularization theories must be reevaluated as religious belief is deeply relevant to the public, political and educational domain in Europe. Further he suggests that religion should not be considered exclusively as an individual or private affair. Suzanne Dillon, in Chapter Three, focuses closely on her own experience as a classroom teacher as well as the classroom practice of teachers teaching Religious Education. She examines different approaches to teaching, learning and assessment in Religious Education in post-primary schools. This chapter highlights the advantages and limitations of the 'learning about' and 'learning from' approaches to teaching Religious Education and contains interesting reflections on the NCCA syllabuses for Junior and Leaving Certificate cycle and the NCCA *Guidelines on Inclusion*. Finally, in this section, in Chapter Four Andy McGrady explores the complexity of language and the proliferation of terms such as Religious Instruction, Religious Education, Religious Nurture, Catechesis, etc. He documents the evolution of meanings and methodologies ascribed to various terms before selecting the term 'Teaching Religion' as the least inadequate way of speaking about enabling the learner to learn about, from and within belief traditions. He overviews recent landmark developments in Irish education such as the phenomenological, confessional and religious studies approaches.

The four chapters in Section II contain the keynotes presentations from the second TMG conference. In Chapter Five Marie Parker Jenkins overviews her own considerable body of research as well as the research of other key theorists in the area of race and ethnicity. She explores the complex relationship between religion and identity. The chapter focuses initially on the experiences of Muslim and Jewish students in schools in the UK before profiling the religious and cultural diversity of students in Irish schools. She concludes by exploring the implications of religious diversity for educational policy and practice in Irish schools. The Catholic theologian, Gavin D'Costa, notes that through learning from other religions the task of finding common ground and learning to be fully human is enhanced. He argues, in Chapter Six, that in order to find mutual ground with other religions, Catholics are required to become more fully Catholic. D'Costa acknowledges that this appears to be an arrogant and paradoxical statement, and he considers counterarguments to his proposal. He suggests that for Catholics to be more Catholic involves them being more fully human. The chapter focuses on Catholic teaching and acknowledges that the Catholic Church does not have a monopoly on the truth and that Catholics find truths in other religions. In Chapter Seven Anne Looney begins with a reflection upon story telling. She explores the big stories or grand narratives of religion as well as the little stories that get told in the queue in Tesco. Looney highlights the importance of the selection and usage of words when speaking or teaching about religion and beliefs. Reflecting on recent terrorist events in France she argues that religion can easily become a proxy for something else such as race, class or privilege. Furthermore she suggests that lessons from the chalkface, from teachers and learners in school settings, suggest that what happens in educational practice may defy the best of policymakers' intentions. Finally, in this section Elżbieta Osewska presents a broad outline of the cultural and religious composition of countries in Central and Eastern Europe. In Chapter Eight she states that since 2004 the religious map is getting more and more complex and diversified, when some countries previously controlled by the Soviet Union joined the European Union. These countries have experienced powerful political, ideological, educational, economic and financial transformation. The author of this chapter refers to a whole range of aspects, which may be identified as crucial for the position of religion in society and explores key questions such as what is the difference between religious pluralism in Western and Central/Eastern Europe? She explores the role of the Roman Catholic Church as well as other churches and faith communities in Poland as they engage in ecumenical and inter-religious dialogue. Her chapter concludes with a reflection on how Religious Education may need to adapt to help younger generations to function meaningfully in a pluralist society.

Sections III and IV contain selected workshop presentations from the second TMG conference. In Section III, *Pluralism and Religious Education in Irish Schools*, Gareth Byrne outlines the context and framework for evangelisation, catechesis and religious education in contemporary Ireland from the perspective of the Catholic Church at national level. As writer and editor for the Bishops' Conference of their National Directory for Catechesis in Ireland, *Share the Good News* (SGN), Gareth presents an overview of the relationship between Church and State as well as key themes such as dialogue, proclamation, pluralism and secularism. Chapter Nine articulates a vision of Catholic education and addresses what it means for a school to have a Catholic ethos in our diverse world as well as the intimate link between home, parish and school working in partnership. Chapter Ten explores religious pluralism in the context of Northern Ireland's educational system. Niall Coll suggests that in the Northern Irish context, because of its history of 'The Troubles' and the peace process, religious pluralism refers primarily to promoting more mutual knowledge and understanding between different Christian traditions. He profiles educational provision in Northern Ireland and Religious Education curricula, as well as the role of religious groups, including the Catholic church's involvement, in faith based schools. He concludes that in a divided society there needs to be greater acknowledgement of the importance of fostering good religious education. In Chapter Eleven Anne Hession explores inter-religious learning as an integral aspect of Christian Religious Education. Hession stresses that one of the purposes of Catholic primary Religious Education and formation is the development of authentic Christian identity in a religiously plural and diverse world. She suggests ways in which teachers might organise systematic inter-religious learning in the context of formal Religious Education in the Catholic primary school.

The final section of the book, *Religious Pluralism and Diversity: Critical Perspectives*, consists of three chapters which raise critical questions and suggestions about religious pluralism and education. In Chapter Twelve Jones Irwin argues that a significant group of children, parents, teachers and teacher-educators are alienated by the lack of choice and paternalism of a denominationalist approach to education in Ireland. He questions whether the rhetoric of 'respect for difference' can have any teeth in an Irish educational system with an overwhelmingly denominational ethos. Irwin calls for significant change to the denominationalist ethos in schools (and in Colleges of Education) in Ireland, which involves faith formation in school time, preparation for sacraments and the foregrounding of the symbolism of a particular religion. He welcomes the beginnings of change and reflects on the challenges of implementing the recommendations of the Forum on Patronage and Pluralism in the Primary Sector. The theme of the need for change to Ireland's educational system is continued in Chapter Thirteen where Michael Nugent and Jane Donnelly raise the key question of whether an educational system is exclusively a means of satisfying the desires of the majority of parents or whether the rights of all parents, children and teachers, including atheist parents, children and teachers, should be respected equally. They argue that the only way to protect everybody's rights in a pluralist society is through a secular state. The chapter outlines the rationale for a secular education system which would be neutral on the question of religion and non-religion and it argues that such a system should be available in Ireland. Furthermore the authors suggest that if a secular educational system were established by the State in Ireland then further educational options could develop as a supplement to, and not a replacement of, that secular system. In Chapter Fourteen Rik Van Nieuwenhove reflects critically upon pluralist and non-denominational perspectives. Van Nieuwenhove suggests that the pluralist paradigm is self-contradictory and self-subversive for to claim that 'There is no truth' is indeed to assert a truth. Further he explores the pluralist paradigm in Irish schools and examines the limitations of teaching children about religion from a detached perspective that fails to capture the complexity and nature of religious belief. In effect he sees that multi-denominational approaches tend to make all religions a matter of indifference. He argues that genuine inclusivity does not mean standing for everything (and thus, ultimately nothing). True inclusivity is presented where learners are steeped in their own tradition where 'one engages in respectful and tolerant dialogue with people of different traditions'.

The concluding chapter by Gareth Byrne synthesises key themes which emerge from the book, outlining ten criteria which might guide dialogue participants in the search for mutual ground.

This book testifies to the fact that the search for a common area of interconnection, which takes the distinct beliefs of people and groups seriously, is a complicated and difficult process. It brings together the voices of those who would like to see a non-denominational educational system in Ireland as well as those passionately committed to denominational and multi-denominational education. Finally this book is unique in that it is the first time that any publication has sought to help merge the mutual ground underpinning such a wide cross-section of commentators with a range of attitudes toward religion, education and pluralism. It is hoped that it will contribute to a rich, respectful and dynamic debate.

NOTES

1.   *Toledo Guiding Principles on Teaching about Religions and Beliefs in Public Schools* (Warsaw: OSCE ODIHR, 2007); UN Alliance of Civilizations, Education About Religions and Beliefs <http://erb.unaoc.org/about/overview-of-erb/> [accessed 7 Jan. 2013].

2.   *The Toledo Guiding Principles*; J. Keast, ed. *Religious Diversity and Intercultural Education: A Handbook for Schools* (Strasbourg: Council of Europe, 2007). DES, *The Report of the Forum on Patronage and Pluralism in the Primary Sector* (2012) <http://www.education.ie/en/Press-Events/Conferences/Patronage-and-Pluralism-in-the-Primary-Sector/The-Forum-on-Patr onage-and-Pluralism-in-the-Primary-Sector-Report-of-the-Forums-Advisory-Group.pdf> [accessed 7 Jan. 2013]. The whole volume of the Taylor and Francis, *Religion and Education Journal*, 39/3 (2012), explores pertinent issues. Also see the United Nations Alliance of Civilizations, *Education about Religions and Beliefs Journal* which provides a variety of

scholarly articles. Religious freedom is one of the fundamental principles underlying the Italian Government's *Charter of Values for Citizenship* (2007). In France, President Sarkozy shocked many secularists with his repeated emphasis on religion as a significant factor in shaping a society's morals and attitudes. In 2007, in an open letter to all those involved in education, he questioned and some would say undermined, France's ancient secular tradition by suggesting that it was inappropriate to leave religion at the door of the school. In 2008, Tony Blair launched a Faith Foundation with the aim of promoting inter-religious collaboration and the advancement of faith as an alternative to conflict, in the modern world. Countries such as Norway, England, Ireland and Switzerland, have engaged in recent debates about the role of religion in society and in particular in their educational systems.

3.   The REDCo project examined and compared the role of religion in the educational systems of selected European countries <http://www.redco.uni-hamburg.de/web/3480/3483/index.html> [accessed 7 Jan. 2013].

4.   For a recent account of intolerance of religion see Martha Nussbaum, *The New Religious Intolerance* (Harvard: Harvard University Press, 2012).

5.   *Religious Diversity and Intercultural Education: A Reference Book for Schools.*

6.   EU's Sixth Framework Programme for Research and Technological Development, Priority 7: *Citizens and Governance in a Knowledge Based Society.*

7.   TRES is a trans-national cooperation project in the form of a thematic network funded by the Socrates Programme which started in the autumn of 2005. The TRES launching conference took place in Uppsala, Sweden, in 2006. For further examples of research groups and networks see the Oslo coalition's project on education for freedom of religion or belief; the European Community Framework 6 project on Religious Education, Dialogue and Conflict involving ten Universities (REDCo); The European Network for Religious Education through Contextual Approaches and the International Seminar on Religious Education and Values (ISREV); Co-ordinating Group for Religious Education in Europe (CoGREE); European Association for the Study of Religions (EASR).

8.   *The Times*, 29 May 29 2008.

9.   84 per cent in the 2011 Census. See Central Statistics Office <http://www.cso.ie/en/census> [accessed 7 Jan. 2013].

10.   The first conference *Toward Mutual Ground: Education, Religious Education and Diversity*, took place at Mater Dei Institute of Education (MDI), a College of Dublin City University, on 21 Oct. 2011 and was the inaugural conference of the newly-established Irish Centre for Religious Education (ICRE). The second *Toward Mutual Ground: Religious Pluralism in Educational Practice in Irish Schools* conference, took place on Friday 23 Mar. 2012 at Mary Immaculate College (MIC), a College of the University of Limerick, and it echoed and responded to the first conference.

11.   MacLure, M., *Discourse in Educational and Social Research* (Maidenhead: Open University Press, 2003).

12.   *Toledo Guiding Principles*, p. 13.

13.   Ferdinand de Saussure, *The Course on General Linguistics* (Peru, Illinois: Open Court Publishing, 1983).

14.   Roland Tormey, *Teaching Social Justice and Development Education Perspectives on Education's Context, Content and Methods* (Dublin: Ireland Aid and CEDR, 2003), pp. 26–7.

15.   Eds. Moody, Martin and Byren, *The Course of Irish History* (Dublin: Mercier Press, 1967), p. 43.

16.   Moody, Martin and Byren, *The Course*, p. 35.

17.   See John Mc Donagh, *Narrating the Nation? Post-Colonial Perspectives on Patrick Kavanagh's The Great Hunger (1942) and Brendan Kennelly's Cromwell (1983)*, unpublished PhD, Warwick University, 1998, p. 49.

18. Indeed the 2002 census figures reveal that while almost ninety per cent of the population cite Catholicism as their religion, Ireland was home to more than twenty different religious traditions as well as those of 'No Religion'.

19. CSO, *Census 2011*, Profile 6, Migration and Diversity <http://www.cso.ie/en/media/csoie/census/documents/census2011profile6/PR%20xxxx%20Profile%206%20Migration%20a...pdf> [accessed 20 Dec. 2012].

20. CSO, *This is Ireland: Highlights from the Census 2011*, Part 1 (Dublin: Stationary Office, 2012), p. 42. See Central Statistics Office <http://www.cso.ie/en/census/> [accessed 7 Jan. 2013].

21. <http://www.cso.ie/px/pxeirestat/Statire/SelectVarVal/Define.asp?maintable=CDD35&PLanguage=0> [accessed 20 Dec. 2012]. It is interesting to note that the inauguration of Ireland's ninth president, Michael D. Higgins, in Nov. 2011 celebrated this diversity with an inter-faith service and a Humanist reflection.

22. J. Coolahan, C. Hussey and F. Kilfeather, *The Forum on Patronage and Pluralism in the Primary Sector: Report of the Forum's Advisory Group* (Dublin: Department of Education and Skills, 2012), p. 1. Ireland is also distinguished by the 'very high number of primary schools per head of population' and it has 'one of the highest proportions of small schools among developed countries'.

23. For example in Malta only majority faith schools receive funding, see *Religious Education in a Multicultural Society: School and Home in Comparative Context*. Final Report available at <http://www.esri.ie/research/research_areas/education/Remc/final_report_publishabl/REMC_Final_Report_Publishable_Summary.pdf> [accessed 20 Dec. 2012]. Henceforth REMC. In Malta Islamic schools receive no financial support from the State. REMC, p. 15.

24. There are 3,165 primary schools (excluding special schools) in Ireland of which 2,888 are under Catholic patronage. The Irish Human Rights Commission in their report 2012 stressed that the state should define legally the terms non-denominational, denominational, multi-denominational and interdenominational in the Irish context.

25. Department of Education and Skills, 2010. The multi-denominational schools: 56 under the patronage of Educate Together; 2 Community National Schools under the patronage of the VEC; 8 Gaelscoileanna under the patronage of An Foras Pátrúnachta; 1 John Scottus School and 2 Steiner Schools.

26. There is one privately funded college, Hibernia, which provides a post-graduate blended learning course in pre-service teacher education.

27. Darmody, M. and Smyth, E., 'Religious Diversity and Schooling in Ireland', in *The Changing Faces of Ireland: Exploring the Lives of Immigrant and Ethnic Minority Children*, ed. by M. Darmody, N. Tyrrell and S. Song (Rotterdam: Sense, 2011).

28. IPPN Survey, *Religion in Schools* (June 2008) <http://www.ippn.ie/index.php?view=article&id=643:28th-june-2008-religion-in-schools-what-750-principals-say&option=com_content&Itemid=50> [accessed 7 Jan. 2013].

29. More than half of women aged 25–34 have a third-level qualification, compared with 39 per cent of men in the same age group (CSO 2010).

30. Áine Hyland, *A Review of The Structure of Initial Teacher Education Provision in Ireland* (Dublin: HEA, 2012).

31. Address of the Minister for Education and Skills, Ruairi Quinn, TD, 10 Apr. 2012 <http://www.education.ie/home/home.jsp?maincat=&pcategory=10861&ecategory=10876&sectionpage=12251&language=EN&link=link001&page=1&doc=56996> [accessed 10 Dec. 2012].

32. Ruairi Quinn, TD, 10 Apr. 2012.

33. For some within the Catholic Church it is a serious threat to the very fabric of Catholic schooling. It has been described as a 'wake up call for the Catholic Church and its role in the Irish Education system'. Eamonn Conway, 'The Future of Catholic Schools: The Forum on Patronage and Pluralism – Cultural Marker and Wake-Up Call', *The Furrow*, June 2012, pp. 369–377.

34   Tom Hickey writes 'The patronage report was always doomed, because it was set up to "respect parental preferences" and "diversity" as if the State could ever provide the range of schools in each community needed to cater for the particular beliefs of all parents within that community,' *The Irish Times*, 24 Apr. 2012.

35.   Irish Human Rights Commission, *Religion and Education: A Human Rights Perspective* (Dublin: IHRC 2011).

SECTION I: EDUCATION, RELIGIOUS EDUCATION AND DIVERSITY

CHAPTER ONE

WHY EDUCATION ABOUT RELIGIONS AND BELIEFS?
EUROPEAN POLICY RECOMMENDATIONS AND RESEARCH

Robert Jackson

Introduction

Speaking in Ireland at the new Irish Centre for Religious Education, I recall my first visit to Dublin was 25 years ago in 1986, when Ireland hosted a wonderful meeting of the International Seminar on Religious Education and Values. Uniquely for ISREV, a serving prime minister, in this case the Taoiseach, Dr Garret FitzGerald, attended the conference and spoke of the importance of understanding religions as part of education. In the same spirit it is a pleasure to have an opportunity to share with you some of the work in which I have been participating in Europe in recent years, for the Council of Europe, the Organisation for Security and Cooperation in Europe, and a European Commission Framework Six research project on issues concerned with religion, education, dialogue and conflict – REDCo. The work being done by the Council of Europe and the European Wergeland Centre in promoting discussion of the Council of Europe's Ministerial Recommendation concerning the religious dimension of intercultural education is worthy too of particular note. However, before I introduce these various European projects, it is important to clarify terminology and to set the scene for recent developments.

The Term 'Religious Education'

The field of religious education is fraught with difficulties and misunderstandings. Not least, the terminology of the subject causes a great deal of confusion. What in the United States and the Republic of Ireland is usually called 'religious education' in England is often called 'religious nurture' or 'religious instruction'.[1] What in England is called 'religious education', generally seen as an impartial study of religions in fully state-funded schools, is often called 'religion education' in the USA and South Africa.[2] In attempting to broaden the subject to include non-religious belief systems as well as religious beliefs (in order to be consistent with the human rights principle of freedom of religion or belief), the United Nations Alliance of Civilization programme uses the term 'Education about Religions and Beliefs' – abbreviated to ERB (http://erb.unaoc.org), while the Organisation for Security and Co-operation in Europe refers to 'Teaching about Religions and Beliefs' (TaRB).[3] Some countries combine religious education or religion education with values education. Thus, in the Canadian province of Québec, we find a syllabus on Ethics and Religious Culture taken by all pupils, while in Scotland, for some levels of schooling, we have Religious and Moral Education.[4] In France, where in public education there is still a deep suspicion of the place of studies of religion, we find what has been sometimes translated into English as 'education about religious facts', taught through various subjects rather than appearing as a separate field of study.[5]

Some educational systems include both education about religions and religious nurture within the state system and provide state funding for both. Thus, in England and Wales, there are both fully state-funded community schools which have a form of religious education which aims to be impartial, and mainly state-funded voluntary aided schools, which have a religious character, and are permitted to practise religious nurture of one form or another.[6]

Religious Education in Faith-Based Schools

With regard to faith-based schools, I agree with Archbishop Silvano Tomasi, the Apostolic Nuncio in the Holy See Mission to the United Nations, that part of the role of faith-based schools should be to 'promote tolerance of differences leading to developing mutual respect and understanding'.[7] In other words, faith-based schools in democracies should be outward looking and promote tolerance and understanding of religious diversity. Archbishop Tomasi also spoke of the need for faith schools to be sensitive to minorities. It is also important that those involved with religious nurture should be in dialogue with those involved with education about religions and beliefs, rather than in conflict with them. In recent times in England, there has been good conversation between 'religious education' and 'religious nurture', especially through the work of the Religious Education Council of England and Wales.

Why Study Religious Education?

It is instructive to step back from the activity of religious education, and the debates surrounding it, to remind ourselves of different justifications for the subject. Within fully state-funded education, concentrating on education about religions, many of the reasons given in support of the subject are instrumental. These vary according to place and time, but they include the idea that religious education should *promote knowledge and understanding of culture*. This argument is expressed in a variety of ways. In France, I have heard this view expressed in relation to understanding history and the arts.[8] Without an understanding of religion or religions, historical understanding, artistic understanding, etc. are impoverished. In the Council of Europe, this argument is articulated more broadly in relation to intercultural education, and I will go into more detail about that later. Another argument is concerned with promoting the *social development of students*. This is really a range of arguments, sometimes referring to education for democratic citizenship, sometimes to human rights education and sometimes to the promotion of social or community cohesion.[9] Under the last (Gordon Brown) Labour Government in the UK, community cohesion was a major item on the agenda, affecting various curriculum subjects including religious education.[10]

A further argument is concerned with enhancing the *personal development of students*. In English community schools, this is expressed as 'learning from religions' – the idea that religious education should not simply be concerned with learning information about religions, but should involve a reflective and discursive element. In my own work, I refer to 'reflexivity', seen as demanding both careful, sensitive and well-informed critique and 'edification', the capacity to identify aspects of tradition which have relevance, and can provide insight to others, beyond that tradition. This picture of 'edification' is quite different from *adopting* the religious stance being studied, and has some features in common with Michael Grimmitt's idea of 'learning from religion'.[11] It is also my view that activities concerned with 'understanding religion' can contribute very positively to the 'religious understanding' of young people from within faith traditions or who have a form of personal spirituality.[12]

We also should recall work from the philosophy of education in the 1960s which was more concerned with intrinsic reasons why particular areas of knowledge and experience should be included in the curriculum, and are essential to a liberal education. In the UK, for example, Paul Hirst spoke about distinct forms of knowledge or areas of human experience, including the religious.[13] In the United States, Philip Phenix wrote about distinct 'realms of meaning' essential to the educational process, including what he called 'synoptics' – such as history, religion and philosophy.[14] In both cases, education was seen to be impoverished if it excluded any distinctive area of experience, including religion or spirituality. However, it is inevitable that governments and intergovernmental organisations should respond to social needs by providing instrumental justifications. But these need to be combined with the wider liberal education argument. The UNESCO report on education – the Delors Report – combines intrinsic and instrumental reasons well when it says education is about learning to know, to do, to live together and to be. The religious and spiritual dimension is an element of all of these – especially 'learning to live together' and learning 'to be'.[15] Justifications for publicly funded faith-based education are rather different of course, although there is likely to be some overlap with the points made above.

Taking the example of England, and stepping back from particular policies of governments, we can see a change over time in the way religious education has been understood in the context of fully state-funded schools. The period starting roughly in the late 1960s was influenced by a number of trends. One of these was the process of secularisation, which influenced a wide range of fields and disciplines as well as popular culture.[16] Another was the rise of religious studies in universities, offering an academic approach to the study of religions drawing on methods from the humanities and the social sciences, including the study of several religions and bringing a global awareness to studies of religion.[17] There was also the pluralisation of society through migration.[18] Following the independence of former British colonies, migrants came to the UK in response to labour shortage and later as refugees, mainly from newly independent African states who wished to Africanise their countries. Some of you will recall the case of Uganda, in which President Amin gave residents of South Asian origin 90 days to leave the country. Many of these refugees were British passport holders and came to the UK. Instead of male migrants coming to work in order to send money back home, whole families came to the UK, from grandparents to young babies.[19] There was a very quick expansion of the presence of Hindu, Sikh and Muslim activity in many British cities, as well as the presence of less familiar styles of Caribbean and South Asian Christianity. All of these factors influenced the gradual shift from what had been a form of non-denominational, mainly Bible-based Christian teaching to a more open study of religions in fully state-funded schools.

A second phase began in the late 1990s, marked by the election of the first Blair government, and acknowledging more directly the place of religion in the public sphere. A policy which had previously allowed Catholic, Church of England and a few Jewish schools within the state voluntary aided system, was expanded to include a wider range of faith-based schools, including modest numbers of Muslim and Sikh schools, and a Hindu school.

However, it was 9/11 that marked a significant change. There was much more awareness of Islam as a global religion, but it was heavily stereotyped and misrepresented in the press and other media. The rise in Internet use also extended global awareness. Governments became concerned with the use of curriculum subjects to promote community cohesion. To be fair, in relation to religious education in England, community cohesion was never perceived by government to be the only aim for religious education, but it did dominate for some time, only to be dropped almost instantly – at least in terms of language and terminology – on the election of the coalition government in May 2010. The point here is that it is impossible to isolate a curriculum subject like religious education from these wider trends and pressures. We should always have the intrinsic argument as a reference point.

The Council of Europe

Moving to the wider European scene, it is important to consider the work of the Council of Europe post-9/11 in the field of religions and education. By way of introduction, the Council of Europe currently includes 47 European member states, plus various Observer states both from inside and outside Europe. Although its buildings are situated close to the European Parliament, it is a rather older and an entirely distinct institution. It was founded in 1949, with the aims of protecting human rights (the Universal Declaration of Human Rights had appeared a year earlier), pluralist democracy and the rule of law. Its role was also to promote awareness and development of Europe's cultural identity and diversity, aiming to promote common values whilst, at the same time, retaining distinctive national and sub-national identities. It also sought solutions to social problems, such as discrimination against minorities, xenophobia and intolerance. The Council of Europe is both a political institution and a project-based one. It has a Parliamentary Assembly which includes Members of Parliament from the member states (currently four from Ireland), not Members of the European Parliament. Its most powerful political body is the Committee of Ministers, consisting of the Foreign Ministers of the member states, including the Irish Foreign Minister, of course. Each member state has a diplomat based in Strasbourg who conducts business on behalf of the Minister for much of the time. Education is included in the brief of one of the Directorates of the Council of Europe, and there is a Head of Education who oversees educational projects and their relationship with the political domain of the Council's work. Projects produce publications and other outputs. If the findings of a project are considered significant, then the Committee of Ministers might make a Recommendation to the member states, encouraging its discussion in the formation of policy at a national or regional level. Such Recommendations are not made lightly and receive much deliberation and revision before being finalised. However, they are essentially discussion documents and carry no legal obligation, but they have to be agreed by all Foreign Ministers. I shall return later to a particular Recommendation from the Committee of Ministers.

As with individual states, European institutions, such as the Council of Europe, were influenced by the events of 11 September 2001 and their consequences. The Council of Europe, being based in Strasbourg, had been influenced by the French view of *laïcité*, and concentrated its work in public education on such fields as intercultural education, human rights education and education for democratic citizenship, as well as on curriculum subjects such as history and modern languages. The study of religion was regarded as part of the private sphere and concerned religious bodies rather than the state. Thus, prior to 9/11, there was no project on religions based in the Council of Europe. I was at a meeting in 2002 in Strasbourg in which the then Secretary

General, Walther Schwimmer, referred to 9/11 as a 'wake-up call' for the Council of Europe in relation to religion and education. It was eventually agreed that the Council of Europe should have a project addressing issues in the study of religious diversity in school settings. This was most certainly *not* an attempt to interfere with the role of religious organisations in the nurture of young people from those backgrounds into faith, but rather to promote understanding of religious diversity for *all* young Europeans, regardless of their background.

The way in which the Council of Europe works is to introduce new aspects of study in relation to its core areas of concern. Thus, on the basis that all should be able to agree that, at the very least, the existence of religion in society is a part of culture, learning about religious diversity could be seen as contributing to intercultural education – intercultural education being one of the Council of Europe's key priorities. There was no intention here to *reduce* religion to culture; this conceptualisation was a strategy for including the study of religions in the Council's educational programme. Of course, this approach is a subset of 'education about religions'; it is distinct from religious instruction or religious nurture, but I would argue that some of its aspects, especially the cultivation of sensitivities and competences needed to understand the positions of others, are highly relevant to the development of an outward looking faith-based education.

Thus, a project was established in 2002 entitled Intercultural Education and the Challenge of Religious Diversity and Dialogue. There were various milestones in the project. One was a meeting in Paris in 2003 in which religious education specialists worked together with specialists from intercultural education. This was a highly productive meeting in which many misunderstandings were removed, and it saw the birth of some fruitful, ongoing collaborative work. Another was a large-scale conference in Oslo in 2004, including members of faith groups, educators and policymakers from many member states.[20] As a result of this conference, the Council of Europe established a specialist group to write a reference book for schools in Europe, introducing some techniques and pedagogical principles for handling religious material in the classroom.[21]

The most important document to appear was a Recommendation from the Committee of Ministers. A team was brought together to draft the Recommendation on behalf of the Committee of Ministers on the management of religious and 'convictional' diversity in schools, based on the project's approach, and incorporating ideas from the White Paper on Intercultural Dialogue.[22] The Recommendation was adopted by the Committee of Ministers in December 2008, and provides a set of principles that can be used by all member states. The Recommendation can be used as a tool in discussing policy in religious education and related fields and should be studied and discussed in all member states. Regardless of the level of experience in the subject, and regardless of the type of religious education traditionally offered in member states (if any), there is a good deal to learn from its discussion.

I will give an indication of the dialogical ethos of the document. For example, its underlying principles include the view that intercultural dialogue and its dimension of religious and non-religious convictions are an essential precondition (although not a sufficient condition) for the development of tolerance and a culture of 'living together' and for the recognition of different identities on the basis of human rights.

Its objectives include:
- developing a tolerant attitude and respect for the right to hold a particular belief … (recognising) the inherent dignity and fundamental freedoms of each human being;
- nurturing a sensitivity to the diversity of religions and non-religious convictions as an element contributing to the richness of Europe;
- ensuring that teaching about the diversity of religions and non-religious convictions is consistent with the aims of education for democratic citizenship, human rights and respect for equal dignity of all individuals;
- promoting communication and dialogue between people from different cultural, religious and non-religious backgrounds;

Its educational preconditions include:
- sensitivity to the equal dignity of every individual;
- recognition of human rights as values to be applied, beyond religious and cultural diversity;
- communication between individuals and the capacity to put oneself in the place of others in order to establish an environment where mutual trust and understanding is fostered;
- co-operative learning in which peoples of all traditions can be included and participate;
- provision of a safe learning space to encourage expression without fear of being judged or held to ridicule;

With regard to teacher training, member states are requested to:
- provide teachers with the training and means to acquire relevant teaching resources with the aim to develop the … skills (*for teaching about*) religions and non-religious convictions;
- provide training that is objective and open-minded;
- develop training in methods of teaching and learning which ensure education in democracy at local, regional, national and international level;
- encourage multiperspectivity in … training courses, to take into account … different points of view in teaching and learning;

The 'human rights' ethos of the document is clear. Of course, there are issues surrounding the UN Universal Declaration on Human Rights (1948), including its Western and European Enlightenment pedigree, and its cultural relativity. Nevertheless, written in the shadow of totalitarianism that produced the

Holocaust, it still provides a powerful statement of Western democratic values, and a reference point for ongoing discussion and clarification of concepts such as 'human dignity'. Article 18 concerns freedom of religion or belief, and this value underpins the Council of Europe Recommendation.

The European Wergeland Centre

The European Wergeland Centre (EWC), named after Henrik Wergeland, a nineteenth-century Norwegian poet who stood up for religious freedom, is a European resource centre on education for intercultural understanding, human rights and democratic citizenship, incorporating cross-cutting topics such as religion, history, language and gender. The idea for the Centre came from the Council of Europe, where separate proposals for a European Centre concentrating on citizenship and human rights and another concentrating on religion and education were merged.[23] The Norwegian Government offered to establish the Centre in co-operation with the Council of Europe. The EWC, which caters for all the member states of the Council of Europe, and uses English as its working language, is situated in Oslo and was opened officially in May 2009. The main client groups are teachers, teacher trainers, decision makers and multipliers within education for intercultural understanding, human rights and democratic citizenship across Europe. An important feature of the EWC is its 'Share & Connect' database through which teachers, teacher trainers and researchers can form networks and contact one another. A joint project currently being conducted by the European Wergeland Centre in collaboration with the Council of Europe is concerned with encouraging discussion of the Recommendation, CM/Rec (2008) 12, in member states; the present chapter aims to facilitate that dialogue in the case of Ireland.

The Organisation for Security and Co-operation in Europe and the Toledo Guiding Principles

Independently of the Council of Europe, a second major European institution concerned with human rights also considered the place of the study of religions and beliefs (non-religious world views) in public education. This is the Organisation for Security and Co-operation in Europe (OSCE), based in Vienna. The OSCE is the largest regional security organization in Europe. Its 56 participant states include most European countries plus the United States and Canada. It was set up in the 1970s to create a forum for dialogue during the Cold War. The OSCE employs the idea of 'three dimensional security'. Security is not only considered in politico-military terms but also through its human dimension and an environmental and economic dimension.

Because of the human dimension to security, OSCE has an Office for Democratic Institutions and Human Rights (ODIHR), which is based in Warsaw. As with the Council of Europe, the ODIHR conducted a project to identify principles on which participant states could develop policy and practice for teaching about religions and non-religious beliefs in schools across its huge geographical region. The result was the production of a standard setting document, the *Toledo Guiding Principles on Teaching about Religions and Beliefs in Public Schools*, named after the city in which the drafting team first worked on the text, and in recognition of Toledo's historical role in communication between those of different religions.

The Toledo Guiding Principles complement the Council of Europe Recommendation. They were produced as a contribution to an improved understanding of the world's increasing religious (and philosophical) diversity and the growing presence of religion in the public sphere. Their rationale is based on the view that there is positive value in teaching that emphasises respect for the individual's right to freedom of religion and belief, and that teaching about religions and beliefs can, in principle, help to reduce misunderstandings and stereotypes.

The primary purpose of the Toledo Guiding Principles is to assist OSCE participating States in promoting the study of religions and beliefs in schools. They also aim to offer criteria that should be considered when and wherever teaching about religions and beliefs takes place.[24] They offer guidance on preparing curricula for teaching about religions and beliefs, preferred procedures for assuring fairness in the development of curricula, and standards for how they could be implemented. The Toledo Guiding Principles were developed by an inter-disciplinary team including members of the ODIHR Advisory Council of Experts on Freedom of Religion or Belief. The members were picked for their particular expertise, not as representatives of different religions or world views. However, they happened to be from a cross section of religious and philosophical backgrounds. Thus there were Christians, Jews, Muslims and Humanists plus one member of a 'new religious movement'.

The underlying argument for the inclusion of the study of religions and beliefs in public education has a human rights emphasis. The first premise is that freedom of religion or belief predicates plurality: if freedom of religion or belief is a given for society, then society inevitably will be plural. The next premise is that, if society is to be cohesive, plurality requires tolerance of difference. The conclusion is that tolerance of difference requires *at least* knowledge and understanding of the beliefs and values of others. Thus, the document supports the inclusion of a just and fair approach to religious difference, whatever the system of religious education or education about religion in particular states.

The Toledo Guiding Principles include a substantial chapter on the human rights framework – including useful discussions of legal issues in relation to the state and the rights of parents, children, teachers and minorities, as well as chapters on preparing curricula and teacher education, plus conclusions and recommendations. The *Toledo Guiding Principles* were approved by the Ministerial Council and launched at the 15th OSCE Ministerial Council meeting held in Madrid in November 2007.

In concluding this section, it should be clear that both the Council of Europe and OSCE documents are intended as tools for those discussing the place of religion in education within European democracies. They are not intended as finished programmes, curricula or syllabuses, and are expected to be discussed, adapted and developed in different ways within different systems of education.

European Research: the REDCo Project

There have been a number of collaborative European research projects in religious education. However, the first to obtain substantial funding from the European Commission for a major mixed methods study was the REDCo (Religion, Education, Dialogue, Conflict) project, funded by the Framework 6 initiative. REDCo was a three-year project (2006–9) involving universities from eight European countries (University of Warwick, England; Universities of Hamburg and Münster, Germany; VU University, the Netherlands; University of Stavanger, Norway; Russian Christian Academy for Humanities, St Petersburg, Russia; Tartu University, Estonia; the Sorbonne, Paris, France and the University of Granada, Spain). The project aimed to establish whether studies of religions in schools could help to promote dialogue and reduce conflict in school and society. The main research focused on young people in the 14–16 age group, but there were also some studies of primary pupils and some action research studies in secondary schools and teacher training using the interpretive approach.[25] The key concepts of the interpretive approach were used as a stimulus to method and theory throughout in the REDCo Project.[26] Core studies included a mapping exercise of religion and education in Europe; a qualitative study of teenagers' views on religion in schools; a cross-national quantitative survey of young people's views in the eight countries; studies of classroom interaction; and a study of teachers.[27]

Selected Findings from Qualitative and Quantitative Studies

Each of the REDCo national studies gives a flavour of the particular national situation where it was located and needs to be examined in some detail. However, some broad trends emerged from the data. Qualitative questionnaires and interviews completed by 14–16 year olds and a quantitative survey, conducted with the same age group in the eight countries participating in the REDCo Project, revealed some general trends that are of relevance to the evaluation and implementation of the policies advocated by the Council of Europe and the Office for Democratic Institution and Human Rights of the OSCE. These might be summarised very briefly as follows:

- Students wish for peaceful coexistence across differences, and believe this to be possible.
- For students peaceful coexistence depends on knowledge about each other's religions and world views and on sharing common interests/doing things together.
- Students who learn about religious diversity in school are *more willing* to have conversations about religions/beliefs with students of other backgrounds than those who do not.
- Students wish to avoid conflict: some religiously-committed students feel vulnerable.
- Students want learning to take place in a safe classroom environment where there are agreed procedures for expression and discussion.
- *Most* students would like school to be a place for learning *about* different religions/world views, rather than for instruction *into* a particular religion/world view (respondents tended to support the system of which they had personal experience).[28]

Dissemination of the REDCo Project continues (Jackson 2012a), including by the European Wergeland Centre, who organised dissemination workshops and conferences in Austria, Norway and Germany during 2010, and in Spain in 2012. Dissemination work has shown a synergy between the findings of the REDCo project and the Council of Europe Recommendation and there is scope for developing materials and training programmes drawing on the REDCo findings and the Ministerial Recommendation.

Having made these points, the various REDCo studies suggest that approaches to the study of religious diversity would need to be implemented differently in particular national contexts. For example, in some countries (e.g. England), religious diversity would be covered mainly in a *separate subject* devoted to the study of religion, while in others (e.g. France) religious diversity would be covered through *several* subjects, with none dedicated specifically to religion. In some countries, religious diversity could be linked to students' discussion of their *personal views* (e.g. the Netherlands, Norway, England, Germany), while in others, this would be more difficult (e.g. France and Estonia). In some countries (e.g. Estonia, France, Norway) religious diversity would be covered in a non-confessional setting, while in others (e.g. Spain), religious diversity would be taught in a confessional context, and steps would need to be taken to ensure fairness, balance and objectivity in teaching and learning. In some countries, religious diversity would be taught in *both* confessional and non-confessional contexts (e.g. the Netherlands, England).

Conclusion
European policy development and research concerning religious education have contributed positively to discussion about the rationale for the study of religions in public education, building networks of communication for exchanging ideas on pedagogy and policy and for collaborative research.

European research is highly relevant to discussions at a national level. For example, research from REDCo and on comparative religious education shows that the relationship between theory, policy and practice in particular countries is complex; it is not simply 'top down', and also includes a range of supra and sub national influences which should be taken into account.[29]

In the case of Ireland, a distinction has been made at the first conference of the Irish Centre for Religious Education between 'mutual ground' and 'neutral ground' in relation to 'teaching religion'. Discussion should take account of the need to balance children's, parents' and teachers' rights in relation to freedom of religion and belief, together with the interests of patrons and of the state. The promotion of a shared public understanding concerning the contribution of teaching religion and beliefs to personal and social development, for conceptual and legal clarity in defining key terms, and for 'the responsibility of all schools to respectfully and creatively accommodate the actual diversity of religion and beliefs manifest within their educational communities' was argued for by Andrew McGrady at the conference.[30] I hope sincerely that both the standard setting documents from the Council of Europe and the OSCE, together with the findings of European research, are of service to educators and others in the Republic of Ireland in pursuing these tasks and taking forward the important discussion of the study of religions in schools.

NOTES

1. A.G. McGrady, 'Religious Education in the Republic of Ireland', in *Religious Education in Europe: Situation and Current Trends in Schools*, ed. by E. Kuyk et al. (Oslo: Iko & ICCS, 2007), pp. 107–113.

2. B. Grelle, 'Defining and Promoting the Study of Religion in British and American Schools', in *International Handbook of the Religious, Moral and Spiritual Dimensions of Education*, ed. by M. de Souza et al. (Dordrecht: Springer Academic Publishers, 2006), pp. 461–474; D. Chidester, 'Religious Education in South Africa', in *International Handbook*, ed. by De Souza et al., pp. 433–448.

3. *The Toledo Guiding Principles on Teaching about Religions and Beliefs in Public Schools*. (Warsaw: Organisation for Security and Co-operation in Europe, Office for Democratic Institutions and Human Rights, 2007.) Full text available at <http://www.osce.org/odihr/29154> [accessed 10 Feb. 2012].

4. Ronald W. Morris, 'Cultivating Reflection and Understanding: Foundations and Orientations of Québec's Ethics and Religious Culture Program', *Religion & Education*, 38 (2011), pp. 188–211' S.J. McKinney and J.C. Conroy, 'Religious Education in Scotland', in *Religious Education in Europe*, ed. by E. Kuyk et al., pp. 223–229.

5. M. Estivalezes, 'Teaching about Religion at School in France', in *International Handbook*, ed. by de Souza et al., pp. 475–486; J.P. Willaime, 'Teaching Religious Issues in French Public Schools: From Abstentionist *Laïcité* to a Return of Religion to Public Education', in *Religion and Education in Europe: Developments, Contexts and Debates*, ed. by R. Jackson et al. (Münster: Waxmann, 2007), pp. 87–101.

6. Department for Children Schools and Families (DCSF), *Faith in the System: The Role of Schools with a Religious Character in English Education and Society* (London: Department of Children Schools and Families, 2007); A. Dinham and R. Jackson, 'Religion, Welfare and Education', in *Religion and Change in Modern Britain*, ed. by L. Woodhead and R. Catto (London: RoutledgeFalmer, 2012), pp. 272–294.

7. S. Tomasi, 'Freedom of Religion or Belief in Education', OSCE Supplementary Human Dimension Meeting, Vienna, 9–10 Dec. 2010. Final report of the meeting available at <http://www.osce.org/odihr/75755> [accessed 9 Feb. 2012].

8. Régis Debray, *L'enseignment du fait religieux dans L'École laïque: Rapport au Ministre de l'Éducation nationale* (Paris: Odile Jacob, 2002).

9. *International Perspectives on Citizenship, Education and Religious Diversity*, ed. by R. Jackson (London: RoutledgeFalmer, 2003); *The Toledo Guiding Principles; Materials Used to Teach about World Religions in Schools in England*, ed. by R. Jackson et al. (London: Department for Children, Schools and Families, 2010) <http://www2.warwick.ac.uk/fac/soc/wie/research/wreru/research/completed/dcsf> [accessed 9 Feb. 2012].

10. Department for Children, Schools and Families, *Guidance on the Duty to Promote Community Cohesion* (London: Department of Children, Schools and Families, 2007); *Religious Education in English Schools: Non-statutory Guidance 2010* (London: Department for Children, Schools and Families, 2010).

11. R. Jackson, *Religious Education: An Interpretive Approach* (London: Hodder and Stoughton, 1997), pp. 131–32; R. Jackson, *Rethinking Religious Education and Plurality: Issues in Diversity and Pedagogy* (London: RoutledgeFalmer, 2004).

12. E. Cox, 'Understanding Religion and Religious Understanding', *British Journal of Religious Education*, 6 (1983), pp. 3–13.

13. P. Hirst, 'Liberal Education and the Nature of Knowledge', in *Philosophical Analysis and Education*, ed. by R.D. Archambault (London: Routledge and Kegan Paul, 1965), pp. 113–138.

14. P.H. Phenix, *Realms of Meaning* (New York: McGraw-Hill, 1964).

15. *Learning: the Treasure Within (the Delors Report), The Report to UNESCO of the International Commission on Education for the Twenty-first Century* (Paris: UNESCO, 1996).

16. E. Cox, *Changing Aims in Religious Education* (London: Routledge, 1966).

17. Ninian Smart, *Secular Education and the Logic of Religion* (London: Faber, 1968).

18. W. Owen Cole, *Religion in the Multifaith School*, first edn (Yorkshire: Yorkshire Committee for Community Relations, 1972).

19. R. Jackson and E. Nesbitt, *Hindu Children in Britain* (Stoke on Trent: Trentham, 1993).

20. Council of Europe, *The Religious Dimension of Intercultural Education* (Strasbourg: Council of Europe Publishing, 2004).

21. R. Jackson, 'The Interpretive Approach', in *Religious Diversity and Intercultural Education: A Reference Book for Schools*, ed. by J. Keast (Strasbourg: Council of Europe Publishing, 2007), pp. 79–85.

22. Council of Europe, *White Paper on Intercultural Dialogue: 'Living Together as Equals with Dignity'* (Strasbourg: Council of Europe Publishing, 2008).

23. R. Jackson, 'European Institutions and the Contribution of Studies of Religious Diversity to Education for Democratic Citizenship', in *Religion and Education in Europe*, ed. by R. Jackson et al., pp. 27–55.

24. *The Toledo Guiding Principles*, pp. 11–12.

25. U. McKenna, J. Ipgrave, and R. Jackson, *Inter Faith Dialogue by Email in Primary Schools: An Evaluation of the Building E-Bridges Project* (Münster: Waxmann, 2008); *Religious Education Research through a Community of Practice: Action Research and the Interpretive Approach*, ed. by J. Ipgrave, R. Jackson, and K. O'Grady (Münster: Waxmann, 2009).

26.   R. Jackson, *Religious Education: An Interpretive Approach* (London: Hodder and Stoughton, 1997); R. Jackson, *Rethinking Religious Education and Plurality: Issues in Diversity and Pedagogy* (London: RoutledgeFalmer, 2004); R. Jackson, 'The Interpretive Approach as a Research Tool: Inside the REDCo Project', *British Journal of Religious Education*, 33 (2011), pp. 189–208; R. Jackson, 'The Interpretive Approach as a Research Tool: Inside the REDCo Project', in *Religion, Education, Dialogue and Conflict: Perspectives on Religious Education Research*, R. Jackson (London: Routledge, 2012), pp. 84–102.

27.   *Religion and Education in Europe*, ed. by R. Jackson et al.; *Encountering Religious Pluralism in School and Society: A Qualitative Study of Teenage Perspectives in Europe*, ed. by T. Knauth et al. (Münster: Waxmann, 2008); *Teenagers' Perspectives on the Role of Religion in Their Lives, Schools and Societies: A Quantitative Study*, ed. by P. Valk et al. (Münster: Waxmann, 2009); *Dialogue and Conflict on Religion: Studies of Classroom Interaction in European Countries*, ed. by I. ter Avest et al. (Münster: Waxmann, 2009); *Teachers Responding to Religious Diversity in Europe: Researching Biography and Pedagogy*, ed. by A. van der Want et al. (Münster: Waxmann, 2009).

28.   The various presentations made in Brussels at the European Parliament by REDCo members, plus summaries of findings, can be read at <http://www.redco.unihamburg.de/web/3480/4176/index.html> [accessed 9 Feb. 2012].

29.   *Encountering Religious Pluralism in School and Society*, ed. by T. Kanuth et al.; Oddrun M.H. Braaten, 'A Comparative Study of Religious Education in State Schools in England and Norway' (unpublished PhD Thesis, University of Warwick, 2010).

30.   See Chapter Four of this volume: A.G. McGrady, 'Teaching Religion': Challenges and Opportunities for Educational Practice in a Pluralist Context.

CHAPTER TWO

RELIGION, EDUCATION AND THE APPEAL TO PLURALITY: THEOLOGICAL CONSIDERATIONS ON THE CONTEMPORARY EUROPEAN CONTEXT

Terrence Merrigan

Religion: The Problem of Definition

The first problem confronting those who seek to reflect on the nature and significance of 'religion' is the very meaning of the term. Precisely because the notion of religion is so multifaceted, it is important to establish clearly what an author or institution understands by this term, especially if what is at stake is public – and educational – policy.

Religion, for the purposes of this paper, is understood as 'a form of life',[1] constituted by a complex 'set of practices, images, stories, and concepts',[2] that 'seems to those who belong to it to be comprehensive, incapable of abandonment, and of central importance to the ordering of their lives'.[3] This 'form of life' will almost inevitably comprise patterns of thought and behaviour which are simply incompatible with 'at least some alternative options'.[4] Moreover, the religious man or woman will regard their lifestyle and beliefs as 'constitutive of a final human fulfilment' and as the most appropriate (if not the only available) means 'of achieving that fulfilment.'[5] Religion is, then, in the words of one commentator, 'the great circle that seems to religious people to contain all the small circles representing their non-comprehensive forms of life.'[6]

This approach to religion has its roots in the thought of Paul Tillich (1886–1965) who famously described religion as the 'experience of ultimate concern'.[7] The question of the legitimacy of the claims of religious traditions regarding what they portray as matters of 'ultimate concern' need not deter us here (though, to do him justice, Tillich addressed this issue quite directly). What is of greater interest, for us, is the recognition that the acknowledgement (or experience) of an 'ultimate concern' has an impact on much more than the inner life of the religious person. According to Joachim Wach, a noted historian of religions (who influenced, and was influenced by Tillich), religious experience inevitably manifests itself in the development of distinctive patterns of thought, behaviour and communitarian forms of life. That is to say, the person who has identified their 'ultimate concern' will give public expression to – and seek public support for – their convictions concerning what they regard as 'unconditionally important'[8] for their life and well-being, and they will do so in ways that have an impact on the intellectual, the ethical and the socio-cultural life of a society.[9] Indeed, Wach insisted that it is precisely this 'activistic note' which distinguishes religious experience from aesthetic experience.[10] Wach points out that 'action' here 'should be understood, in a very broad sense, as opposed not to contemplation but to sluggish inaction or indifference'.[11]

Religion, in this view of things, is not a cultural artifact; it is a cultural phenomenon in its own right with a distinctive rationality, ethic, and ritual. The goal of the religious man or woman is to immerse themselves ever more deeply in their tradition, with a view to appropriating its world view, its ethical norms, and its religious object. Bernard Lonergan described this as a threefold process of 'conversion' that is played out on the level of cognition (intellectual conversion), action (moral conversion) and devotion (religious conversion). The reasoning of the religious person is then, ideally, the reasoning of the whole person, the thinking, willing, feeling, imagining subject who draws upon every 'faculty' to orient herself in the world. Religion's power over its adherents is rooted precisely in the depth and breadth of its *existential* claim, that is to say, its claim to address the question of 'the meaning and fulfilment of [its adherents'] lives'[12] and to provide them with the cognitive, practical, and symbolic tools to find that meaning and fulfilment.

The question which must be asked is whether this view of religion is still possible within the European context and what this might mean, both in the short and long term, for the future of religious education.

The Approach to Religion: The Challenge for European Policymakers

For a number of years now, a debate has raged among sociologists of religion about whether Europe qualifies as an 'exceptional case', as a region where the fate of religion and religious practice deviates from the global norm. Initially, it was European sociologists of religion who described the United Sates as a special case, perplexed as they were by the fact that the population of a Protestant (and capitalist), liberal democracy with roots in the European Enlightenment persisted in being so publicly religious. In time, the tables were turned and the claim was advanced that it was Europe that was out of step with the rest of the world. American sociologists highlighted the distinctive character of the European process of 'secularization', that is to say, the process by means of which religion retires – or is forcibly removed – from public life and, barring its outright demise, takes up residence in the privacy of people's minds and hearts.[13]

José Casanova, for example, pointed out that the European experience of the union between throne and altar (or church and state) and the European churches' resistance to the Enlightenment's cognitive and political critiques of religion were not part of the American experience. The upshot of this was that the culture of hostility to religion that was so characteristic of the development of modern Europe was foreign to the Americas where religious affiliation often proved to be a powerful force for good among immigrant populations.[14]

In the 'New World', religion had been obliged, from the outset, to accommodate itself to a liberal, democratic regime and to accept that its sphere of influence was something to be earned and continually renegotiated in a complex and multilayered society. In sociological terms, this meant that religion was obliged to come to terms with the fact of 'functional differentiation', that is to say, the division of labor among a variety of social actors. Religion's ability to secure a piece of the social fabric, so to speak, ensured that it was neither marginalized nor condemned to terminal decline.

In Casanova's view, European theorists have tended to conflate the process of functional differentiation with both the decline and the marginalization or privatization of religion. These three uneven and quite distinctive movements (differentiation, decline, and privatization) are lumped together in the word, 'secularization', and meaningful discourse about the nature and future of religion is made nearly impossible. The claim that we live in a 'secular' society is taken to mean that religion has had its day, that where it persists it is a marginal and transitory phenomenon, a matter for the individual subject, and that – in the best of all possible worlds – it should have no claim on the public's attention or the public purse.

In the case of Europe, in particular, Casanova contends that there is a 'secularist self-understanding built into modern European identities,' and that this self-understanding 'affects the handling of "religious" issues, turning them into paradoxes' of the kind which haunt, for example, the question of Turkey's accession to a European Union that is ostensibly blind to religious differences.[15] This 'secularist self-understanding' is a corollary of the European understanding of secularization discussed above, and consists of the view that 'the decline [of religion in Europe] [is] "normal" and "progressive",' that is to say, 'a quasi-normative consequence of being a "modern" and "enlightened" European.' Elsewhere, Casanova describes 'the basic premise of the secularisation paradigm' as the view that 'the more modern a society the more secular it becomes.'[16]

According to Casanova, 'secularization became a self-fulfilling prophecy in Europe,' or a 'taken-for-granted belief,' from the moment that 'large sectors of the population of Western European societies, including the Christian churches,' came to regard secularization as the inevitable outcome of modernity.[17] The secularist mindset which, according to Casanova, has 'the European mind' and the social sciences in its 'spell',[18] refuses to acknowledge 'the "really existing" religious and secular pluralisms and the multiple European modernities,' and insists instead on 'the idea of a single secular modernity, emerging out of the Enlightenment'. According to this view, 'only secular neutrality is supposed to guarantee liberal tolerance and pluralist multicultural recognition in an expanded European Union'.[19]

This gives rise to what Casanova calls 'the secularist paradox,' namely, 'that, in the name of freedom, individual autonomy, tolerance, and cultural pluralism, religious people – Christian, Jewish, and Muslim – are being asked to keep their religious beliefs, identities, and norms "private" so that they do not disturb the project of a modern, secular, enlightened Europe'. This 'secular' identity is 'shared by European elites and ordinary people alike'. It gives rise to the view that 'it is best to banish religion from the public sphere' where it will inevitably serve as a source of conflicts and tension.[20] Increasingly, it would seem, Europe's discourse is one of 'global secular cosmopolitanism'.[21] And it is characteristic of this discourse that it cannot accommodate religion.

It is this secularist paradox which led the British sociologist of religion, Grace Davie, to inquire whether the paradigm that such presuppositions engender can actually serve 'to create and to sustain a truly tolerant and pluralist society ... a society which goes well beyond an individualized live-and-let-live philosophy; a society able to accommodate "that unusual phenomenon" in contemporary Europe, the person (of whatever faith) *who takes religion seriously*' [our emphasis].[22]

Casanova objects to the notion that the European experience justifies the formulation of 'a prescriptive normative theory of how religious institutions ought to behave in the modern world'. The European paradigm must, therefore, be critiqued. According to Casanova, such a critique ought to focus on three 'particular, historically based – that is, ethnocentric – prejudices' that characterise modern secularization theory. These are '[i] its bias for Protestant subjective forms of religion, [ii] its bias for "liberal" conceptions of politics and of the "public sphere", and [iii] its bias for the sovereign nation-state as the systemic unit of analysis.'[23]

What is being called for here is a re-conceptualization of religion, one that seeks to uncover – or perhaps more accurately, recover – its communitarian dimension, its rootedness in culture, and its resistance to abstraction. Put more simply, what is needed is a reconsideration of religion's communitarian, cultural and irreducibly plural character. In what follows, I will consider these three dimensions of religion and, in each case, attempt to formulate a proposal regarding what such a re-conceptualization implies for anthropologists, theologians and educators.

RETHINKING RELIGION AND RELIGIOUS EDUCATION

The Communitarian Character of Religion

The idea that religion is a comprehensive 'form of life,' constituted by ritual, normative practices, established patterns of behaviour, and so forth would probably sound foreign to many of our contemporaries.

From a historical perspective, it should – in theory – sound most foreign to those from a Protestant background. The principle of *sola fide* determined that the Protestant religious trajectory would be directed inwards. And Hegel did indeed famously declare that the 'distinctively Protestant principle' was 'interiority' or 'inwardness,' a principle which inevitably brought with it the 'rejection' of 'externality and authority' as 'impertinent and lifeless'.[24] The nature of the Enlightenment and post-Enlightenment critique of religion in Protestant lands was adapted to this trajectory. There, it was the very idea of God (and hence of religion) that came under attack.

The *sacramental principle* determined that the Catholic religious trajectory would be directed outwards, in the direction of the visible Church with its teaching and ritual. As St Cyprian expressed it, 'He cannot have God for his father, who has not the church for his mother.' The nature of the Enlightenment and post-Enlightenment critique of religion in Catholic lands was adapted to this trajectory. There, it was the politicized institutional Church and its doctrinal system that came under attack.

In both cases, the upshot of the critique was the reinforcement of the growing conviction that religion was best left to the individual to do with as he or she pleased. In both cases, too, the response, on the part of those charged with defending religion, was rather predictable. Schleiermacher sought to turn the tables on the Protestant despisers of religion by situating it in the heart of subjective experience, namely, the (universal) feeling of 'absolute dependence'. And Rome sought to reassert both its power and its doctrinal tradition by means of, for example, the dogma of papal infallibility.

In the time that has passed since Schleiermacher's defense of religious experience and Rome's assertion of tradition and authority, the modern turn to the subject has been radicalized by the post-modern questioning of the subject's own essential identity. Somewhat paradoxically, the threat to the subject has brought about a renewed interest, among Protestant theologians, in tradition. So, for example, we find the Lutheran theologian, George Lindbeck, writing that, 'There are numberless thoughts we cannot think, sentiments we cannot have, and realities we cannot perceive unless we learn to use the appropriate symbol systems ... Unless we acquire language of some kind, we cannot actualize our specifically human capacities of thought, action and feeling. Similarly ... to become religious involves becoming skilled in the language, the symbol system of a given religion.'[25]

In his celebrated essay, 'Religion as a Cultural System' (1966), Clifford Geertz lamented the fact that anthropologists spent far too much time investigating the impact of a particular religion on 'socio-structural and psychological processes,' and far too little examining 'the system of meanings embodied in the symbols which make up the religion proper'. The study of the specifics of a religion (and Geertz means a species of religion, not the generic type) is, according to Geertz, 'what most needs to be elucidated'.[26] While Geertz acknowledges that every 'description' of the culture, religious or otherwise, of the 'other' is to some degree subjective, the goal remains to do justice to 'the interpretations to which persons of a particular denomination subject their experience, because that is what they profess to be descriptions of'.[27]

The Protestant turn to the so-called 'cultural-linguistic' character of religion is not unproblematic and it is certainly not equivalent to the Catholic view of tradition. Nevertheless, it does reflect a shared realization that cuts across denominational lines, namely, that religion (for the religious) is not reducible to a collection of 'data' to be assessed, or a series of propositions that can be taught, or to a set of practices that effect predictable results. In this regard, we might say of religion in general what John Henry Newman said of Catholicism in particular, namely, that it is 'a deep matter – you cannot take it up in a teacup'.[28]

To acknowledge the complexity of religion, that is to say, to recognise that it is the fruit of communitarian life, that its 'logic' is only fully comprehensible within a communitarian framework, and that its claims to truth are part of a complex communitarian discourse, is to acknowledge that distinctive religious traditions cannot be treated in a monolithic fashion. Islam, for example, is a multifaceted reality, and to ignore or minimize its internal divisions may make the work of the sociologist or the educationalist neater, but it will also make it largely irrelevant to those who wish to understand the so-called 'Islamic' world.

'Thick description' of a specific denomination or movement within a religious tradition is essential to the comprehension of that tradition.[29] In fact, I would argue that, in the case of religions, the starting point must be the species and not the genus. The upshot of this claim might be formulated as follows: *All those who would seek to interpret or present a religious tradition ought to endeavour to do justice to the interpretations offered by adherents of that tradition since, in the final analysis, what is at stake is their particular experience of reality, an experience that is only accessible through their 'descriptions' of it.*

The Cultural Character of Religion

The father of modern sociology, Emile Durkheim, predicted that the cult of the individual would become modern society's new religion. It is not at all surprising that this new 'religion' has proved extremely useful as a means of legitimating and reinforcing 'the autonomy of the primary institutions' that are vital to the organization of the modern state and the modern economy, as opposed to voluntary or secondary institutions.[30] Thomas Luckmann, who diagnosed the privatization of religion and coined the phrase 'invisible religion' to describe the modern emphasis on 'the pursuit of individual autonomy through self-expression and self-actualisation' regarded the social trends that promote this process as most probably 'irreversible'.[31] Casanova challenges the presumption that privatization is a 'modern structural trend'. In his view, this represents a 'historical option' or 'a modern "preferred option"', but ... an option nevertheless'. Privatization is encouraged by modern differentiation. It suits the modern taste for individualism and subjective experience, but, and this is more problematic, it is 'mandated ideologically by liberal categories of thought which permeate not only political ideologies and constitutional theories but the entire structure of modern Western thought'.[32]

Modern secularization theory displays a 'bias for "liberal" conceptions of politics and of the "public sphere"'. As far as religion is concerned, liberalism means the insistence, indeed the determination, that religion, as far as possible, be kept out of public debate and even public life.[33] This demand is an extension of the view that religion is a private matter. This view is evident, in 'secularised' Europe, in proposals such as the one made recently by 'Liberal' Belgian politicians to remove all religious symbols, including the many large crosses that are characteristic of Belgian cemeteries, from public view, and a recent court case in Italy that was centred on a request to remove crucifixes from publicly-funded schools. The irony of such cases is that they appeal to the pluralistic character of contemporary European culture to demand the removal of those particular signs and symbols which make plurality visible. On the basis of such debates, one might be forgiven for concluding that whatever else modern European culture may be, it apparently does not allow for a great deal of manifest particularity.

We shall return to the theme of plurality and particularity in the following consideration. What is of interest at this point is the claim, whether implicit (as in the debate about the 'preamble' to the so-called European Constitution) or explicit (as in the cases just mentioned) that religion ought to have no significant role in the determination of European self-understanding.

As we have already indicated, from a theological point of view such a claim is simply indefensible because of its outright denial of the essentially communitarian nature of religion, in the sense that it is both a communitarian activity and a bearer of communitarian wisdom. From a political point of view, however, the claim is much more insidious because it is a demand to leave the public sphere to other actors. (The economic crisis now rolling over Europe [and the rest of the world] should give us 'cause to pause' as regards the competency and perhaps even the sincerity of some of those actors.) To the degree that religion is communitarian, it is inevitably political, and the political potency of religion is currently very much on display in non-European regions of the world (such as Myanmar, the Islamic nations, India, etc.). Of course, the political impotency of 'European' religion is problematic but might it not be the case that this is a peculiarly European development, and one that it may well be wrong to regard as an inevitable (or universal) process?

Casanova has contended that 'the European "norm" of secularization warrants some more critical scrutiny'.[34] Indeed, he has stated quite categorically that,

> It is time to abandon the Euro-centric view that modern Western European developments, including the secularization of Western Christianity, are general universal processes. The more one adopts a global perspective, the more it becomes obvious that the drastic secularization of Western European societies is a rather exceptional phenomenon, with few parallels elsewhere other than in European settler societies such as New Zealand, Québec, or Uruguay [and perhaps, most recently, Brazil].[35]

Where religion retains its communitarian power, it is also able to exercise its political power. Clearly, it has not always done this in ways that correspond to some of its most basic claims. Nevertheless – and history can be invoked here as well – religion manifestly does have the potential to serve as a corrective to, or at least to enable resistance to, the hegemonic and homogenizing forces that are characteristic of liberal, consumer-driven societies. It does so by providing the religious individual with a focus that is not reducible to the ever-changing – because 'new and improved' – products of the worldwide marketplace.[36] From the perspective of Tillich's notion of 'ultimate concern', that focus, while it necessarily comes to expression in some 'concrete embodiment,' is never reducible to a particular worldly object though it does orient the religious man or woman toward the totality of worldly experience.[37] In his words, 'If religion is the state of being grasped by an ultimate concern, this state cannot be restricted to a special realm. The unconditional character of this concern implies that it refers to *every* moment of our life, to every space and every realm [our emphasis] … In all preliminary concerns, ultimate concern is present, consecrating them. Essentially the religious and the secular are not separated realms. Rather they are within each other.'[38]

Tillich is aware that the permeation of the everyday (or the secular) by religious commitment is an ideal that is never fully realised, and that both the secular and the religious tend to reify into 'special realms'. Nevertheless, the religious impulse cannot but come to expression in cultural forms and can never be understood apart from culture. In view of this fact, one must ask whether contemporary Western representations of religion have even begun to do justice to the complexity of religion as a cultural phenomenon and as an essential factor in the shaping of all those civilizations within which it is manifest. Indeed, one must ask whether much modern European discourse on religion is irredeemably skewed in favour of a so-called liberal and even anti-religious agenda that presents itself as the disinterested wisdom of a world come of age.

The upshot of these considerations might be formulated as follows: *All those who would seek to interpret or to present a religious tradition, ought to be prepared (i) to engage in a thoroughgoing reconsideration of their own fundamental presuppositions regarding the nature and function of religion, and (ii) to do so with an openness to what is happening at the global level, where religion's many faces are manifest in sometimes frightening relief.*

The myriad faces of religion are the subject of our third and final consideration.

The Plural Character of Religion

One of the most striking reflections on the West's failure to appreciate the inherent diversity of religion and its multilayered appeal is contained in the book written by the former American secretary of state (1997–2001), Madeleine Albright, entitled *The Mighty and the Almighty: Reflections on America, God, and World Affairs*, and published in 2006. Therein, Albright describes the determined efforts of the Clinton administration to resist or even ignore the 'prediction', made by Samuel Huntington in 1993, that 'the era following the cold war might well witness an interreligious "clash of civilizations".' In her words, 'We did all we could to distance ourselves from that theory.' Religious conflicts in the Balkans and the Middle East, Ireland and South Asia seemed to the government of the day to be 'the echoes of earlier, *less enlightened* times, not a sign of battles still to come' [our emphasis].[39] However, the terror attacks of 9/11 made Albright 'realise' that 'it may have been [she] who was stuck in an earlier time'. She goes on to muse that,

> In contrast to Michael Novak's observation four decades ago [that religion was not a matter for 'serious conversation'], people now talk (and argue) about God all the time. Even in Europe, which seems otherwise exempt from the trend toward religious growth, the number of observant Muslims is rising quickly, and a pope – named for Benedict of Nursia, the continent's patron saint – was determined to re-evangelize its Christian population.[40]

Our recent history, then, has alerted politicians and indeed all of us to the fact that religion is a global reality, that it can rear its head when and where we least expect it, and that it can acquire a significance we thought it had long since lost. This new – because threatening – reality calls for an adequate response, and governments and educational authorities have provided at least a partial one by promoting the idea of a truly 'pluralist' society. The upshot of this call has been the development of a range of positions, in the political, the social and the religious realms which sail under the flag of 'pluralism'. The precise meaning of this term is, however, by no means self-evident and one would do well both to examine the somewhat disparate cargo this word carries and the port of call it is designed to reach.

The terms 'pluralism' and 'pluralist' are intended to describe, in the first place, the factual plurality of religions and world views that now characterises Western culture in particular. But they are also often used to refer to what can only be described as an ideological programme. Nearly two decades ago, Peter Donovan proposed a distinction between pluralism as an epistemological principle, and ideological pluralism. In the first case, to be a 'pluralist' is to recognise the (right to) existence of contradictory truth claims, in view of the conviction that the cause of truth is best served by discussion and argument. It the second case (i.e. ideological pluralism), to be 'pluralist' is to pursue an ideological project that has, as its ultimate goal, the neutralisation of all heterogeneity by the imposition of a totalitarian understanding of truth. In this scenario, there is only one truth, namely, the truth of pluralism.[41]

In this scenario, too, pluralism may well become, in the words of David Tracy, 'simply a passive response to more and more possibilities, none of which shall ever be practiced. That kind [of pluralism] is, as Simone de Beauvoir insisted, the perfect ideology for the bourgeois mind. Such a pluralism masks a genial confusion in which one tries to enjoy the pleasures of difference without ever committing to any particular vision of resistance and hope.' Tracy continues by noting that, 'The great pluralists in the history of Western thought [such as, for example, William James] knew that any worthy affirmation of plurality was the beginning, but never the end, of a responsibly pluralistic attitude.'[42] That is to say, 'any worthy affirmation of pluralism' must be marked by the determination to take plurality seriously, to acknowledge real and perhaps even insurmountable difference, and to allow oneself to be challenged by that difference.

The advent of the postmodern age may have made the possibility of an existence that consists of nothing more than the contemplation of 'more and more options' somewhat more plausible, but one hopes – indeed expects – that those committed to the cause of religion will reject such postmodern posturing for what it is. That being said, Tracy's reflections do point up the fact that the mere profession of a 'pluralistic attitude' is no guarantee that one takes the 'other' really seriously. As we noted earlier, liberal Western democracies, despite their protestations to the contrary, do not always look kindly on religions that lay claim to cultural space in the name of their communities.

The picture in theology and religious education may not be all that different. Here, too, the profession of a pluralist agenda does not always translate into a genuine respect for otherness or for plurality. Here, too, those who sail under the flag of pluralism should be challenged to explain what precisely they mean by the term and what they hope to achieve.

Since the 1960s the theology of religions (or the theology of interreligious dialogue, as it is now usually called) has sought to come to terms with the challenge of the religious other. It is beyond the scope of this paper to examine the recent history of this discipline. For our purposes, it is enough to note that, at least until fairly recently, so-called 'pluralist' paradigms of interreligious dialogue and interreligious learning have dominated the discussion. One of the foremost reference points for such theories has been the work of so-called 'pluralist' theologians such as John Hick. In some places, Hick's theology of religious pluralism has been more or less uncritically appropriated in order to ground a so-called '*inter*religious' approach to religious education. This approach is then opposed to so-called '*mono*religious' approaches (which are portrayed as attempts to 'initiate' students into one tradition), on the one hand, and so-called '*multi*religious' approaches (which are portrayed as relativistic and inimical to any sort of religious commitment at all), on the other. A critical analysis of this facile typology (and its many variants) makes clear that it was developed with little or no attention to the import of the term 'pluralist' as this is used by Hick and those who followed his lead.[43]

The more or less self-evident character of the transition from the recognition that the contemporary culture is pluralistic to the option for an educational model based on pluralist theology is remarkable. How are we to account for the ease of the transition? In my opinion, three factors are at work here: (i) a rather careless use of the term 'pluralist'; (ii) insufficient knowledge of the content of so-called 'pluralist' theology; and (iii) an unfounded prejudice with respect to other theological options. The upshot of all of this is a sort of intellectual *coup* by means of which a complex term is hijacked and turned into a vehicle for the sort of ideological pluralism mentioned above.

The pluralist theology developed by Hick, which has roots in the work of Wilfred Cantwell Smith and has found a Catholic voice in Paul Knitter, culminates in a programme to subordinate all particularity to a universalistic vision that claims to know what all religious traditions are 'really' about. So, for example, pluralist theology claims to know that the truth about the transcendent reality is greater and perhaps even very different from what the religions claim to know. In making this affirmation, so-called pluralist theologians neutralise the particular claims of every religious tradition and implicitly claim for themselves an omniscience that most religions only credit to God. In the case of Christianity, this pluralistic presupposition translates into a refusal to take seriously the tradition of Christian self-understanding that comes to expression in the doctrine of incarnation. It is not surprising, therefore, that Hick has devoted considerable time and energy to deconstructing precisely this doctrine and explaining to Christians what it 'really' means.[44] More dramatically perhaps, pluralist theologians have insisted that those who do not share their theological presuppositions cannot really engage in authentic dialogue at all. This is truly breathtaking. A theological position that prides itself on its tolerance and respect for particularity has apportioned to itself the right to determine what will be the subject of interreligious dialogue and who is entitled to take part in it!

To my mind, to take religious plurality seriously is to realise – and to acknowledge – that meaningful interreligious dialogue has yet to begin. Such dialogue will be characterised, in the first place, by the frank admission of difference, of 'otherness', and the recognition that the engagement with the 'other' may issue in the abandonment of one's own most cherished beliefs. A step in the direction of this sort of dialogue was taken, in Catholic circles, with the 1991 declaration, *Dialogue and Proclamation*, which was issued jointly by the Pontifical Council for Interreligious Dialogue, and the Congregation for the Evangelization of Peoples.[45] Among other principles, this document declared that genuine dialogue implies a willingness to allow oneself to be 'questioned' by one's dialogue partner (§32) and 'to be transformed by the encounter' (§47), to acknowledge the deficiencies in one's own tradition and one's practice of that tradition, and even to run the risk of abandoning one's 'previous spiritual or religious situation in order to direct oneself towards another' (§41). As the document puts it, 'sincere dialogue implies, on the one hand, mutual acceptance of differences, or even of contradictions, and on the other, respect for the free decision of persons taken according to the dictates of their conscience' (§41).

The danger threatening our ostensibly pluralistic culture is the sort of insipid pluralism that Tracy decries, a pluralism that does not truly take 'difference' or 'otherness' or 'plurality' seriously, or worse still, appeals to 'plurality' as a means of emptying the 'particular' of its irreducible – and challenging – content.

The upshot of these considerations might be summarized as follows: *All those who would seek to interpret or to present a religious tradition ought to be prepared (i) to allow that 'a worthy affirmation of plurality' is not incompatible with commitment to the irreducible particularity of that tradition, and (ii) that such commitment does not vitiate the possibility of authentic interreligious encounter (or dialogue).*

Conclusion

The aim of this paper was to inquire whether European approaches to religion and religious education do justice to the experience of 'religious' people and to the undeniable role that religion has played – and continues to play – in the lives and cultures of men and women throughout the world. Such an inquiry inevitably involves the question of whether Europe's much vaunted claim to promote and practice pluralism really bears careful and critical scrutiny, or whether Europe's real attitude toward religion was best captured in the words of one of the characters in Sean O'Casey's *The Plough and the Stars* (1926), to the effect that, 'We ought to have as great a regard for religion as we can, so as to keep it out of as many things as possible.' If that is the case, then, it would seem, Europe is well and truly an 'exceptional case' but one that probably belongs at the back of the (religion) class.

NOTES

1. Paul Griffiths, *Problems of Religious Diversity* (Malden, MS: Blackwell, 2001), p. 12.
2. S. Mark Heim, *The Depth of the Riches: A Trinitarian Theology of Religious Ends* (Grand Rapids, MI: W.B. Eerdmans, 2001), p. 21.
3. Griffiths, p. 12.
4. Heim, p. 22.
5. Heim, p. 21.
6. Griffiths, p. 12.
7. Paul Tillich, *Theology of Culture* (Oxford: Oxford University Press, 1959), p. 9.
8. Paul Tillich, *Ultimate Concern: Dialogues with Students*, ed. by D.M. Brown (London: SCM, 1965), p. 20.
9. Joachim Wach, *Essays in the History of Religions*, ed. by J.M. Kitagawa, G.D. Alles (London: Macmillan, 1988), p. 139. For a critical assessment of Wach's entire oeuvre, see C.K. Wedemeyer and W. Doniger, eds, *Hermeneutics, Politics, and the History of Religions: The Contested Legacies of Joachim Wach & Mircea Eliade* (Oxford: Oxford University Press, 2010).
10. Joachim Wach, *Types of Religious Experience: Christian and Non-Christian* (Chicago: University of Chicago Press, 1951), p. 33.
11. Joachim Wach, *The Comparative Study of Religions*, ed. by Joseph M. Kitagawa (New York: Columbia University Press, 1958), pp. 36–37, 98–99.
12. Tillich, *Theology of Culture*, p. 28.
13. On this topic, see José Casanova, *Public Religions in the Modern World* (Chicago: University of Chicago, 1994); 'Public Religions Revisited,' in H. De Vries, ed., *Religion: Beyond a Concept* (New York: Fordham University Press, 2008), pp. 101–119; 'Religion, European Secular Identities and European Integration,' in T.A. Byrnes and P.J. Katzenstein, ed., *Religion in an Expanding Europe* (Cambridge: Cambridge University Press, 2006), pp. 65–92; Thomas A. Howard, *God and the Atlantic: America, Europe and the Religious Divide* (Oxford: Oxford University Press, 2011).
14. Casanova, *Public Religions*, pp. 11–39.
15. Casanova, 'Religion, European Secular Identities and European Integration,' p. 90 n. 1.
16. Casanova, 'Religion, European Secular Identities and European Integration,' pp. 66, 69.
17. Casanova, 'Religion, European Secular Identities and European Integration,' pp. 84–85.
18. Casanova, 'Religion, European Secular Identities and European Integration,' p. 70.
19. Casanova, 'Religion, European Secular Identities and European Integration,' p. 66.
20. Casanova, 'Religion, European Secular Identities and European Integration,' pp. 66–67.
21 Casanova, 'Religion, European Secular Identities and European Integration,' p. 90.
22. Grace Davie, *Religion in Modern Europe: A Memory Mutates* (Oxford: Oxford University Press, 2000), p. 14. Davie refers to O. Leaman, 'Taking Religion Seriously,' *The Times*, 6 Feb. (1989), p. 18.
23. Casanova, *Public Religions*, pp. 38–39.
24. Erich Przywara, 'St. Augustine and the Modern World,' in M.C. D'Arcy, ed., *Saint Augustine* (New York: Meridian, 1957), p. 251. Przywara refers to Hegel's *Werke* (Stuttgart, 1928), vol. 19, p. 328.
25. George Lindbeck, *The Nature of Doctrine: Religion and Theology in a Postliberal Age* (Philadelphia: Westminster, 1984), pp. 34–35.
26. Clifford Geertz, *The Interpretation of Cultures: Selected Essays* (New York: Basic Books, 1973), p. 125.
27. Geertz, p. 15.
28. C.S. Dessain, ed., *The Letters and Diaries of John Henry Newman* (Oxford: Clarendon Press, 1961), vol. 11, p. 110.

29. For the notion of 'thick description,' see Geertz, pp. 6–7.

30. Casanova, *Public Religions*, p. 37.

31. Nicholas Abercrombie et al., eds, *Dictionary of Sociology* (London: Penguin, 2000), p. 185.

32. Casanova, *Public Religions*, p. 215.

33. Casanova, *Public Religions*, pp. 38–39.

34. Casanova, 'Religion, European Secular Identities and European Integration,' p. 69.

35. Casanova, 'Religion, European Secular Identities and European Integration,' pp. 84–85.

36. Richard Roberts, 'Globalized Religion?', in Robin Gill, ed., *Theology and Sociology: A Reader* (London: Cassell, 1996), pp. 471–485.

37. Tillich, *Theology of Culture*, p. 28.

38. Tillich, *Theology of Culture*, p. 41.

39. Madeleine Albright, *The Mighty and the Almighty: Reflections on America, God, and World Affairs* (New York: HarperCollins, 2006), pp. 8–9.

40. Albright, p. 10.

41. Peter Donovan, 'The Intolerance of Religious Pluralism,' *Religious Studies* 29 (1993), 218–221.

42. David Tracy, *Plurality and Ambiguity: Hermeneutics, Religion and Hope* (New York: Harper & Row, 1987), p. 90.

43. Terrence Merrigan, '"Interreligious Learning" in the Light of the Contemporary Catholic Theology of Interreligious Dialogue,' in D. Pollefeyt, ed., *Interreligious Learning* (Leuven: Peeters, 2007), pp. 183–207.

44. 'The Image of the Word: John Henry Newman and John Hick on the Place of Christ in Christianity,' in T. Merrigan and Ian T. Ker, eds, *Newman and the Word*, Louvain Theological and Pastoral Monographs (Grand Rapids: W.B. Eerdmans, 2000), pp. 1–47.

45. The text of the document and critical reflections on it are contained in William R. Burrows ed., *Redemption and Dialogue: Reading 'Redemptoris Missio' and 'Dialogue and Proclamation'* (Maryknoll, NY: Orbis, 1993). To allow readers to consult other editions of the text, all references will be to the numbered paragraphs of the original document.

CHAPTER THREE

RELIGIOUS EDUCATION AT SECOND LEVEL IN IRELAND: INCLUSIVE PRACTICE

Suzanne Dillon

This chapter explores the question of inclusive practice in Religious Education from the perspective of classroom practitioners in Ireland. It frames the discussion around three key questions:

1. What is it that teachers want to teach in Religious Education? What do teachers want children to learn?

2. What do teachers need to be doing in the classroom to help children to learn in Religious Education?

3. What criteria of success are being utilised by teachers? How will teachers know that children have learned?

From the outset, it is important to acknowledge that it is possible to provide multiple answers to each of these questions and that the first is perhaps the most contested.

What is it that Teachers want to Teach in Religious Education?
There are at least two ways to address the question of what teachers want to teach in Religious Education. The first is summarised in the terms 'teaching about/teaching for' used by Grimmitt and Read (1975) and now familiar in discussions of Religious Education. That approach accommodates conversation about perspective and context which is pertinent to the consideration of inclusive practice and which will be explored later in this chapter.

The second approach is tightly curriculum focused. It is about content, themes and topics and has relevance when considering inclusive practice in Religious Education.

Questions number two and three above depend on the answers provided to the first question to a great extent, because inclusive practice is about a lot more than the particular teaching and learning strategies employed in a lesson.

Inclusive practice in Religious Education is not just about the methodology or strategies used, it is about the hearts and minds, the values and understandings, which underpin those strategies. In this chapter these are explored, not through an academic or philosophical lens, but through story, drawing on my observations of teaching and learning in Religious Education lessons and on my own experience as a teacher.

Grimmitt and Read's terms 'learning about' and 'learning from',[1] though their meaning has been contested, provide a useful way into this question. They are helpful in positioning approaches which might be described as 'experiential' and those described as 'rational' along one dimension for enquiry; and confessional or liberal perspectives along another. 'Learning about' religion can be understood as shorthand for an approach that emphasises knowledge and understanding. It includes inquiry into the nature of religion, its sources, ways of life, religious practice and expression. It provides learners with a vocabulary through which they can communicate what they have learned. It takes a descriptive and historical approach to religion and can draw heavily on phenomenology (Smart 1968) and ethnography (Jackson 1997).[2] An approach to teaching Religious Education in this way has validity from a confessional perspective. It provides children and young people with a body of knowledge and a language (including concepts and schema), with which to both explore and express faith. 'Learning about' is also attractive from a liberal perspective. It recognises religion as a cultural phenomenon, worthy of study; it avoids the risk of conferring preference on any one religious tradition; and done well, it can challenge stereotype and prejudice, contributing significantly to the aims of an intercultural education.

There are problems with 'learning about', however, where it is done poorly. A focus on the content of religion can lead to very shallow learning where the positioning of the learner as 'outside' religion is ontologically suspect. On the other hand, if both teacher and learner are insiders, 'learning about' does not expand the cognitive horizons of the learner. Finally, the risk of missing the life-experiences of children and young people is very real, thereby limiting the impact of education in Religious Education on the values and attitudes they form.

'Learning from' religion addresses some of these concerns, particularly where it is understood as that learning which is directed toward the affective domain of education, where the lived world of the child is at the centre. In the context of cultural plurality, there are dangers in a 'learning from' approach. Audrey Bryan's (2010)[3] recent criticism of interculturalism in Ireland as a kind of 'symbolic violence', though I do not accept her arguments, surfaces at least one of these dangers. It is the danger of hegemony of the dominant voice in religious education, such that 'learning from' religions, other than the dominant religion, positions the minority group as at worst, objects of curiosity, about whom it is interesting to learn and from whom we can learn our own superiorities. I am being harsh here, but to make a point – 'learning from' can be exclusive rather than inclusive, despite the content which is explored.

On the other hand, 'learning from' provides rich opportunities to engage learners where they are at in their own lives. I do not want to over-emphasise the experiential in Religious Education, I am mindful of Wright's difficulties in this regard and am persuaded that there is value in his religious literacy approach to Religious Education.[4] I accept that an approach which leaves Religious Education at the level of learner experience is only a disservice to learners. It limits their understanding to the immediate and the proximate. However, 'learning from' is a richer conception of Religious Education – it is about religion enriching the experience of the learner.

A fundamental principle of inclusive practice is that all children should learn together. They learn with and from each other. A number of approaches facilitate this such as the interpretive approach developed by Professor Jackson and his colleagues in Warwick, including Ipgrave's dialogical approach.[5] Where 'learning from' captures the insider/outsider position as a fluid one, such that the learner is variously an 'outsider', standing back in an attitude of constructive criticism and an 'insider', engaged in reassessing his or her own experience and understanding, there lies the space where inclusive practice in Religious Education can be realised.

The second route into the question of what we want to teach in Religious Education is curriculum focused. The NCCA, in consultation with a wide range of partners, has provided syllabuses for Religious Education for post-primary study in the Republic of Ireland. Both syllabuses are optional and they share a set of common aims.

The syllabuses set out a range of knowledge, understandings, skills and attitudes which learners should acquire through the study of Religious Education. These might be accommodated, for the purposes of this chapter, within the 'learning about' approach just described. Verbs like 'engaging with'; 'recognising'; 'respecting'; and 'appreciating' appear in the descriptions of the attitudes to be developed. The skills include 'identifying'; exploring'; 'analysing'; 'differentiating'; and 'comparing and contrasting'.

The approach advocated in the NCCA *Guidelines For Teachers* for both syllabuses is one supportive of inclusion and that position is reinforced by the *Guidelines on Inclusion* for primary and post-primary schools. It is clear that Religious Education is not just about religions and attitudinal orientations in general. It is intended to foster a specific orientation which recognises the plurality of religious expression and understandings and which critically engages with religion as highly relevant to society and to individuals. The contribution which Religious Education makes to developing acceptance, understanding, respect and mutuality, attitudes which define inclusiveness in practice, is predicated on an understanding of Religious Education as both informative and formative.

What do Teachers Need to Do in the Classroom to Help Children to Learn in Religious Education?

All of this takes us to consideration of the second fundamental question: What do teachers need to do in the classroom to help children to learn in RE? This question can be answered through the medium of a story. A teacher showed her young students – second-year boys – a short video on First Communion. It was a kind of 'Reeling in the Years' production, made in the late 1990s, tracking the stories of three children preparing for first communion in the Catholic tradition. The lads loved it, particularly because they recognised two 'extras' in the documentary as boys from their neighbourhood. Following the video presentation, the boys shared their own first communion stories and it was clear that three had none to share – not being Christian. That did not dampen their spirits as long as other boys had brought their communion photographs into the class, generating a lot of amusement. The thirty-five minute lesson time flew by and the boys were genuinely disappointed by the interruption of the bell, begging the teacher to allow them return to this topic for the next lesson.

The level of enthusiasm and enjoyment evident in the lesson was high. One might well ask if this was a good lesson. Well, that depends on how one interprets the teacher's intention; to connect with the life-world of the boys? The lesson certainly did that and it provided them with opportunities to consider a range of issues, from how fashion/hairstyles had changed to how financially lucrative the occasion had been. This latter sparked comparison with confirmation and the notion that getting older brought some rewards! What the lesson did not do was get under the experience of the boys to explore its meaning at a deeper level than immediate gratification. Neither the Christian nor the non-Christian perspective was captured. Both the teacher and I were aware that the opportunity once lost, is lost. Despite their keenness, the boys were unlikely to be motivated to work at this deeper level in the next lesson – their enthusiasm was for the chat.

The teacher may well have intended to ask the boys to consider questions exploring how ritual and worship are expressions of the human response to life; to include the outsider perspective available in the class group; to consider the meaning of the photographs for the boys and their families; to explore patterns of behaviour common across all cultures and traditions. Those questions are ones which would help the boys to find their own positions regarding ritual, observance, community of faith and community of faiths and, from that position, to consider alternative understandings of the same.

I am reminded of the wisdom of Confucius: 'Learning without thought is labour lost; thought without learning is perilous.' The strategies used in inclusive classrooms are ones which provide the learner with critical skills for interpreting religious phenomena and their own experiences of religion. They engage children and young people in *talking* about and through difference. So, inclusive classrooms are noisy places. They are places where there is a lot of debate and discussion, where co-operative learning strategies provide opportunities for moving beyond superficial hearing to genuine listening. Role-play and case studies introduce the learners to the complex nature of plural interpretations of situations and multiple answers to the same questions. Arts and communications media are used to expose children and young people to experiences, however vicarious, which prompt discussion of how understandings of God, religious traditions and non-religious perspectives have impacted on personal lifestyle, inter-personal relationships and relationships between individuals and their communities.

The inclusive classroom is also a place of quiet. A second story may help to illustrate this point. Imagine yourself in a classroom with twenty-eight boys and girls, just weeks before the Junior Certificate. Leaning precariously against the whiteboard is a large, framed print of a work of art entitled *The Confession*, by Alphonse Legros. The teacher had taken this from the wall on one of the school's corridors, where students had *not* been seeing it on a daily basis. The lesson opened with an invitation to the students to suggest what it was about and they suggested a range of topics including dying; begging for mercy; power; being exposed. As they explained their ideas, they started to focus more on the other characters and the ideas changed. They suggested community support; mercy; openness (to supplication); and freedom. The teacher then told them the title of the painting and where she had found it. She asked them to write for a few minutes about their initial impressions and whether the information she had provided had changed them. (Quiet.) Then in small groups – three or four – they shared to the extent that they wanted to. (Not so quiet now.) The plenary at the end was enriched by what was clearly an established practice in this classroom – the students shared not just what they had thought and how their thinking had changed during the lesson – they critiqued the processes they had engaged in while arriving at those ideas. So one student said (and I paraphrase), 'I wasn't paying attention, not at the beginning of the class when you showed us it, all I saw was a dusty dark thing. And I wasn't paying attention in the corridor because I don't ever remember seeing that before, even though you've said where it was. And not paying attention meant I couldn't really talk to the others.' (Quiet – but not the quiet of 'oops, now he's in trouble'. The quiet of acknowledgement, we've all failed to pay attention sometime.)

Approaches to religious education which engage learners in critical consideration of the content being explored and which support personal reflection on the meanings of what is learned and *how* it is learned, are approaches which are likely to foster attention to self and other. This attention makes possible the achievement of the attitudes and skills necessary for meaningful dialogue with others whose traditions and cultures are different. That is inclusive practice.

How will we know that Children have Learned?

And so to my third question: What are our success criteria? How will we know that children have learned? In short it is relatively easy to measure the knowledge aspects of any syllabus – simple recall tests suffice to an extent. By asking students to provide explanations, we can begin to get at understanding. If we provide an opportunity to explore, discuss and evaluate, and require learners to both demonstrate the process and their learning, perhaps through performance or project report, we can get much closer to discovering their learning.

The summative evaluation arrangements made by the State Examinations Commission provide one measure of success in Religious Education. It should not, in an inclusive classroom, be the only measure. Teachers of Religious Education should and do, regularly assess the progress made by their pupils and students. But how do they do so inclusively? That brings us right back to the first question – they need to be clear about what it is they want to teach; to identify the learning outcomes for a specified unit of work, such as a module, course or programme. If 'engagement with' and 'understanding of' and 'respect for' are key terms in those outcomes, teachers need to avoid decontextualised recall of terms, definitions and descriptions. Imaginative approaches to assessment are needed, which allow learners to demonstrate that they have achieved those outcomes. Forms of assessment such as practical activity, presentation, and portfolio work, where mind-maps, rough drafts, reflective notes and the finished paper are presented to demonstrate the learner's journey through the issue, are evident in inclusive classrooms. Feedback on assessment becomes the impetus for further learning and discussion. Throughout, the emphasis is on supporting children and young people in developing skills in self-reflection and self-monitoring, so that they can travel from a strong, positive sense of their own identity and worth into a conversation with other, equally strong and valued, members of the community in which they live now and in those communities they have yet to encounter.

Finally, I believe, and research into effective teaching and learning supports my belief, that at the heart of good teaching in any subject is a faithful teacher. What do I mean by 'faithful'? The word faithful has connotations of 'dedicated' and 'committed', suggesting teachers who, in addition to having the requisite subject knowledge and expertise, are enthusiastic and have a desire to make a difference in the lives of young people. In their communication of the subject, they are 'authentic' and 'true to life'. They teach in a fair and balanced way, respecting both the content and intention of the Religious Education syllabus and the various experiences of the children and young people with whom they work. Faithful teachers of Religious Education give their students the confidence to live out of their own faith, or non-faith, interpretations of life, and to respect and value the perspectives of others.

NOTES

1. M. Grimmitt, 'Contemporary Pedagogies of Religious Education: What Are They?' *Pedagogies of Religious Education* (Great Wakering, England: McCrimmons, 2000), pp. 24–52.
2. N. Smart, *Secular Education and the Logic of Religion* (London: Faber and Faber, 1968); R. Jackson, *Religious Education: An Interpretative Approach* (London: Hodder and Stoughton, 1997).
3. A. Bryan, 'Corporate Multiculturalism, Diversity Management and Positive Interculturalism in Irish Schools and Society' in *Irish Educational Studies* 29/3 (2010), pp. 253–69.
4. A. Wright, 'Language and Experience in the Hermeneutics of Religious Understanding', *British Journal of Religious Education* 18/3 (1996), pp. 166–180; A. Wright, 'Contextual Religious Education and the Actuality of Religions', *British Journal of Religious Education* 30/1 (2008).
5. J. Ipgrave, 'Dialogue, Citizenship and Religious Education', in R. Jackson, ed., *International Perspectives on Citizenship, Education and Religious Diversity* (London: RoutledgeFalmer, 2003). Discussion and debate are important elements in Ipgrave's threefold approach to dialogue. Primary dialogue is the acceptance of diversity, difference and change. Secondary dialogue involves students in engaging with difference and being open to learning from others. 'Tertiary dialogue' is the term Ipgrave uses to describe the actual dialogue between children which then results.

CHAPTER FOUR

'TEACHING RELIGION':
CHALLENGES AND OPPORTUNITIES FOR EDUCATIONAL
PRACTICE IN A PLURALIST CONTEXT

Andrew McGrady

Introduction

> 'When I use a word,' Humpty Dumpty said in rather a scornful tone, 'it means just what I choose it to mean – neither more nor less.' 'The question is,' said Alice, 'whether you can make words mean so many different things.' 'The question is,' said Humpty Dumpty, 'which is to be master – that's all.'
>
> (Lewis Carroll, *Alice's Adventures in Wonderland*)

What we name, who determines a name, the name we use, and the meanings ascribed to the name are complex realities as is well captured in the oft-quoted above extract from Lewis Carroll. Humpty Dumpty also expresses well the power relationships between the 'namer' and the 'hearer' concerning that which is being 'named'. Throughout this chapter the term 'Teaching Religion' will be used with a view to locating a relatively neutral term to designate what happens when religion and belief are brought to school in a curriculum context. Of course no term is fully neutral but the alternative terms currently in use, or coming into use, such as 'religious instruction', 'religious education', 'Education about Religion and Beliefs' (ERB) or 'Ethics programmes' all express a particular approach and, in some cases, have different meanings both in the Irish and global contexts. There is a need for a shared public understanding of the contribution of Teaching Religion and for clarity concerning the terms used. It is further acknowledged that the relationship between schooling and religion is broader than a curriculum subject dedicated to religion and relates to the characteristic spirit or ethos of a school being expressed in symbols, rituals and the wider life of the school as an educating community. These however are not the immediate concern of this present contribution.

Teaching Religion

Teaching Religion in the Irish context has become a matter of intensifying public and educational debate. Key moments in this debate have been:

- The new Primary Curriculum (1999) which is based upon seven areas comprising of groups of subjects but in which the development and implementation of the curriculum in religious education in primary schools remains the responsibility of the relevant patron bodies rather than the National Council for Curriculum and Assessment (NCCA)

- The introduction of optional state syllabuses for Religious Education at second level (developed by the NCCA) as part of the Junior Certificate (1999) and Leaving Certificate (2003) examinations

- The May 2011 report of the Irish Commission for Human Rights (IHRC) on *Religion and Education: A Human Rights Perspective*

- The April 2012 report from the Forum's Advisory Group concerning the *Forum on Patronage and Pluralism in the Primary Sector* established in 2011 which included the recommendation for the introduction of Education about Religion and Beliefs (ERB) and Ethics in all primary schools.

Teaching Religion and Religious Instruction

Over the past 60 years the meanings ascribed to Teaching Religion have exhibited distinctive patterns in the Irish context. At the time of the introduction of free second-level education in 1966 it was most commonly understood through a 'catechetical' lens. Thus in the Catholic school a Catholic teacher taught about the Catholic faith to Catholic pupils with the express intention of deepening their understanding and commitment to that faith tradition and community. The focus within the curriculum, which was approved by the Church rather than the state, was mainly on a single religion and a single set of religious beliefs. The pupil was seen as one who, through baptism, had been graced with the gift of faith and who had been sent by his or her parents to a Catholic school in order to be formed for an adult and mature faith. This approach is that which is classified as 'religious instruction' in the Irish Constitution or to use the framework outlined by Hull 2001 'teaching for religion'.[1] Such an approach was, and is, founded upon a view of the human person as free and rational and is often summarised as 'faith seeking understanding'. The work of the school is seen as an extension of the work of the parish and of the family. Religious instruction is not 'neutral' in terms of its understanding of revealed truth and related values; on the contrary, it is seen as part of the evangelising mission of the Church. It flows from commitment and invites a freely accepted and informed commitment on the part of the learner through incorporation into the life of the religious community providing the religious instruction. The consent for the child to participate in such faith formation comes from the parent. In a submission to the

Forum on Patronage and Pluralism the present author defined religious instruction as follows:

> The term 'religious instruction' refers to the educating 'into' religion structured as a timetabled subject in which pupils of a particular religious faith or tradition are brought together separately from other pupils in the school (either during the school day or on the school premises after the regular school day, or by some approved system of pupil release during the school day) and are offered a programme based upon a curriculum defined by the relevant religious authority of their faith tradition and inspected by that authority, which largely (though not exclusively) uses the traditions of that faith community as learning resources and which, while seeking to be respectful of all faiths, does seek to promote the faith development of each pupil in that particular religious tradition. The term 'religious instruction' should not be regarded as outdated or pejorative. It is required to meet the usual standards of educational provision (it may not be reduced to 'indoctrination') and the teacher must be recognised by the relevant authority as qualified to teach religion.

The Irish Constitution, related state instruments and international instruments clearly permit schools to provide 'religious instruction'. While the term 'religious instruction' may no longer be the preferred term among such educators it does have legal and constitutional currency. Religious institutions have a constitutionally acknowledged right to provide and manage schools. Such schools have been provided historically by the Churches in Ireland for many reasons chiefly as a means of promoting the good of individuals especially the marginalised and the poor and serving the common good. In this context religious instruction is seen as an essential, integrating component of full human development. The right to provide religious instruction is carefully balanced in the Irish Constitution, and other international instruments, by the right of parents to withdraw their child from such religious instruction. The Irish Constitution (Article 44.2.4) states that: 'Legislation providing State aid for schools shall not discriminate between schools under the management of different religious denominations, nor be such as to affect prejudicially the right of any child to attend a school receiving public money without attending religious instruction at that school'. Thus the Constitution allows in a carefully balanced manner, for both the provision of religious instruction and the parental right of withdrawal from such religious instruction. In Ireland a formative approach to Teaching Religion remains the predominant paradigm in primary schools under denominational patronage.

Teaching Religion and Educational Religious Education
From the mid-1980s a second lens was applied to Teaching Religion which is often described as the 'Educational' or 'Educational Religious Education'. This lens focused on the unique context in which Teaching Religion took place – the

school – a place with different educational goals to the family or a parish. The growing secularization of Ireland also prompted educators, particularly at second level, to question whether a curriculum that was based upon the assumption that all pupils had, or wished for, a firm faith commitment was credible. Outside of the Irish context this led, mainly at second level, to the emergence of a phenomenological approach which sought to be neutral and objective by teaching comparative factual information about the world's religions. This approach was influenced by the work of Ninian Smart, a sociologist of religion, and is described by Hull (2001) as 'teaching about religion' using descriptive and historical methods, aiming neither to promote nor to erode religious faith but to provide information. This approach was also influenced by the emergence of departments of Religious Studies in Western Universities. Within the Irish context 'teaching about religion' had little influence as an approach. What gradually developed was what Hull (2001) describes as 'teaching from religion' which introduces pupils to the world's religious and belief traditions as a gift to the pupil's spiritual and ethical imagination and a resource for their search for meaning and values. The historical development of such Educational Religious Education (as distinct from confessional Religious Instruction) in second-level schools in Ireland has been clearly mapped by Looney (2006).[2]

Perhaps the clearest statement of the 'Educational' Religious Education approach evident in the Irish context is that provided for the second-level Junior Certificate and Leaving Certificate syllabuses which are designed to be open to pupils of all faiths and none. Here it is not assumed, or even necessary, that the teacher and pupil share the same faith commitment. There is no explicit intention (for assessment and examination purposes) to promote adherence to a particular faith or belief tradition although there is an acknowledgement that schools will continue to provide faith development initiatives in accordance with their ethos. Thus in the context of a State syllabus a teacher who is an Anglican can teach about Islam to 15-year-old pupils of all faiths and none in a VEC Community College with no intention of converting the pupils to Islam. Both the Junior Certificate and Leaving Certificate syllabuses state in their introductions that the aims for religious education for assessment and certification in the post-primary school are:

1. To foster an awareness that the human search for meaning is common to all peoples of all ages and at all times.

2. To explore how this search for meaning has found, and continues to find, expression in religion.

3. To identify how understandings of God, religious traditions, and in particular the Christian tradition, have contributed to the culture in which we live, and how they continue to have an impact on personal lifestyle, inter-personal

relationships, and relationships between individuals and their communities and contexts.

4. To appreciate the richness of religious traditions and to acknowledge the non-religious interpretation of life.

5. To contribute to the spiritual and moral development of the student.

Thus in English-speaking countries which have a 'State' schooling sector the term 'religious education' largely refers to:

> educating 'about' and 'from' religion structured in the school context as a timetabled school subject in which the curriculum is defined by a State agency (either alone or in partnership with communities of faith and/or communities of conviction), forms the basis of a 'common programme' taught at the same time to all pupils (of all religious faiths and none) as part of the school day, which is inspected by the relevant State authority, which uses the traditions of more than one faith community as learning resources, and which, while seeking to be respectful of all faiths, does not seek to promote any single faith.
>
> (submission from present author to Forum on Patronage and Pluralism)

Lest the distinctions between 'religious instruction' and 'religious education' be misinterpreted as intrinsically mutually exclusive it should be noted that both can be related in an approach to Teaching Religion. Both occur in a public arena (while both are personal, neither is private), both seek to develop the learner personally, socially, spiritually and ethically, both seek to promote critical reflection, understanding and appreciation, both require dialogue with the learner's life experience and invite personal appropriation and both require the free assent of the learner to participate. In terms of Catholic schools the 2007 document on Catholic Primary Schools: *A Policy for Provision into the Future*, issued by the Irish Catholic Bishops' Conference states (section 4.3):

> The Catholic school welcomes diversity and strives for inclusivity. It is open to people of other denominations and other faiths, welcomes them into its community and respects their beliefs … While it maintains its own ethos and provides religious instruction and formation in the Catholic Faith, the Catholic School sees this diversity as an opportunity for dialogue and understanding with those of different faiths. It seeks to co-operate with parents of other traditions who wish to provide religious instruction for the children in their own tradition.[3]

The 2009 statement from the Sacred Congregation for Catholic Education in Rome[4] also makes a lesser distinction between 'faith formation and catechesis' on the one hand and 'religious education' on the other:

> Religious education in schools … is different from, and complementary to, parish catechesis and other activities such as family Christian education or initiatives of ongoing formation of the faithful. Apart from the different settings in which these are imparted, the aims that they pursue are also different: catechesis aims at fostering personal adherence to Christ and the development of Christian life

in its different aspects … whereas religious education in schools gives the pupils knowledge about Christianity's identity and Christian life.

Teaching Religion and Intercultural/Interreligious Education
The tragic events associated with the 9/11 attacks on New York in 2001 and subsequent attacks around the globe raised awareness that religion and belief could not be regarded as a purely private concern of the individual when incidents like these were having such a profound effect on society and on global security. Governments and international bodies began to question their stance of strict neutrality toward Teaching Religion and to focus on how the exploration of religions and beliefs as social and cultural 'facts' could be included within formal schooling as a means of promoting mutual understanding, tolerance and minimising religion-and-belief-related violence. Parallel to this, large scale migration, especially into the economically-developed countries of the West including Ireland, the ever-present revolution in communications technology and accelerating globalisation have raised urgent questions about identity, nationality, culture, pluralism and social cohesion. In response Teaching Religion began to draw upon the frameworks developed as part of inter-cultural dialogue and inter-religious engagement. Lane (2011) provides a high-level description of inter-religious education[5] while Jackson in this volume and McGrady (2006)[6] provide an overview of the development of initiatives at the level of the United Nations and the Council of Europe.

Teaching Religion and Freedom of Religion and Belief
In recent years in Ireland there has also been a growing awareness that Teaching Religion must also be situated within a human rights frame of reference. Of particular importance is the right to freedom of religion and belief. In 1966 the United Nations General Assembly adopted the *International Covenant on Civil and Political Rights* (ICCPR) which came into force from 23 March 1976. Ireland signed the covenant on 1 October 1973 and ratified it on 8 December 1989. Article 18 states:

1. Everyone shall have the right to freedom of thought, conscience and religion. This right shall include freedom to have or to adopt a religion or belief of his choice, and freedom, either individually or in community with others and in public or private, to manifest his religion or belief in worship, observance, practice and teaching.

2. No one shall be subject to coercion which would impair his freedom to have or to adopt a religion or belief of his choice.

3. Freedom to manifest one's religion or beliefs may be subject only to such limitations as are prescribed by law and are necessary to protect public safety, order, health, or morals or the fundamental rights and freedoms of others.

4. The States Parties to the present Covenant undertake to have respect for the liberty of parents and, when applicable, legal guardians to ensure the religious and moral education of their children in conformity with their own convictions.

As has been repeatedly pointed out freedom of religion relates to both freedom 'for' religion and freedom 'from' religion. Both must be acknowledged and accommodated. There is also increasing reference to both 'religion' and 'belief' in related documentation where 'belief' is regarded as inclusive of non-theistic world views held by communities of conviction. The *Convention on the Rights of the Child*, adopted by the UN General Assembly in November 1989 and in force from September 1990, also applied these rights to the child (normally a person under 18 years of age). Of particular interest is the wording of Article 14.2 which states that 'States Parties shall respect the rights and duties of the parents and, when applicable, legal guardians, to provide direction to the child in the exercise of his or her right in a manner consistent with the evolving capacities of the child.' The reference to the 'evolving capacities of the child' is of direct relevance to the right of withdrawal from provision of Teaching Religion. The Committee on the Rights of the Child (CRC) monitors the implementation of the convention and in November 2006 made a recommendation relating to Ireland as follows:

60. The Committee reiterates the concern raised by the Committee on the Elimination of Racial Discrimination (CERD/C/IRL/CO/2) that non-denominational or multi-denominational schools represent less than 1 per cent of the total number of primary education facilities.

61. The Committee encourages the State party to take fully into consideration the recommendations made by the Committee on the Elimination of Racial Discrimination (CERD/C/IRL/2, Para 18) which encourages the promotion of the establishment of non-denominational or multi-denominational schools and to amend the existing legislative framework to eliminate discrimination in school admissions.

In February 2011, in an address to the Cambridge Group for Irish Studies at Magdalene College, the Catholic Archbishop of Dublin, Dr Diarmuid Martin, stated that 'The Irish Government has an obligation to ensure that parents who do not want a religious ethos in the formation of their children can, as far as possible, exercise their rights … I believe that there is need for a national forum to debate the issue. Plurality in management is needed to address the changed Irish culture.' In March 2011 the Minister for Education and Skills, Mr Ruairi Quinn TD, announced the establishment of a *Forum on Patronage and Pluralism in the Primary Sector*, the terms of reference of which included advising the Minister on 'how it can best be ensured that the education system can provide a sufficiently diverse number and range of primary schools catering for all religions and none'. Following consultation the Advisory group to the Forum submitted its report to the Minister in April 2012, the recommendations of which included measures for promoting diversity of school provision by facilitating the Catholic Church to divest itself of the patronage of some schools and a proposal relating to the provision of Education about Religion and Beliefs (ERB) and Ethics education in primary schools.

The Minister for Education and Skills responded to the report on 20 June 2012[7] and stated his intention to draw up a White Paper for consideration by Government which would ensure that the education system can provide a sufficiently diverse number of schools, catering for all religions and none. In this context the Minister announced a public consultation process on the findings and recommendations in the Forum Report with regard to promoting more inclusiveness in schools. He also noted the Forum's recommendation that all children should have the right to receive Education about Religion and Beliefs (ERB) and Ethics and recommended the development of ERB and Ethics programmes for all pupils not just those who are withdrawn by their parents from religious instruction. He stated his view that any new programmes could be supplementary to what is already provided with ERB and Ethics being in addition to, and not in any way a replacement for, faith formation in denominational schools. In a significant departure from the previous practice as stated in the new Primary Curriculum in which the state had no involvement in religious education at primary level, he announced that the National Council for Curriculum and Assessment (NCCA) will immediately explore with the education partners and religious interests the development of ERB and Ethics programmes.

Part of the difficulty in the current debate concerning Teaching Religion, patronage and diversity is the lack of an agreed definition of 'denominational', 'multi-denominational', 'interdenominational' and non-denominational schools as well as the lack of designation of any school as a 'secular' school. In a submission to the Forum on Patronage and Pluralism the present author proposed the following definitions:

- *Denominational patronage*: a school under the patronage or trusteeship of a single religious faith community (e.g. a Catholic national school, a Muslim national school or a voluntary secondary school under the trusteeship of a religious congregation or one of the new lay educational trusts). Such a school provides religious instruction according to the traditions, practices and beliefs of the specified religious community. It should also provide a wider religious education and work with parents of other faith traditions to enable them to provide for religious instruction.

- *Inter-denominational patronage*: a school under the patronage or trusteeship of more than one religious faith community. Such a school provides a common religious education and should provide for a variety of religious instruction opportunities.

- *Multi-denominational patronage*: a school under the patronage of a body (such as a VEC) in which members of religious communities have a right to sit on a Board of Management. Such a school should also provide a common religious education and should provide for religious instruction.

- *Non-denominational patronage*: a school under the patronage of a secular body or a body in which religious communities have no right of membership of a Board of Management and which has an explicitly secular ethos. Such a school should provide for an appropriate form of religious education (learning about religions and beliefs) and nurture knowledge, understanding and appreciation of the religious, the ethical and the spiritual as part of human development. However it clearly would not provide religious instruction and thus the issue of 'opting-out' of 'religious instruction' does not arise. (It might assist parental wishes relating to religious instruction by making the school premises available outside of normal hours but without committing its financial or staffing resources to this activity – parents would 'opt-in' for this.)

It is worth making mention here also of the contribution of the *Toledo Guiding Principles on Teaching about Religions and Beliefs in Public Schools* issued in 2007 by the Organisation for Security and Cooperation in Europe (OSCE).[8] These Guidelines, which are explored in greater detail by Jackson in this volume, situate Teaching Religion in the context of commitment to religious freedom and human rights focussing solely on the educational approach that seeks to provide teaching about different religions and beliefs as distinguished from instruction in a specific religion or belief. Toledo suggests ten Guidelines including:

> Teaching about religions and beliefs must be provided in ways that are fair, accurate and based on sound scholarship. Students should learn about religions and beliefs in an environment respectful of human rights, fundamental freedoms and civic values (Principle 1).

> Teaching about religions and beliefs is a major responsibility of schools, but the manner in which this teaching takes place should not undermine or ignore the role of families and religious or belief organizations in transmitting values to successive generations (Principle 3).

The Toledo Guidelines relate primarily to the teaching about religions and beliefs in state schools. The majority of schools in Ireland are not technically state schools but private schools aided by substantial state funding (constitutionally in Ireland the state 'provides for' rather than 'provides' education). However it is useful to regard such private schools as common schools serving the needs of the wider community and society. The Guidelines are most usefully seen as providing minimum criteria for the provision of Teaching Religion in order to promote democratic citizenship, mutual understanding and the common good. Thus teaching about religions and beliefs in the context of religious freedom should not be regarded as identical to 'religious education' but as a necessary aspect of it. Neither should the Guidelines be interpreted as stipulating that there must be a separate curriculum subject dedicated to teaching about religions and beliefs. The Guidelines allow for this to be approached in an interdisciplinary or thematic manner across curriculum subjects depending upon the circumstances obtaining in a particular situation.

The Guidelines cannot be interpreted as ignoring the need for pupils to come to a critical awareness and understanding of their own religious or belief tradition. They clearly state that (p. 19) 'learning about religions and beliefs contributes to forming and developing self-understanding, including a deeper appreciation of one's own religion or belief'. Social cohesion and tolerance requires mutuality – a balanced understanding of both 'my religion and belief' and 'the religion and belief of others'.

Finally the Guidelines present an opportunity to reflect upon the parental right of withdrawal from Teaching Religion. Such a right is upheld in a qualified manner. If teaching about religions and beliefs are necessary to promote the common good then the parental right to withdraw from such 'informational' rather than 'faith formational' curriculum elements does not serve that common good. Thus, 'where compulsory courses involving teaching about religions and beliefs are sufficiently neutral and objective, requiring participation in such courses as such does not violate freedom of religion and belief (although States are free to allow partial or total opt-outs in these settings)' (Toledo Conclusion 7). It is of course not possible, or even desirable, to attain absolute neutrality and objectivity in courses involving teaching about religions and beliefs. What is called for is fairness, accuracy of representation and balance in the context of freedom of religion and belief. Religion and belief have a strong affective component as well requiring critical and free appropriation.

Challenges and Opportunities for Educational Practice
The above survey provides an insight into Teaching Religion by indicating one way of describing the evolution of meanings ascribed to it from religious instruction, to educational religious education, to intercultural and inter-religious dialogue to promoting freedom of religion and belief. An alternative framework, that provided by Hull 2001, of teaching *for* religion, to teaching *about* religion, to teaching *from* religion was also identified. Central to the current public debate are issues related to parental school choice, withdrawal from aspects of Teaching Religion, identity, truth and values, freedom of religion and belief and the patronage or trusteeship of a publicly funded education system. Responding to the complexity and inter-relatedness of these issues requires that Teaching Religion will differ depending upon the particular circumstances of a school but will always require an approach that draws, in

an appropriate yet distinctive manner, on all of the above understandings including the informational, the formational and the transformational.

Recent debates about schooling in Ireland have often seemed to be based upon the simplistic notion that schools under denomination patronage do not include within their community, teachers and pupils of other faith traditions and none and that respect for religious diversity is only a characteristic of multi-denominational or non-denominational schools. This is not the case. All schools in Ireland now exhibit diversity as educational communities in terms of the pupils, teachers and parents and strive for inclusivity. In this sense all schools are multi-cultural and 'multi-religious/multi-faith/multi-world view'. It is confusing to interpret terms such as 'denominational' or 'multi-denomin-ational' as referring chiefly to student intake. It is more helpful, as argued above, to regard such terms as referring primarily to the patronage/ management body of the school and to highlight the responsibility of all schools to respectfully and creatively accommodate the actual diversity of religion and beliefs manifest within their educational communities while maintaining their ethos and authenticity and being of service to parents who have chosen the school as an expression of their particular denominational identity. Further the rights of patrons should not be regarded as absolute. Patrons are accountable to the Minister of Education and Skills for their patronage and stewardship of public resources and must act for the common good as well as for the good of the faith communities or associations they represent. Creativity and generosity will continue to be required of all patrons particularly when a full plurality of patronage is simply not viable economically or demographically. The White Paper announced by the Minister for Education and Skills in June 2012 will make an important contribution in this regard.

Any approach to 'teaching religion' that does not embrace inter-religious and inter-cultural dialogue is educationally limited. A plurality of world views must be appreciatively yet critically considered as part of the search for meaning and values and as a foundation for responsible active citizenship, mutual respect, tolerance and social cohesion. The June 2012 announcement of the Minister for Education and Skills charging the NCCA with the development of programmes related to Education about Religion and Beliefs (ERB) is the first curriculum initiative by the State relating to teaching religion in Irish primary schools and is a welcome development. It is in continuity with the previous intervention by the State in charging the NCCA with the drawing up of optional state syllabuses for Teaching Religion at second level. The challenge to all patron bodies, denominational and multi-denominational, is to contribute constructively and generously to the shaping of ERB which has the potential to be a shared element across the primary sector, taught to all pupils at the same time in a manner consistent with the ethos of the school. A further challenge to patron bodies is to integrate ERB with the distinctive provisions they make for faith development approaches to Teaching Religion which will legitimately require the separation of pupils into denominational groupings.

Conclusion: The Need for Policy Driven, Transparent, and Audited 'Teaching Religion'
The fullest possible development of the child as an active and responsibly religious citizen is promoted when every school 'provides' or 'provides for' appropriate forms of Teaching Religion in accordance with the patronage structure of the school taking full account of the rights and responsibilities of all involved. The balance and integration between 'religious education' and 'religious instruction' within Teaching Religion will vary between schools reflecting different patronage structures and sectors.

At the start of this chapter reference was made to the conversation between Alice and Humpty Dumpty concerning the meaning of terms and the power relationships involved between those who 'name' and those who use the language so provided. There is always a danger that Teaching Religion becomes associated with power and control rather than serving the full development of the child and the common good. The approach to Teaching Religion forms an essential aspect of school policy and must be formulated in partnership with all stakeholders taking due account of the rights and responsibilities involved. Parents should be aware of this policy at the time of enrolling their child and teachers at the point of application for employment. But policies are only as good as their implementation and the school's policy for Teaching Religion must be subject to regular and transparent quality assurance mechanisms. These should involve the patronage or management groups associated with the school but should also formally involve the state. Educating in the area of religion and belief are curriculum activities in the public space. The state as guardian of the common good has a legitimate interest in Teaching Religion including religious instruction and faith development since the pupil being educated within their faith tradition remain a citizen being part of a wider secular community and such denominational and confession Teaching Religion must promote solidarity with and respect for all. It is no longer sufficient to regard Religion Teaching as the sole concern of a patronage body or management group.

Notes

1. John M. Hull, *The Contribution of Religious Education to Religious Freedom: A Global Perspective* (2001) <http://www.johnmhull.biz/International%20Association%20for%20Religious%20Freedom.html> [accessed 5 Sept. 2012].

2. Anne Looney, 'Religious Education in the Public Space: Challenges and Contestations', in *International Handbook of the Religious, Moral and Spiritual Dimensions in Education*, ed. by de Souza, M. et al. (Dordrecht: Springer, 2006).

3.   Irish Catholic Bishops' Conference, *Catholic Primary Schools: A Policy for Provision into the Future* (Dublin: Veritas, 2007).

4.   Congregation for Catholic Education, *Circular Letter to the Presidents of Bishops' Conferences on Religious Education in Schools* (2009) <http://www.vatican.va/roman_curia/congregations/ccatheduc/documents/rc_con_ccatheduc_doc_20090505_circ-insegn-relig_en.html> [accessed 12 Sept. 2012].

5.   Dermot A. Lane, *Submission to the Forum on Patronage and Pluralism in Primary Schools in Ireland* (2011) <http://www.education.ie/servlet/blobservlet/fpp_sub_lane_dr_dermot.pdf> [accessed 5 Sept. 2012].

6.   Andrew G. McGrady, 'Religious Education, Citizenship and Human Rights: Perspectives from the United Nations and the Council of Europe', in *International Handbook of the Religious, Moral and Spiritual Dimensions in Education*, ed. by de Souza, M. et al. (Dordrecht: Springer, 2006).

7.   Ruairi Quinn TD, *Response to Report of the Advisory Group on the Forum on Patronage and Pluralism in the Primary Sector* (20 June 2012) <http://www.education.ie/home/home.jsp?maincat=&pcategory=10861&ecategory=11469&sectionpage=12251&language=EN&link=link001&page=1&doc=57707> [accessed 5 Sept. 2012].

8.   Organisation for Security and Cooperation in Europe, ODIHR, Advisory Council of Experts on Freedom of Religion and Belief, *Toledo Guiding Principles on Teaching about Religions and Beliefs in Public Schools* (2007) <http://www.oslocoalition.org/documents/toledo_guidelines.pdf> [accessed 12 Sept. 2012].

Section ii: Religious Pluralism in Educational Practice

CHAPTER FIVE

WHEN 'RACE' AND RELIGION MERGE:
THE SOCIAL, PERSONAL AND SCHOOL CONTEXT

Marie Parker-Jenkins

The Search for Mutual Ground

Searching for mutual ground is a timely topic in light of recent and ongoing religio-political events in the Middle East and elsewhere. This chapter provides an introductory framework which maps out key general themes and concepts which are pertinent to the task of searching for mutual ground between religiously diverse groups. It explores current research in the field of 'race' and ethnicity, while also raising central questions which underpin ongoing discourses on the issue of identity and religion.

Research Background

My own research background lies in the area of social justice with particular reference to ethnicity, religion and gender. An overlapping theme is that of Children's Rights[1] whereby the issues of religion relate to the educational needs of pupils from minority ethnic backgrounds, particularly those based on Islamic traditions.[2] I was motivated to research the educational needs of Muslim children after reviewing the politics of the *Satanic Verses* event.[3] Although the preliminary outrage was based on the inadequacy of the British blasphemy laws in protecting the religious sensitivities of Muslim citizens, one of the major concerns of Muslims living in the UK was the perceived failure of the educational system to respond to the educational needs of their children.[4] As an educationalist, I was interested in the academic success of Muslim children and those of other minority ethnic communities and I established a research project focusing on the perceptions of senior managers in both Muslim and non-Muslim schools.[5] I continued to document the area of ethnicity and education: specifically, the establishment of Muslim schools in the UK and their pursuit of public funding in line with support for other denominational schools.[6]

Discussion of 'race' and religion have relevance to many religious groups and I explored the wider issues of community, culture and identity with reference to new faith-based schools in the UK, i.e. Muslim, Sikh, Hindu, Greek Orthodox.[7] A further theme within these discourses has been concern over the poor academic attainment of pupils from culturally diverse backgrounds, and this body of research formed the basis of a further publication, *Aiming High: Raising the Attainment of Pupils from Culturally Diverse Backgrounds*.[8] More recently, my area of inquiry has included the link between race, ethnicity and children rights and I conducted a UK government-funded project on community cohesion with reference to Muslim and Jewish school communities.[9] In both these projects, the complexity of identity emerges and the overlap between 'race' and religion.

The Merging of 'Race' and Religion

There is often confusion over questions of identity, and from my research I found that teachers were understandably confused as to where 'race' and 'religion' merge or overlap. In other words what part of a child's cultural identity and educational needs is based on their 'race' or ethnic background and which aspects concern their religious convictions?

It is important at the outset to define key terms and the way in which I am using them in this chapter. The term 'race' is used to describe genetic heritage (including skin colour, and associated traits), while ethnicity describes *cultural* background or allegiance.

Ethnicity relates to a person's place of birth, symbolised by visible signifiers such as colour, dress, and lifestyle or birthplace allegiance. Indeed 'culture' is a complex expression of a sense of belonging and the passing on of customs, traditions, etc.[10] Associated with this is the fact that the concept of identity draws on a number of factors such as gender, age and social class. Identity relates to the understandings people hold about who they are and what is meaningful to them. This involves self-designation and designation by others and can be constructed in terms of *either* or *all of religion, race or ethnicity*.[11]

One key question for educationalists is where does religion end and culture start? Or is it the other way around? Within an Islamic perspective, religious identity often takes primacy and is connected to social inclusion: 'No one is excluded from the Islamic community on grounds of race or colour.' Further, for many Muslims 'National identity is a technicality, a passport, I am a member of the umma.'[12]

Having provided a brief conceptual background, I will now explore these concepts with reference to the personal, school and social contexts.

The Personal Context

In the early 1990s, I undertook research of Muslim schools with reference to gender and my research focused on the experience of Muslim girls in a Muslim school. This was in the aftermath of Rushdie's *Satanic Verses* highlighted earlier. I noted that whilst there was criticism of Muslim schools there had been very little research on this area and as a result I negotiated access to a local Muslim school. With the help of a Muslim friend acting as an intermediary, I arranged a preliminary meeting in her home between a senior community leader and myself. The project which evolved from this initial discussion drew on ethnographic techniques to explore the experience of Muslim girls in a Muslim secondary/high school.[13] The research methodology involved administering questionnaires to all pupils, during class time, followed by interviews with 80 per cent of the girls arranged on an individual or group basis according to pupil choice.

The girls in this study were vociferous about the importance of their religion and their Islamic identity. Moving away from the formal interview schedule, one young, British-born teenage girl explained the difficulty of being accepted as the child of an immigrant: 'We're always Asian Miss, never British.'[14] This sense of identity being linked to racial boundaries and the parents' country of origin was echoed in a project I subsequently conducted in Australia in 1995. Again this involved research in Muslim schools but the difference was that these educational institutions were supported by the government. As part of the inquiry, I explored Muslim girls' sense of identity in a state high school in New South Wales. These pupils defined their identity as follows: Lebanese, Arabic speaker, Female, Muslim, Australian.[15] Similarly in Zahid's research the complexity of personal identity is clearly evident in the participants' responses. 'First of all I'm Muslim. After that Pakistani. I wouldn't like to describe myself as English although I was born in this country.'[16]

Recent empirical studies on second and third generation British South Asians have noted an increasing tendency among British Pakistanis and Bangladeshis to assert their Muslim identities.[17] The complexity of personal identities is expressed by a student in a study carried out in the United Kingdom and represents the most detailed description I have found to date:

> I could view myself as a member of the following communities depending on the context and in no particular order: Black, Asian, Azad Kashmiri, Mirpuri, Jat, Marilail, Kungriwaley, Pakistani, English, British, Yorkshire man, from Bradford Moor. Any attempt to define me as only one of these would be meaningless.[18]

If we deconstruct the concept of personal identity further we can describe it as:

- Mono
- Dual
- Multiple
- Layered

- Gendered
- Situational
- Linguistic
- Cultural
- Racial
- National
- Religious
- Dynamic

These descriptors help to explain a person's sense of identity and they may overlap, be combined or vary according to the situation or the age of the individual. For example, senior members of staff in the Australian study noted that their pupils' sense of identity varied according to the context as they mediated the Australian school system and their home community(ies). Similarly, whilst Muslim girls in 1990s studies tended to remove their *hijab* or headscarf as they attended state schools, by the twenty-first century they were not prepared to follow their older sisters nor to compromise their religious convictions. Extending the discussion further, my research has explored the significance of religion and the desire to manifest religious belief from a human rights perspective. *The European Convention on Human Rights*,[19] for example, recognises the right of individuals to express their religious belief in their choice of dress, and this religious conviction should be respected by the state when it comes to school attendance.[20]

The School Context

Individuals may belong to a number of communities during their lifetime, such as family, kinship, school or state, and for some there is also one characterised by their religious belief. For some people, two communities overlap in the form of religion and the choice of school, and decisions concerning membership of these groups are informed by the way they construct their lives.

In a recent study I examined how Muslim and Jewish communities seek to protect themselves against threats of 'identity erosion', or against Islamophobia and anti-Semitism, through influence over the education of their children in faith-based schools.[21] This UK study investigated how anti-Semitic and Islamophobic hostility surfaced toward schools formed by Jewish and Muslim communities and how this bodes in terms of a government agenda aimed at developing greater community cohesion. This was in the context of the British government agenda on social cohesion post 9/11, the riots in northern towns in England in 2001, and bombings in London in 2005. The UK government saw school as the place where 'community cohesion' should be developed. The Department of Children, Schools and Families (2007) in its non-statutory *Guidance on the Duty to Promote Community Cohesion* highlighted educational institutions particularly as helping to achieve political initiatives:

[The] schools' role here is crucial: by creating opportunities for pupils' achievement and enabling every child and young person to achieve their potential, schools make a significant contribution to long term community cohesion.[22]

The main aims of this research were to answer the following questions: why, how, and in what way is religious/cultural sustainability regarded as critical to a school's *raison d'être*; and what are the experiences of engagement and estrangement/alienation with the wider community? This was built on my previous work,[23] which posed the question; 'do we ask enough of faith-based schools in terms of community engagement on behalf of their pupils?' The fieldwork took place between 2007–2008, involving nine schools in the Midlands and Northern England, and over one hundred stakeholder participants were involved including senior managers, governors, teachers, parents, pupil/student focus groups, and members of the wider communities. The study involved a case study of five Muslim schools and four Jewish schools that were representative of primary/elementary and secondary/high school levels, which incorporated a range of independent to state-funded institutions within both religious traditions. The slight discrepancy in the number of schools was based on a decision to include a Muslim girls' school headed by a non-Muslim head teacher thus providing the widest spectrum of perspectives.

Jewish schools in the United Kingdom tend to differentiate themselves through an added nomenclature, such as Liberal/Progressive, Modern Orthodox, Ultra Orthodox, or Zionist, depending on the communities' interpretation of Jewish identity.[24] Conversely, schools based on an Islamic ethos in the United Kingdom are normally identified under the collective term 'Muslim School' although there is huge differentiation within them based on sectarian and cultural factors;[25] elsewhere in Europe they are described as 'Islamic schools'.[26] To ensure a wide spectrum, our research included Liberal/Progressive Jewish schools and those based on a Modern Orthodox Jewish ethos. Within the Muslim sample schools, selection was based on an Islamic ethos, which ranged from 'orthodox' to more 'liberal' in terms of interpretation of religious texts. All five schools were Sunni due to the absence of any based on a Shia tradition.[27] Children in the Muslim schools were predominantly second or third generation British Muslims from a diversity of backgrounds: e.g. Pakistani, Bangladeshi, and Middle Eastern. Those in the Jewish schools were mostly from families established in the United Kingdom for many decades and generally representative of European backgrounds.

For the purpose of this study we defined the concept of Islamophobia as 'unfounded hostility towards Islam, and therefore, fear or dislike of all or most Muslims'.[28] Anti-Semitism was defined as 'a certain perception of Jews, which may be expressed as hatred toward Jews'.[29] Theoretically, we employed Denham's notion of 'self-segregation by choice'[30] as it relates to 'cultural sustainability' within schools. We defined cultural sustainability as the passing on of traditions, customs, and values through the family, and the extent to which it is possible to operate in a non-Islamic or non-Jewish state.

We obtained data from the school stakeholders which informed us about their sense of identity as part of the religious school community and their experience of engagement or disengagement with the wider community. For example, one teenage girl said:

> here we are a community; we are all together in the same situation, so it just builds up your self-esteem. Being in this society ... you are not anything ... here we are together ... and we don't have to face anything.[31]

Similarly, Swain found 'collective identities were built on self-definition as Muslim first, but this was not a fixed identity ... the construction of a collective Muslim identity [was] as a strategic response to the racialised and stigmatised status of being a Muslim in school'.[32] Further, within the school community context a Head teacher explained:

> We are very conscious of thinking of the wider community in 3 levels; the Jewish wider community ... that includes Orthodox, Ultra Orthodox, Non-observant, Progressive, Liberal. A wider community, other faiths, and then a wider general community. English society in its multicultural mixed-up self.[33]

Beyond this view of community engagement, our data revealed a feeling of hostility from the wider multicultural society. Sacks argues that multi-culturalism emerged as a reality based on the large extent of migration toward Western countries from non-Western countries, which in turn led to the idea of 'one nation, one culture'.[34] In our study one Muslim school principal argued:

> Kids have to live and work in a society which they have to know something about. Just celebrating each other's festivals is a very facile approach – it doesn't teach respect. The kids who throw stones at me or spit at me in the street have been through a multicultural education and probably their parents have – you could say the educational system has failed them.

Hostility toward faith-based schools challenges the success in developing community cohesion. As in the USA and in Europe,[35] all schools in the UK have to be vigilant to potential attacks, and there is evidence of an increase in violence in British schools.[36] However, Muslim and Jewish schools are particularly vulnerable to hostility that can be defined as anti-Semitism or Islamophobia,[37] and this was evidenced in our research. For example, a female Muslim teacher working in the North of England stated:

> Here there are many, many Sikh women that have been attacked because people assume they are Muslim. I don't know what your religion is, but if you went out in this dress, people would assume that you are Muslim just because you have a headscarf on and they would have a go at you.

She added with reference to community relations:

> Certainly xenophobia has increased since 9/11 ... and here at the moment there are two issues, one is Palestine and Israel ... and then there is Afghanistan, Iraq and America and so forth, and that is a separate issue. But it seems that they have joined the two together and they are using the word 'terrorist' for everything and anything.

The disproportionate attention that faith-based schools receive regarding cohesion is frequently grounded in a lack of knowledge of what takes place in these schools. As all schools in the UK have been obliged to demonstrate 'community cohesion' since Autumn 2008, there is a need for embedding this concept into the policy framework. However, as this critique of 'community cohesion' suggests there is also a need to challenge policy because previous initiatives have been severely criticised.[38] In terms of disengagement, there is a fear of British society, and this is seen as one of the main factors preventing minority religious groups from integrating fully with the host society:

> There is lots of evidence of anti-Semitism in the wider society ... If I ask most of my parents do they have non-Jewish friends I would say at least 70% probably don't have a single non-Jewish friend. A large number of our families associate within not a religious, but within an exclusively Jewish social community, all the people they see and most of the people they know are Jewish.[39]

UK policy has signalled the role of schools in helping to promote social cohesion in the light of the Stephen Lawrence Inquiry which investigated the murder of a black student. Visiting and connecting with different schools and those of a different faith was an approach used by most of the schools in our study. The idea of twinning has been advocated for many years.[40] However, the impetus to carry this out has been based on individual school response, and the difficulty of overcoming logistical and financial hurdles has meant that in many cases schools have remained culturally isolated and ignorant of 'the Other'. The 'Other' in this case may be within as well as beyond a religious tradition. A deputy head teacher in a modern orthodox school reported:

> We have been trying for some time to find a Muslim school that will engage with us. It's trying to find a liberal Muslim school because we want our children to meet moderates of other religions.[41]

From a UK perspective, The Ouseley Report (2001), in its review of race relations and the failure to prepare young people for life in a multicultural society, highlighted 'a virtual apartheid' between schools. Likewise, the Cantle Report (2001) highlighted how distinct religious or ethnic communities can live within metres of each other but have no social bonds or shared cultural capital. Government is said to be keen to tackle this problem and sees the role of schools as paramount to the agenda, particularly in the light of violent acts of terrorism perpetrated in the name of religion. Resistance to effective engagement between schools will mean that the notion of 'community cohesion' is left to the goodwill of schools, and potentially government inspection at a rudimentary level will mean that the policy may remain at the level of pious but empty rhetoric.

The Social Context

Individuals may choose to select schools on the basis of religious identity and this can provide a safe and culturally sustaining community. However, schools do not operate in a vacuum. Apart from influence by government agencies, there is a level of social interaction with the wider social context. It is this level of social engagement which is particularly challenging for some citizens. This was expressed by a teacher as follows:

> For example, if I go out tonight and burn a shop and someone knew it was me, in the newspaper it would more than likely say a 'Muslim terrorist.' If a non-Muslim, they would say it was an arson attack. Only last week there was a man who said he had a rucksack with a bomb in it, but he was white, so what the police did was shoot him with rubber bullets … this [other] guy was walking up and down and he looked like an Asian. If he had a beard and he actually said he had explosives in his bag, they would have used live bullets on him … that is Islamophobia. (Female Muslim teacher working in the North of England)

Associated with a sense of hostility from the outside community, particularly among Muslim respondents, the notion of a lack of acceptance was also raised. One female teacher commented:

> Muslims feel under quite a lot of pressure … say today news come on and there is an explosion on a bus in London … it could be that a petrol tank exploded but it seems that the fault only lies with Muslims and it doesn't lie with anything else, we are the cause for everything.

In addition, in terms of acceptance by the wider community, she continued:

> I have been here 34 years … those people who have tried to become part of the community have been rejected … at the moment we don't think we have been accepted by the majority of the community because we are always being undermined, and if you are being undermined you have to associate with something else.

This view is replicated in the work of Modood in terms of a lack of belonging expressed by immigrants despite long-term residency in the UK.[42] It is this perception and experience of being unwelcome, rather than of attachment to their country of origin, that diminishes a sense of belonging in British society. For both Jews and Muslims, family ties and the presence of people with similar ethnic or religious backgrounds were seen as an important reason for moving to and valuing the locality in which they lived and for which they chose the school. Recent research shows that both migrants and established Muslim residents stated that they derived a sense of security from the presence of people sharing their religion, ethnicity or country of origin in their locality.[43]

The failure of multiculturalism to deliver equitable outcomes in society and an attempt to look beyond this concept are echoed in Britain and elsewhere. For example, Hollinger and Kincheloe and Steinberg's work on critical multiculturalism[44] highlight the inadequacy of past government policy in this area. Conversely, the emphasis on 'bonding social capital'[45] assists in promoting shared values within the school community and a cooperative practice between the school and the home, which is perceived as lacking in non-faith-based schools.

So far this chapter has drawn on the experience of UK, Australia and other countries in responding to the significance of religious identity. The Republic of Ireland has more recently experienced the reality of cultural pluralism and so the remainder of the chapter will explore 'race' and religion with reference to the Irish context.

The Irish Context

Irish society has experienced unprecedented demographic change since the turn of the twenty-first century. Increasingly educators have to respond to the changing nature of cultural diversity in their classrooms. There has been immigration in Ireland throughout its history but the scale of the phenomenon post-2003 in the Republic of Ireland has meant that issues of cultural diversity and multiculturalism have become more prevalent.

The concept of 'Multiculturalism' is expressed in terms of creating tolerance for minority groups, raising awareness of their religious and cultural practices, celebrating differences, dispelling ignorance and reducing prejudice to create a harmonious society.[46] Closely related is the concept of 'Interculturalism', particularly evident in Irish education policy, which refers to engaging in a dialogue with the other by which both benefits.[47] There is an understanding that there is reciprocity and learning from and with each other, with an active connotation requiring accommodation from all sides; re-configuration of views and beliefs system.[48] 'Cultural diversity' as a concept has been used more commonly in the post-Accession period in the Republic of Ireland (2003) whereby people with different cultural backgrounds live together. The recent Diasporas of people into Ireland from Europe and elsewhere, such as from Poland, Nigeria, Lithuania, Indonesia and East Asia,[49] have created a society, which is more ethnically, linguistically and religiously diverse than in previous years.

In Ireland, diversity is more visible due to the relative size of the country in physical population terms. Minority ethnic groups are identifiably different, through such things as religion or dress, distinguishing them from the majority ethnic population.[50] Migratory movements have always been a feature of European society, mainly due to economic reasons, but also resulting from conflicts and wars. However, people in European societies, as elsewhere do not always view populations with different cultural backgrounds as a source of enrichment for their society, or for their education systems: instead, this difference may provide a challenging situation.[51]

Language is dynamic but for the purpose of this chapter with reference to the Irish context, the terms *cultural diversity* and *interculturalism* reflect recent and appropriate terminology within the Irish context and in light of social, economic and political policy development. Traditionally characterised as 'Catholic, White and Gaelic/Celtic',[52] Irish schools are said to be finding it difficult to 'recognise and acknowledge new expressions of race, culture and religion'.[53]

Historically there has been little recognition of cultural diversity in Ireland with a general myth that it has been a mono-cultural society.[54] However, a parallel indigenous culture has been provided from the Irish Traveller community.[55] There is, therefore, no such thing as a mono-cultural Ireland. Furthermore, a culture by definition is never static; it is constantly evolving through different influences,[56] and there has been evidence of cultural diversity in Ireland over the last number of centuries. The issue today is about the scale and speed of cultural diversity in Ireland.[57] Throughout Irish history there have been a number of minority ethnic–religious groups present such as Jews, Chinese, Muslim and Asian Communities.[58] Yet, since the foundation of the state there has been resistance to and very tight regulation of the immigration of 'ethnic' others.[59]

Within the country, there has also been a range of different languages like Irish, Irish Sign language, and Gammon/Cant – a language historically known to and used by Irish Travellers.[60] Historically, Ireland has not been linguistically homogeneous. The new interest in reviving the Irish language points to a desire by people to sustain Irish language linguistics as well as diversity within the Irish nation.[61] This is manifested in the school curriculum where Irish is compulsory for all pupils from 5–16 (NCCA). Importantly, whilst there is increasing support for the Irish language this does not extend to promoting Travellers language[62] and there is an unwillingness to acknowledge and accept Travellers as a legitimate ethnic group in Irish society.[63] Thus the history of cultural and linguistic diversity in the Republic of Ireland is both complex and politically contentious.[64]

The Department of Education and Skills placed a priority on provision of English language support teachers in response to growing cultural diversity in Ireland. Budgetary cutbacks in late 2008, however, mean that this support is unlikely to continue.[65] Also, whilst a number of reports have been commissioned and published by the DES and others,[66] there has been an emphasis on policy perspectives rather than classroom practice. Similarly, anti-racism and respect for diversity has been included in initiatives organised by the Department for Education and Skills, but there is no anti-racist policy.[67] Under the *Equal Status Act 2000* and *2004*, schools may give preference to a child who is of the schools' religious denomination over a child who is not, or refuse to admit a child not of the school's religious ethos. This can result in children having to travel long distances for their education.[68]

Emigration has always been a feature of Irish history and the Irish Diaspora is one of the largest in the world. What is different now is that there has been a trend of migration into Ireland, and Irish Nationals remained within the country to help build what became a significant economy, know colloquially as 'the Celtic Tiger'.[69]

Table One

Comparison of religious affiliation in Ireland between 2002 and 2006

Denomination	2002	2006	% Increase
Roman Catholic	3,462,606	3,681,446	6
Church of Ireland (Incl. Protestant)	115,611	125,585	9
Muslim	19,147	32,539	70
Buddhist	3,894	6,516	67
Hindu	3,099	6,082	96

Source: (CSO 2006, CSO 2002)

Furthermore, demographic data available from the Central Statistics Office reveals the shifting nature of cultural diversity in the Republic of Ireland as demonstrated in table 1. For example, in the 2002 report, out of a population of just under 4 million, 3,462, 606 people reported to be Roman Catholic, 19,147 Muslim (Islamic), 3,894 Buddhist, and 3,999 Hindu. At the following census in 2006 statistics referring to religious affiliation demonstrated the following; the category of Catholic had increased to 3,681,446 which may be explained by the arrival of significant numbers of emigrants from Poland 63,276. Similarly the number of Muslims doubled to 32,539; Buddhists to 6,516, and Hindus 6,082.

Studies on Ireland's New Religious Movements note that the religious landscape of the island of Ireland has transformed dramatically and that in the Republic, the Catholic Church which has been dominant since the late nineteenth century, has faced a steady decline in levels of practice.[70] As such, people classify themselves in a range of ways, as religious and non-religious, and 'alternative' spiritualities have become more widespread. The World religions of Islam, Buddhism and Hinduism now have a presence as a result of migration and religious conversion, and this has particular significance in Ireland, where religion has historically been bound up with ethnic and political identity, both north and south of the border.

As well as religious affiliation, cultural diversity in Ireland can be demonstrated by the fact that in the 2006 census, 35,326 people gave Africa as their birth place, 46,953 Asian, and 275,775 EU of which the largest groups were from Poland, UK, Lithuania and Latvia. The speed and diversity of these demographic phenomena has impacted on the changing nature of diversity, and challenges in the classroom.[71] Despite changes in the labour market in the downturn of the economy and an exodus of Irish nationals since 2008,[72] non-Irish groups have not appreciably decreased, particularly those with families and it is argued 'immigration and migration are in flux but diversity is here to stay'.[73]

Immigration also means that 'the global becomes local and the local is changed by the global',[74] and as such Ireland has been and will continue to be impacted by wider social forces. Religious affiliation, as demonstrated in the 2006 and 2011 Census reports, highlights religious pluralism in Ireland today as well as ethnic diversity.

Table Two

Comparison of religious affiliation in Ireland between 2006 and 2011

Denomination	2006	2011	% Increase
Roman Catholic	3,681,446	3,861,335	4.8
Church of Ireland (Incl. Protestant)	125,585	129,039	2.7
Muslim	32,539	49,204	50.6
Buddhist	6,516	8,703	33.6
Hindu	6,082	10,688	75.7

Source: (CSO 2011, CSO 2006)

For example, the English were reported to be the largest minority group in the 2006 Census and this group was superseded by the Polish minority in 2011 as demonstrated in Table 2. This latter group began arriving in sizeable numbers after 2004 when Poland accessed to the European Union. Their children operate in Irish schools with a dual heritage, but in terms of personal identity are they Polish–Irish or is it the other way around? How do we decide and who do we mean by 'we'? Hybrid identity is a feature of American society and is well known with nomenclature like 'Irish–American' or 'American–Irish', but this practice is relatively new to Ireland. This will be an emerging issue as we explore what it is to be Irish today and the different forms this might take.

Other implications lie in the significance of religious diversity in terms of policy and practice. Other countries such as Canada, USA and Australia have had many decades to respond to the reality of a multi-cultural, multifaith and multilingual society. This includes pre and in-service education for teachers to develop 'religious literacy', to understand that children's sense of identity may be based on their religious affiliation, and that we have in our classrooms, 'children of all faiths and none'.[75]

From an educational perspective this relates to identity and the achievement of pupils from culturally diverse backgrounds. This involves examining the experience of pupils from minority ethnic groups in Ireland and their academic outcomes.[76] It is not the fact that children of minority ethnic background or their parents do not have high aspirations, but it may be that some teachers and schools do.[77] Research has demonstrated concerns over underachievement in other contexts, for example UK and Northern Ireland.[78] Ireland is in an ideal position to embrace good practice from other countries but also to avoid the pitfalls. For example there is a need to take racism seriously; to celebrate diversity but tackle racism through the curriculum and school practices.[79] As part of the discussion we also need to recognise that we are all 'ethnically located',[80] and for children particularly, there are dual and multiple senses of identity. This means that we need to review the concepts of identity and citizenship in Ireland,[81] and develop the sense of 'belonging'.[82] It is also important to ensure that institutional barriers do not lead to educational disadvantage.[83] These implications refer to groups and communities but it is important to acknowledge the child as an individual, with their own personality, needs and aspirations. Indeed, there is a view that there is no such thing as a Muslim, Catholic or Sikh child but the child of Muslim, Catholic and Sikh parents.[84]

In conclusion educational institutions should be places where all children feel welcome and safe, regardless of their religious/ethnic background or other factors such as class, gender, sexual orientation or disability. But how can you develop the inclusive school and society so all feel valued? That is the challenge that will occupy practitioners in the future if we are to have an equitable, stable and successful society.

NOTES

1. Parker-Jenkins, 1999, 2011. Marie Parker-Jenkins would like to acknowledge the support of her research assistant, Manny O'Grady (PhD) in the preparation of this chapter.
2. Parker-Jenkins, 1995, 2002, 2005, 2008.
3. Qureshi and Khan, 1989; Modood, 1992.
4. Qureshi and Khan, 1989.
5. Parker-Jenkins, 1995.
6. Parker-Jenkins, 2002, 2008.
7. Parker-Jenkins et al., 2005.
8. Parker-Jenkins et al., 2006.
9. Parker-Jenkins, 2011.
10. Giddens, 1995; Parekh, 2000; Werbner, 2002.
11. Giddens, 2001; Hall, 1992; Barth, 1969.
12. Hulmes, 1989, p. 32.
13. ESRC, 1993.
14. UK ESRC Project, Parker-Jenkins and Haw, 1996.
15. Parker-Jenkins, 1996.
16. Zahid, p. 58. Personal identity is also echoed in the work of Shain, 2011.
17. Shain, 2011.
18. Richardson and Wood, 2004, p. 4.
19. Council of Europe, 1947.
20. Parker-Jenkins, 2011.
21. ESRC, 2008, Parker-Jenkins and Glenn, 2011.
22. Guidance on the Duty to Promote Community Cohesion, p. 4.
23. Parker-Jenkins, Hartas, and Irving 2005.
24. Miller, 2001.
25. Parker-Jenkins, Hartas and Irving, 2005.
26. Walford, 2001.
27. Association of Muslim Schools, 2009.
28. Runnymede Trust, 1997, p. 1.
29. European Monitoring Centre on Racism and Xenophobia, 2009, p. 1.
30. Denham's (2001).
31. Muslim Girls' School, Parker-Jenkins and Glenn, 2011.
32. Shain, 2011, p. 77.
33. Progressive-Liberal Jewish School, Parker-Jenkins & Glenn 2011.
34. Sacks, 2007, p. 35.
35. Larkin, 2007 and The Independent, 2007.
36. Parker-Jenkins, 2008.
37. Runnymede Trust, 2008.
38. Troyna and Carrington, 1990; Gillborn, 1995; Gilroy, 1987.
39. Jewish head teacher, Parker-Jenkins and Glenn 2011.
40. Parker-Jenkins, 1995.
41. Parker-Jenkins and Glenn, 2011.
42. Modood, 2005.
43. Jayaweera and Choudhury, 2008.

44.   Hollinger's (1995) 'Post Ethnic America: Beyond Multiculturalism'; Kincheloe and Steinberg's (1997) work on critical multiculturalism.
45.   Coleman, 1994; Pugh and Telhaj, 2007.
46.   Lynch, 1988; Jeffcoate 1981, Parekh 2005.
47.   Tormey and Haran, 2006.
48.   Finkbeiner, 2006; Guilherme, 2003; Fennes and Hapgood, 1997; Kramsch, 1993.
49.   CSO, 2006.
50.   Dadzie, 2001.
51.   Grünberger, 2009.
52.   Torvey and Share, 2003, p. 343.
53.   Mulcahy et al., 2007.
54.   Tyrell et al., 2011; Cosgrove et al., 2011.
55.   Hayes, 2008.
56.   Johnson and Rinvolucri, 2010; O'Dowd, 2005.
57.   Irish National Committee, 2006; Nestor and Regan, 2011.
58.   Tormey and Haran, 2003; Loyal, 2002.
59.   Cullen, 2000.
60.   NCCA, 2006.
61.   Share et al., 2000.
62.   Hayes, 2000.
63.   Fanning, 2007.
64.   Devine, 2011.
65.   DES, 2009.
66.   DES, 2002.
67.   NUIG, 2006.
68.   Educate Together, 2005.
69.   Gardiner, 1994.
70.   Cosgrove et al., 2011.
71.   McGorman and Sugre, 2007; Lyons, 2010.
72.   *The Irish Times*, 2008.
73.   Smyth, 2009.
74.   Devine, 2007, p. 143.
75.   Synod, 2001.
76.   Darmody et al., 2012; Battistich, 2004; Strand, 2011.
77.   Parker-Jenkins et al., 2008.
78.   DES, 2003.
79.   Connolly and Khaoury, 2008; Drudy and Lynch, 1993; Pavee Point, 2005; Knox, 2011; Connolly, 2002a&b.
80.   Hall, 1992.
81.   Tormey, 2009.
82.   Baumeister and Leary, 1995.
83.   Darmody et al., 2012.
84.   Hawkins, 2006.

CHAPTER SIX

CATHOLICISM, RELIGIOUS PLURALISM AND EDUCATION FOR THE COMMON GOOD

Gavin D'Costa

Introduction

We live at a curious moment in the history of the Catholic Church in Western Europe. It makes us blind and causes us to stumble. Historically, the Church has been central in fusing together a cultural vision underpinned by Greek, Roman and Jewish traditions into something called 'Christian civilization' which is responsible for so much that most western Europeans love and cherish. Ironically, those same western Europeans currently equate Catholicism with corruption, sexual abuse, misogyny, and secrecy. Obviously, these elements are present in Catholicism, but their presence has obscured a narrative which would also recount how the Catholic Church is responsible for the emergence of modern science, the security of the rule of law which grew out of canon law, the unique sense of human rights and freedom that apply to all peoples, charity as a virtue, splendid art, music and culture, a philosophy grounded in reason, the invention of the university, and innumerable other gifts that we take for granted.[1] During the 1960s at the Second Vatican Council, the Catholic Church began to deal with its transition from a Church supported by European stately power to a Church within a secular state and a Church within a pluralist society, generating an approach to toleration and liberty that would deeply affect the United Nations (UN). Indeed the UN charter for Universal Human Rights included as one drafter, the French Catholic philosopher, Jacques Martian. In all these momentous changes the Church of course sometimes blocked the momentum that it had set in place.

This chapter will not analyse how this curious state of affairs has come about, or suggest that the Church itself is free from blame in bringing about this crisis. Neither does it suggest that the Catholic Church is a spotless institution without need of internal renewal and reform. The latter would certainly be implausible. Instead this chapter outlines what I, as a Catholic theologian, view as a difficult challenge. It claims that finding mutual ground with other religions requires Catholics to be fully Catholic, because for Catholics this is what being fully human is. Second, through conversations and learning from other religions, both the task of finding common ground and learning to be fully human are enhanced. Having made these two claims I want to defend them in two parts. In part one I want to look at three obvious objections to my claim. I want to suggest that these objections can in principle be refuted, but recognise there is a long-term conversation to be had with Catholicism's 'cultured despisers'. The chapter only sets out a general road map, and clearly much more detailed work would be required to develop these arguments further. If part one is defensive (or in more traditional terms, engaging in apologetics), part two is speculative and constructive, in outlining what a Catholic approach to other religions might look like within a Catholic educational curriculum.

Part I: Three Counter Claims Examined

The first two counter claims to be examined form the heart of a common-sense objection to the Catholic claim that to be fully human is to be fully Catholic.[2] Objectively one might argue that the Catholic claim is sheer arrogance as all around us today we see non-Catholics being more fully human than many Catholics. This might be termed the empirical objection. Many non-Catholics exemplify good and holy lives, work tirelessly for the common good, show love and compassion, and are obviously admirable and amazing. Aung San Suu Kyi, the Dalai Lama and Mahatma Gandhi are just tips of a huge iceberg.

The response to such statements is to agree that they are obviously true and are realities to be celebrated and enjoyed. Anyone who denied the goodness, truth and sanctity are found outside the church would be crazy – and a bad Catholic as well. Vatican II happily acknowledges this in *Lumen gentium* 16 and *Nostra aetate* and *Gaudium et spes*.[3] The Catholic claim however is not an empirical one that all Catholics will be free from sin and that non-Catholics are deeply sinful. It is a claim primarily about Jesus Christ and not about Catholics failing to follow their calling. Secondarily, and dependently, it is about the sacramental Church that mediates Christ to the world not about bad bishops or corrupt Catholics. Not that the latter is not a deep scandal and a call to reform, but the logical point is that the latter is not actually an empirical problem to the claim being made. The primary claim is that Christ teaches us to be most fully human through the power of the Holy Spirit so that our goal, which is union with God and each other in truth and justice, is slowly attained. Being truly human has a trinitarian structure. The structure of *The Catechism of the Catholic Church* (CCC) is revealing.[4] In Part One it sets out the profession of faith concerning the triune God. In Part Two it sets out the celebration of this in the sacraments of the church, and in Part Three shows how this affects every aspect of Christian life, from mental health, media, to the market economy. The paragraph opening this third section puts it well:

> The dignity of the human person is rooted in her creation in the image and likeness of God; it is fulfilled in her vocation to divine beatitude. It is essential to a human being freely to direct herself to this fulfilment. By her deliberate actions, the human person does, or does not, conform to the good promised by God and attested by moral conscience. Human beings make their own contribution to their interior growth; they make their whole sentient and spiritual lives into means of this growth. With the help of grace they grow in virtue, avoid sin, and if they sin they entrust themselves as did the prodigal son to the mercy of our Father in heaven. In this way they attain to the perfection of charity.[5]

Who we truly are and what we are meant to be, both as persons and as a society, is revealed in the trinity, and most specifically in the Son, the crucified, suffering and risen one. Being fully human means that we pursue God together, revealed to us in Christ through the Spirit, with all our mind, heart, body and will, and that we pursue this relationship with love and charity under the guidance of the church. The claim is fundamentally Christological and ecclesiological, not an empirical one about who is the nicest person on the block. Thankfully, Vatican II and the *Catechism* never claim that non-Catholics are going to hell or that they lack goodness, truth, or sanctity. The magisterium never claims that Catholics do not have loads to learn from the beliefs and practices to be found within the religions of the world, for what is good, true, and holy always derives from the one God who is known to us in Christ. However there are new objections to my claim in the light of this answer, but such is the intellectual life.[6]

A second possible objection might be that if we are not talking about people's actions and their orientation, as in an empirical claim, but rather about objective revelation, can or does the Catholic Church really claim Christ is the only revelation of God? This is manifestly not so as we find so many truths in other religions and non-religious movements. The Catholic Church does not have a monopoly on truth, so the claim fails.

In response it is important to recognise that since Vatican II the Catholic Church teaches two very balanced points on this matter. First, the fullness of God is known through Christ who is God's self-revelation. It obviously cannot say other than that without being unfaithful to the truth of the incarnation. It also says, secondly, that God never leaves Himself without witness, either in conscience, nature and cultures (religious and non-religious). This second line freely affirms the grace of God in the world and Pope John Paul II developed a strong doctrine of the Spirit's presence in the hearts of women and men, in their cultures and religions, that draw them toward the good, the true, and the beautiful. Hence, there is no hard exclusivist claim that truth, goodness and holiness cannot be found outside the Church. Between these two balances is the complexity of sin and the fall – where all people, including Christians (sometimes quite surpassing others!), busily spend their time obscuring and blocking the light. Thankfully, those same people also spend some of the time allowing the light to shine and building structures and communities where the light can shine. God works in nature, conscience, and through cultures – and thus through religions and non-religious traditions, drawing all women and men, all societies, toward Christ who is the fullness of God's revelation.

The second objection thus collapses for it works on a binary that does not exist, i.e. the Catholic Church is the sole repository of truth versus a fallen world. However the actual claim I want to defend is that the normative and decisive truth of who God is has been revealed so that we can rejoice in truth, goodness and holiness wherever we find it and it will teach us and lead us deeper into Christ – and deeper into the mystery of his work throughout creation and cultures. What this means in practice, is obviously complex and dependent on various contexts. What it means in the Irish, English or for that matter the Bolivian context is going to differ. Yet exploring it will certainly lead us into a deeper appreciation of other ways of life as well as the religions and cultures of the world. It also leads us into a deeper critique of the ways that block the light of Christ, both by us as a Christian community and by other non-Christian groups. We must always start with ourselves if our critique of others is to have any credibility. And the Vatican II documents on ecumenism[7] suggest this latter principle which obviously applies also to non-Christian religions: let us be self-critical first about reform before we criticise another.

It is important to acknowledge that there are many more objections and that the reader might not even be mildly persuaded by my two skeletal arguments but give me the benefit of the doubt and hear me out. So far I am claiming that to be fully human is to be fully Catholic, because God makes Himself known in the incarnation, and shows us what being human is, and shows that to us in a community of humans. I am also claiming this is a perfectly reasonable epistemological and ontological claim. Finally, I'm also claiming that it is only from such a base that we can work toward discovering mutual ground with other religions.

I should add, as an aside, that actually most religions and non-religions make similar claims. The Dalai Lama actually believes that to gain final release one needs to be a male de Lug Buddhist monk.[8] In this instance to be fully human is to be fully Buddhist. Or, some would suggest, to be fully human and enlightened is to be fully Marxist, so that one can oppose false consciousness that keeps the masses enslaved. Or to be fully human is to be devoted to Lord Krishna, for in that devotion we find the source of what allows us to flourish and serve society. These groups go about locating 'mutual ground' on the basis of standing on the ground which forms who they are. If we forget this, then, like a dog we are always chasing our tails. The dog is just interested in catching his tale until he gets tired and flops. However, unlike dogs we chase our tails with an aspiration toward being neutral and fair to all.

It is here that we meet the final third objection. If our schools (like our society – the argument can easily be extended) are shared by people from many faiths and none, are we not more likely to find common ground by refusing to side with any one religion? Should we not seek together to construct a vision of neutral ground and the common good? Some might argue that we should not give epistemological and ontological priority to any one religion – precisely to serve the common good.

Responses to this argument are found in various forms of modernity that believe that neutral ground exists and one should seek it. The wars of religion that devastated Europe and some argue, Ireland as well, call for this radical shift. Rationalism, technique, democracy, science, and pragmatism have all been possible contenders to provide this neutral ground within the modernist project, but they have been increasingly called into question as they provide procedure but no content. More insidiously, they often provide content under the guise of procedure. I want to argue that there is no starting point without the privileging of some epistemic and ontological presuppositions. This type of modernist neutrality has been called into question by the social, natural, and humanistic sciences in different ways, even if it haunts the popular imagination and the intelligentsia press. It also haunts educational theories that developed in the 1950s and 60s and obviously impacts upon many educators today, possibly upon some of the readers of this chapter.

Let me briefly sketch two problems within the educational context which I'm sure you will be more than familiar with. First, in practice, the study of religions from a neutral vantage point has structurally favoured a secularist agenda, whereby all religions are paraded for the pupil and either described neutrally so that no value judgement is allowed or possible. Yet this means that one of the most important elements in education, critical judgement, is stifled. To fail to engage with the religions critically actually does a profound disservice to them as they make remarkable demands about how to be fully human, how to conduct our lives, how to relate to ultimate questions. So, when this type of neutralist position is pushed hard, the platform from which judgements are made has to be from a non-religious position so that no one religion is privileged. This inevitably means that secular values and judgements are promoted in the process of evaluation. I am not saying that these values are wrong or unhelpful, although some of them are. I am saying that epistemologically, the neutralist position in the study of religions sides with secularism and thus undercuts the primary rationale for adopting the approach of neutralism. This is not neutralism, it is simply one of the voices of the group implicitly claiming a privilege, but insidiously arguing that it has none and believes no one should have such a privilege. Of course there is certainly a touch of caricature here but the work of social theorists like Jürgen Habermas and John Rawls and educational theorists like Don Wiebe and Ninian Smart substantiate this argument, which I have developed in other publications.[9] My tentative conclusion is that there is no neutral standpoint from which to study religions and deal with religious pluralism in the educational context. Consequently Catholics need to show why their standpoint is a good one to do the job of helping to educate the young about religious plurality so that mutual ground and the common good may be sought – and found.

So far this chapter has explored preliminary arguments that help to defend the obvious objections to my starting point assumptions. Now I will try and make those assumptions do some constructive work developing them in relation to schools and to education more generally.

Part II: The Catholic School and Religious Pluralism
I want to argue that the Catholic vision generates the possibility of properly studying religions which will be a benefit to all pupils, both Catholics and non-Catholics. That is in part because the particularity of Catholicism recognises the importance of respecting different starting points. We only recognise the value of true plurality when we take difference seriously as the basis for working toward finding the common ground. If we assume common ground as a given, then we are in danger of seeing it purely as we wish to and perpetuating the tradition of colonialism regarding the other.

Consider Vatican's II's teaching on other religions in *Nostra aetate* in relation to this point. I think this document is a brilliant and important landmark in the Church's acknowledging of the spiritual value and truths within the other of Judaism, Islam, Hinduism, and Buddhism. In *Lumen gentium*[10] the Council clearly marks out the difference between Catholicism, other Christians, the religions of the world, and non-religious world views. Then, with this map in position *Nostra aetate* urges Catholics to 'turn [their] attention chiefly to what things human beings have in common and what things tend to bring them together'.[11] Here it then begins to outline what Catholics have in common with those furthest away from them in terms of beliefs (non-theistic traditions). *Nostra aetate* isolates both elements of beliefs and practices that might be held as common ground. There is a clear asymmetry in the sense that common ground might well be found between those who at first sight have little in common in the area of beliefs. To give an example, I have been involved in the Campaign for Nuclear Disarmament for many years. When I started to actively campaign in this area as a postgraduate at Cambridge, the majority of the people in the campaign were from all walks of life with large numbers of Buddhists and Hindus (mostly white converts) and a large number of Quakers and non-religionists, and only one other Catholic. I learnt hugely from the Buddhists and Hindus because we shared our CND concerns in common. From there we were able to talk about our religious differences without those differences becoming problems as we knew that we shared common ground and common concerns. What was fascinating for me was the discovery that an entirely different metaphysics and cosmology could arrive at similar conclusions in terms of prudential judgement and action. This is a very important point.

When it comes to the theistic traditions of Islam and Judaism, the commonality of beliefs and practices takes up more space in the Council documents. There is a sense in which the shared theism, despite differences on the trinity and incarnation, provides serious common ground in terms of religious beliefs and practices. What is most remarkable about the pontificate of Benedict XVI was the attempt to move gear from comparing beliefs to exploring the ground for common actions in civic society. Of course, there is a role for engaging with each others' beliefs, but what Benedict hit upon, was the importance for religions to cooperate in the public square regarding debates about all manner of things that concern them: poverty, injustice, the ecological crisis, women's and children's rights and so on.

The shortest of all of the documents of the Council, *Nostra aetate*, has had one on the most profound legacies (both problematic, but also wonderful and creative) within the Catholic Church. It has meant that Catholics have been given the mandate to engage with difference, knowing that in this difference there is a source of truth and blessings, as well as an opportunity for evangelism and witness, as well as the chance for serious learning and self-criticism.

Let me turn to one criticism of *Nostra aetate* to develop this point – and it bears upon the school situation. Some Jews after the Council said that while they were delighted that the deicide (Latin: *de-us* 'god' and -*cidium* 'killing') charge against the Jewish people had been dropped by the Catholic Church, they still felt that Judaism only appeared in the document in terms of Catholic theological self-interest. Judaism, in its own right, had no reality in the Council documents. Was this a fair charge and does it bode ill for my proposal? Their charge touches upon the issue of a form of colonialism in relation to religions. Some Jews argue that they are simply interpreted from the viewpoint of the Christian and not valued for who they are in themselves, thus stifling real difference.[12]

Regarding Vatican II, I do not think this Jewish charge really holds as the Council was not trying to present a phenomenology of Judaism, but trying to set its own Catholic house in order. It was trying to address the teachings of contempt toward Judaism that stemmed from interpretations of the New Testament that in part had led toward the Holocaust. Remember, the only reason the Council touched this issue was because of Pope John XXIII's friendship with the eminent French, Jewish historian, Jules Isaac. Isaac had a personal audience with John where he urged the pontiff to address the deicide charge that was at the basis of so much theological and then political anti-Semitism. Isaac, a profoundly learned and wise man, was utterly clear that there could be no shift in the basic doctrinal positions of Catholic Christianity, but had carefully argued that the deicide charge was not part of the doctrinal heritage of Christianity. However what the Council also did, which counters the charge I am looking at, was set the theological basis for why Catholics should attend to the Jewish people: that their election is still operative, that they are the roots upon which the wild gentile branch of the Church has been grafted, and that their final coming in will be outside the control of the Church. All this was based on a fresh reading of Romans 9–11 which dominated Cardinal Bea's vision that underpinned the documents.[13] So it is precisely because of this positive theological vision that we find in the middle of paragraph 4 on the Jews this remarkable passage:

> this synod wishes to promote and recommend that mutual knowledge and esteem which is acquired especially from biblical and theological studies and friendly dialogues.

The study of Judaism for its own sake can only follow from a theological argument that underwrites the importance of such study, for knowledge in itself can be used for any and many purposes. *Nostra aetate* and the subsequent founding of the Secretariats for the Jewish people and the non-Christian religions developed this project along tandem lines, for the theological rationale for the importance of Judaism was of course different from the importance of the other religions.

What does all this tell us about the possible study of the world religions within a Catholic framework? I would suggest it tells us at least four things. First, the study of the other is always based in the knowledge that the other is made in the image of God and thus, the material culture generated by the other is worth very close investigation, for the theological reason that God never leaves Herself without witness. Our study of other religions and non-religions does have a theological rationale: love one another, discover that of the divine in each other's traditions, respect truth, beauty and goodness wherever you find it, and enjoy the delight of diversity for God's truth is always beyond our own little conception of it.

Second, if we are to truly respect the other, than we do need to understand them in their own terms as well. This is where the phenomenological grasp of the religions is vital. This is where it is absolutely important to allow the other to speak in their own words and with their own concerns. We should not colonise the other and make that which is alien and challenging, easy and domesticated. Hence, in this demanding educational process we require very well trained teachers in theology, religious studies and religious education. This of course calls for generations of training and curriculum design at higher education institutions that form Catholic teachers as well as training and curriculum design within actual Catholic schools, where local populations of non-Catholics require special attention. If for example, a Catholic school is made up of 75 per cent Muslims and 25 per cent Catholics, which is the case in England in some places, then Islam must play a major role in that 'special attention'. And of course, we need to train children to be aware of a radically pluralist world which might be beyond their immediate experience in a small rural area. Even in these areas the internet operates, so the global village does exist wherever we find internet cafes!

Third, bringing together the theological and phenomenological is the real task of the next generation of Catholic schools. In one sense it is not just the task of schools, but also churches, families, universities, hospitals, and any institution which is marked by a culture aspiring to be Catholic. Nonetheless schools have the vital charge as the educational demands are so high. Parents have the job, along with the parish, to encourage the faith and its practice. Schools have to relate this faith and practice to a complex and bewildering world with hope, realism and real regard to the common good, to which the Catholic Church is irrevocably committed. You are no doubt asking, as you should, but will this lead to criticisms of other religions? Since religions are so diverse, it is difficult to give clean-cut answers. It is also clear that one cannot criticise a religion for teaching caste (Hinduism), for example, if that part of the tradition is wedded to caste on the basis of its interpretation of sacred texts. The teacher might have a number of related tasks here: to show the pupil that some Hindus have tried to give careful justifications of caste based on their sacred texts; to show the pupils that some Hindus have a different estimation of caste than other Hindus – i.e. they reject it; to show the pupils that many Catholics from India still perpetuate caste divisions within Catholicism; to show the pupils that there have been analogical similarities to caste within their own Catholic traditions; and to show the pupil how the Catholic Church in India has dealt with caste. In this complex process truth is always complex as well as simple, the student learns about their own religion, the religious complexity of the other, and the social dimensions of the two religions. But in all this, I am arguing, the steering light must be Christ. So yes, there is no learning without critical questions to self and to other, but that is part of the process of attaining the common good.

Fourth, the other obvious concern will be that regarding mission. Are pupils and religions other than Catholics safe in a Catholic school from the pressures of mission? I put it bluntly as the fear is a serious one. Interestingly, some of the Catholic schools in London have large Muslim populations and there is very little evidence of missionary activity other than truthful witnessing, by both Catholics and Muslims students to each other. It would be contrary to Catholic teaching to present the gospel with any pressure or force against a person's conscience. This was the central concern of both Vatican II documents on Religious Freedom and Missionary Activity. One thing we need to rethink is the bad press related to the word 'mission'. If instead we see it as a sharing of what we love and cherish, then we equally are open to mission from others while at the same time living out a missionary witness. Secularists and non-religionists do the same and there is nothing to be ashamed about.

Conclusion

I realise that there are many different positions in this debate. I have sought to put forward one of them that makes the Catholic claim that to be fully human is to be fully Catholic, because in Christ, we have the fullest vision of the good of the human person and human community. Unpacking all this is complex and takes time, patience, and serious self-criticism. I have also argued that this vision of the good must be unfolded in dialogue with the religions and other world views of our society. And this dialogue has, for the Catholic Christian, a theological basis. It is not founded on just trying to be nice to others, but is founded on the reality that God works in cultures and religions and we as Catholic Christians have a duty to be attentive to God in whatever way God acts. I have finally argued that the study of religions must form part of the educational curriculum in a Catholic school as this is the basis of learning about others and seeking the common good. Without seeking the common good together we are lost. Finally, all this activity takes place within the context of the outrageous claims that I started with and not despite them: that Christ and his sacramental Church are God's gift of God's self to all women and men and children.

NOTES

1. See Thomas E. Woods, Jr, *How the Catholic Church Built Western Civilization* (Washington DC: Regnery Publishing, 2005).
2. There are of course other common-sense objections and many non-common-sense objections as well.
3. *Lumen gentium* 16; *Nostra aetate*; *Gaudium et spes*.
4. See *Catechism of the Catholic Church* <http://www.vatican.va> [accessed 12 May 2012].
5. *Catechism of the Catholic Church* <http://www.vatican.va/archive/ENG0015/_INDEX. HTM From the Vatican Website> [accessed 12 May 2012], with minor changes by me in the translation; CCC 1700.
6. For an elaboration of this, see *The Catholic Church and the World Religions*, ed. by Gavin D'Costa (London: Continuum, 2010).
7. *Unitatis redintegratio*, 4.
8. See an elaboration of this claim in Gavin D'Costa, *The Meeting of Religions and the Trinity* (Edinburgh: T&T Clark, 2000), Chapter Three.
9. See Gavin D'Costa, *Christianity and the World Religions* (Oxford: Blackwell, 2010), chapters 5–6.
10. *Lumen gentium* 14–16.
11. *Nostra aetate* 1.

12.   See for example the highly nuanced and interesting comments from David Berger on 'Dominus Iesus: A Jewish Response' <http://www.bc.edu/dam/files/research_sites/cjl/texts/cjrelations/resources/articles/berger.htm> [accessed 29 Jan. 2011].

13.   See Augustin Cardinal Bea, *The Church and the Jewish People* (London: Geoffrey Chapman, 1966), for an excellent background and commentary from the man so closely involved with the document through its many stages.

CHAPTER SEVEN

WHAT POLICY CAN LEARN FROM PRACTICE: LESSONS FROM THE CHALKFACE

Anne Looney

About Pluralism and the Big Story ...

The great storyteller of the Blasket Islands, Tomás Ó Criomhthain, an t-Oileánach (The Islandman), captured life and living on those islands and shared his stories with Robin Flower who in turn shared them with the rest of the world. However, as he grew older, his stories became fewer and fewer. Flower asked him why. The island man is reported to have said: 'They came from the mainland with their newspapers full of little stories. And all the little stories have driven the big story out of my head.'

I've retold that story as a resource for many reflections: about the importance of grand narrative; about the importance of children knowing why they learn; about the hazards of eight thirty-five-minute lessons in a day and the dangers of what becomes in that context, drive-by teaching and a student experience akin to an anthology of brief unconnected stories.

However, in preparing this paper, and reading the proceedings of a conference on Pluralism and Education held at Dublin City University in 1996, I came across the story used in a somewhat different way by Geraldine Smyth, to make an interesting point about a particular understanding of pluralism, a concept she rightly identifies as semantically elusive yet of normative power.[1]

Smyth refers to the experience, which seems to be that of Ó Criomhthain, of being driven without a compass through a maelstrom, of random, incommensurable and rival versions of reality, morality, culture or society ... until all sense of direction is lost and silence seems a preferable option to shouting over the storm. In such a context, in such a storm, without a compass, there is no chance of *safe*, let alone *mutual* ground. Silence of course, means that there can be no dialogue, no critique, no listening, no engagement, no questions, and therefore, little prospect of mutual ground or any safe landing place at all in the storm of multiple voices and perspectives.

Smyth's storm image reminded me of the events at Union Hall earlier this year around the loss of fishing vessel the *Tit Bonhomme*. The media captured some of the remarkable scenes of mutual ground and mutual grief:

> At the centre of keeping up morale was the Union Hall-born priest Fr Pierce Cormac. He had gone to the pier at about 7 a.m. on the Sunday that news of the tragedy began to break. Over the next month he was a constant figure on the pier, supporting the families.
>
> That first Sunday Ui hAodha asked him if he would say a rosary on the pier, and over the next 25 days the multifaith prayer service became a constant feature, the echo of voices rising above wind and rain to mark the end of another day of searching.
>
> Morad Gharib says: 'We would have said our own prayers anyway, but it was brilliant when Fr Pierce approached us and asked if we would like to join in the prayers. Every step of the way, they asked how we wanted things done, and we could not have asked for more.'[2]

This piece points to two 'big stories' united by a third, tragic story, and presents us with different voices but one hope.

This conference and the earlier gathering on the theme at Mater Dei Institute of Education in Dublin has set out to gather and raise many voices, recognising that all of us have a 'big story' that cannot nor should not be driven out of our heads. Since education is a process by which big stories are handed on (someone once described the curriculum in schools as the set of stories one generation tells to the next), we are rightly interested in questions of what stories to tell, who chooses the stories and who tells them?

Interestingly, looking back at the earlier conference sixteen years ago at Dublin City University, the focus was as much about culture and identity as it was about religion, and, religious education got very little coverage in the conference papers. The then Minister for Education in the Republic of Ireland, Niamh Bhreathnach spoke about education for democratic citizenship, and about diversity in curriculum through the new Leaving Certificate Applied.[3] The Chief Inspector at the Department of Education in Northern Ireland discussed how drama was important for dealing with cultural differences.[4] Of course there were inputs on the ethos of Catholic, Protestant, Educate Together and integrated schools but little emphasis was placed in those presentations on religious education.

Move along to the recent Forum on Patronage and Pluralism and the contrast could not be more marked. Culture and identity was almost absent from deliberations, and religion and religious education dominated the submissions and the debates. We are in different times, of course with different themes, but it is noteworthy that debates about pluralism in education have shifted focus somewhat over the past decade and a half. It is particularly striking that this shift in emphasis in our debates has happened when Ireland has never been more ethnically or linguistically diverse or when institutional religion has been at such a low ebb in terms of numbers participating, or presenting for ministry or leadership roles. Of course the emergence of a genuinely secular space in Irish society has probably been the most significant change in the last 16 years, a new 'big story' to tell and be heard. However, the near-to-silence at the Forum on issues of culture and identity remains noteworthy.

Religion and Education – Two More 'Big Stories'
The title of the second TMG conference *Toward Mutual Ground: Religious Pluralism in Educational Practice in Irish Schools* brings together two of the most highly contested concepts in contemporary culture and society – Religion and Education. On its own, each is a source of endless debate and polemic. Both are the focus of public, professional, political and academic scrutiny. They also feature on the Tesco list – things that get debated in the queue in Tesco by the general public, and are not the sole preserve of the *commentariat* who sit on TV and radio panels and write letters to newspapers or compose blogs. Nonetheless, each is a favourite media topic, and together, offer an attractive synergy that can fill hours of actual and virtual comment time.

Both education and religion matter a great deal to a great many people. Both evoke passionate and committed responses. Both are imbued with a powerful nostalgia for an imagined golden age. In the case of religion, particularly in Ireland, it is a golden age of full churches and a *faithful* faithful. In education it is a golden age of silent classrooms filled with diligent committed and respectful students. Sharing space with the imagined golden age, is the rhetoric of reform. Education and religion both find themselves the focus of a rhetoric focused on the symbolic power of the twenty-first century. *Schools for the twenty-first century. Religion for the twenty-first century.* Finding their place and their time is a challenge for both religion and education. Put religion and education *together*, and begin to think about the relationship between them and the debates get twice as interesting, twice as challenging and probably ten times more complex.

A few years ago I wrote about the differences between the debates in the United States on issues of religion and education, which I classified as largely about theology, in contrast with the debates in the United Kingdom which, I suggested, were largely about ideology.[5] I contrasted some of the debates going on about intelligent design, evolution, science and creationism, in the US curriculum with the faith schools debates happening in the United kingdom, and the criticism by A.C. Grayling of what he termed 'the indoctrination of intellectually defenceless children' that occurred, he claimed, in faith-based primary schools and the consequent segregation that inevitably undermined national cohesion.

It is interesting to speculate where our Irish debates about religion and education are positioned on an imagined continuum between theology and ideology. It is ironic that the theological debates are so loud in a country with a public school system that is overtly secular. And the ideological debates are loudest in a country with a constitutional monarch who is also the supreme governor of the Church of England. As I was preparing for this event, a frenzy was breaking out in France over Halal and Kosher meat in the Paris area. In summary, Marine Le Pen, the leader of the extreme right in France, suggested that all the meat sold in the Paris area was now being slaughtered to meet the requirements of Halal or Kosher customers, and that innocent Parisians were now buying meat of this kind without their knowledge. President Sarkozy rowed in and called for the labelling of all meat, and the prime minister suggested that Jews and Muslims should put their dietary laws behind them and embrace modernity.

Perhaps the reader missed that story from France, because their attention was caught by the horrific events in another part of France in March 2012, where, over a period of eight days, Jews and Muslims were shot in cold blood by a person who is generally accepted now to be a deranged psychopath. But listen to the analysis offered by Fiachra Gibbons of *The Guardian*:

Today in Toulouse we have been given a horrific illustration of where such delirious cynicism can lead. All of those who have been shot or killed in and around the city in the past eight days have had one thing in common. They are from visible minorities. They had names or faces that marked them out as not being descended, as Jean-Marie Le Pen would say, from 'our ancestors the Gauls'. Their roots – both Jewish and Muslim – were in the Maghreb or the Caribbean. They were, in short, a snapshot of *la France metissée* – the mixed race, immigrant France that works hard and 'gets up early' to empty bins and look after children; the people who die disproportionately for France yet who are also most often locked up in its prisons and crumbling banlieues.

As one father said this morning as he hugged his son to him outside the school, 'They are attacking us because we are different.'

Police are a long way yet from catching, never mind understanding, what was going through the head of someone who could catch a little girl by the hair so he wouldn't have to waste a second bullet on her. But some things are already becoming clear. He shouted no jihadist or anti-Semitic slogans, going about his grisly business in the cold, military manner oddly similar to Anders Behring Breivik, the Norwegian gunman who massacred 77 people at a social democrats summer camp last summer [2011].

As with Breivik, politicians will be quick to the thesis of the lone madman. Another lone madman influenced by nothing but his own distorted mind, like the lone gang of neo-Nazis who had been quietly killing Turks and Greeks in Germany for years unbothered by the police, who preferred to put the murders down to feuds or honour killings.

What could be the link, they ask, between Jewish children and French military personnel? The link is they are both seen – and not just by a far-right fringe – as symbols of all that has sabotaged *la France forte*, to borrow Sarkozy's election slogan. Confessional schools, be they Jewish or an informal weekend madrassa, are seen as actively undermining the secular Republic by activists of groups like the Bloc Identitaire and the Front National, as well as some members of Sarkozy's UMP, and even some on the left.[6]

One thing is clear from his analysis, whether you agree with it or otherwise. Words, whether in the Tesco queue or in the media, in a blog or at a political rally, really matter. We need to pay attention to the words we use because religion can easily become a proxy for something else – race, class or privilege perhaps. Marine Le Pen's concern was not with the dietary requirements of orthodoxy. She was not worried about food. Her words were about food. Her meaning was something else entirely.

Can 'religion' become a proxy for something else? A widely reported outcome of the Celtic tiger has been a polarisation of the school system, especially at second level. In other words, we have more schools with lots of advantaged children and more with lots of disadvantaged children, and fewer with a mix. Current discussions about 'greater diversity' in the primary school sector can seem benign at first hearing. Listen more carefully, to whispers of concern about what 'more diversity' means and about whether Catholic schools will be popular with parents not because of their religious ethos but because their religious ethos might make them 'less diverse'. One of the lessons from the chalkface is that what happens in practice can defy the best of policy intentions. Ironically, we can spend an endless amount of printer ink on differences between multi-denominational, denominational, non-denominational and inter denominational at a policy level and miss entirely that the real big story can be quite simply about 'same' and 'other'.

Beginning in Practice – Four Other Lessons from the Chalkface
Of note, our book title invites us to begin in practice, in the 'doing' and 'acting' of religious pluralism, rather than in the legislation or design of policy for or about it. Our tendency in Ireland has been to focus on the latter and to pay little enough attention to the practice as it emerged and shaped itself. In reality, children, young people and their families find themselves sharing meaning and interpreting events with and for children, young people and families, in an increasingly diverse and multi-storied world. Throughout this chapter you have heard many stories from the chalkface of practice that may well have much to teach policy. Four are presented here. There are and will be others.

The first feature of the practices we have encountered that seems important for policy is *the centrality of children and young people*. While espousing the maxim that curriculum is the set of stories one generation choses to tell the other, it is tempting to focus on what stories and who chooses, and to fail to focus on those who engage with the stories in schools and classrooms. The public good of education resides not in the policy rhetoric but in the experience of children and young people. It may sound like a truism to say that education is about children and young people, but we can get so worked up about our big stories that we can forget about *theirs*, and their far more cosmopolitan identities which are almost pluralist by definition. Children manage diversity with relative ease, until they learn from adults those categories of *same* and *other*. So school governance which has traditionally been seen as an outreach of a religious or state institution, might be usefully reconfigured more around children and their learning, around all children, not just mine or yours. The state's interest is in all children, because they are children, not because they belong or don't belong to any religious group. As noted earlier, the recent Forum debates and submissions seem to have lost that civic focus of earlier debates about pluralism and education.

The second lesson connects to a point previously made about public discourse generally, but worth re-visiting as a lesson we can learn from the chalkface. This is the point that *words matter*. We need to learn from the experience of the Community National Schools which listened to their communities and began to use the term *multi-belief* instead of *multi-faith*, not because they had a policy that guided them, but because they engaged with the many voices in the school community. And while there will be pages written about definitions and terms, what is of interest is that in practice, it is not the definition that counts, it is the meaning as it is experienced in the school or classroom that needs to inform the 'label'.

The third lesson we can learn is *that schools are places for engagement*. If we want, as was suggested at the conference on pluralism sixteen years ago, active engaged citizens, an idea that still informs our vision of twenty-first-century education, then the idea of an objective or dispassionate study of anything seems a pedagogical contradiction. The students we heard from in the course of the conference were engaged and passionate. In debates about twenty-first-century learning we talk about young people having a set of skills that include problem solving, critical thinking, resilience, communication skills, the ability to work in groups and teams, creativity and imagination and the ability to come up with new and innovative solutions to old problems. The idea of an objective engagement with 'facts' or a neutral presentation of content, which is sometimes mooted by policymakers looking for new directions for learning about religions, for example, was ridiculed even by Dickens.

Similarly, emerging discourse on teacher professional identity highlights the new public demands on, and expectations of, teachers and teaching which have little to do with 'objectivity'. The work of Christopher Day for example, focuses on what he calls the new moral purposes of teaching, describing teachers as 'potentially the single most important asset in the achievement of a democratically just learning society'.[7] Andy Hargreaves explores a similar theme in his recent work on the role of teaching and teachers in the knowledge society. He discusses the need to reassert teaching as a 'moral, visionary profession' once more.[8]

Day talks about passionate, engaged teaching:

> To be passionate about teaching is not only to express enthusiasm but also to enact it in a principled, values-led, intelligent way. All effective teachers have a passion for their subject, a passion for their pupils and a passionate belief that who they are and how they teach can make a difference in their pupil's lives, both in the moment of teaching and in the days, weeks, months and even years afterwards.[9]

In this context, it is not reasonable to suggest that any aspect of the school life or of a child's learning should be disengaged, or disconnected from any sort of affective response.

A final lesson from practice is its focus on *the pragmatic and the solution*. Again, a lesson from the Community National Schools is that local solutions generally work, and when there are problems, they can be solved in dialogue and mutual respect. It does not always take a shipwreck or a storm. And sometimes the way to work out a solution is to try it. We can find that so much energy goes into formulating the details of a policy document, that we have neither the energy nor the motivation to enact it.

And Finally, A Lesson From Finland

Any self-respecting paper on an education theme must refer to Finland. Since their chart-topping success in the PISA tests, Finland has become something of a holy grail for anyone who wants to shape a successful school system. One of the most striking things about Finland is that it has a big story about education. The purpose of schooling is to contribute to a society characterised by equality and the development of each child as a thinking, active and creative person. That big story acts as the organiser for a system characterised by local autonomy and flexibility. What is Ireland's big story? What is our organising principle for education? Are we clear about our education 'big story', about what we want from our school system?

The closest we get is probably the introduction to the widely regarded Primary School Curriculum developed in 1999 from the previous 1971 curriculum. It emphasises education as public project in the three general aims of primary education. The first of these is to 'enable the child to live a full life as a child and to realise his or her potential as a unique individual'. The second is 'to enable the child to develop as a social being through living and co-operating with others and so contribute to the good of society'. The final aim of primary education, as set out in the introduction to the 1999 curriculum is 'to prepare the child for further education and lifelong learning'.[10] In support of these aims, a set of key issues is offered by way of context. Under the heading 'the spiritual dimension', the introduction to the curriculum includes the following:

The importance that the curriculum attributes to the child's spiritual development is expressed through the breadth of learning experiences the curriculum offers, through the inclusion of religious education as one of the areas of the curriculum, and through the child's engagement with the aesthetic and affective domains of learning.[11]

However, a significant qualifier is added in the introduction to the curriculum areas where it states that 'the development of curriculum for religious education remains the responsibility of the different church authorities.'[12] Nonetheless a rationale for religious education is offered, and the responsibility of every school in this regard is signalled:

It is the responsibility of every school to provide a religious education that is consonant with its ethos and at the same time to be flexible in making alternative organisational arrangements for those who do not wish to avail of the particular religious education it offers. It is equally important that the beliefs and sensibilities of every child are respected.[13]

Interestingly, the rationale begins with a reference to *every* school and ends with *every* child. A number of years ago, I suggested that religious education had become too important to leave to the Churches.[14] It is tempting to suggest that, in an Irish context, it has now become too complex to be undertaken by the state. That would be to ignore the fact that practice in some Irish schools has already moved to respond to local contexts, often quietly, usually successfully, and sometimes, remarkably so. As they construct their 'big story', policymakers need to listen to and learn from these 'little' stories from the chalkface.

NOTES

1. G. Smyth, 'Foreword' in *Pluralism in Education: Conference Proceedings* 1996, pp. 3–7.

2. *The Irish Times*, 21 Mar. 2012.

3. N. Bhreathnach, 'Realities for Schools in 2000 AD: 1' in *Pluralism in Education: Conference Proceedings* 1996, pp. 15–18.

4. T. Shaw, 'Realities for Schools in 2000 AD: 2' in *Pluralism in Education: Conference Proceedings* 1996, pp. 21–25.

5. A. Looney, 'Religious Education in the Public Space: Challenges and Contestations', in *International Handbook of the Religious, Moral and Spiritual Dimensions in Education. Part Two*, ed. by M. de Souza, K. Engebretson, G. Durka, R. Jackson, and A. McGrady (Dordrecht: Springer, 2006), pp. 949–966.

6. *The Guardian*, 19 Mar. 2012.

7. C. Day, *A Passion for Teaching* (New York: RoutledgeFalmer, 2004).

8. A. Hargreaves, *Teaching in the Knowledge Society: Education in the Age of Insecurity* (New York: Teachers College Press, 2003), p. 160.

9. Day, 2004, p. 12.

10. Government of Ireland, *The Primary School Curriculum: Introduction* (Dublin: The Stationery Office, 1999), p. 7.
11. Government of Ireland, 1999, p. 27.
12. Government of Ireland, 1999, p. 40.
13. Government of Ireland, 1999, p. 58.
14. Looney, 2006.

CHAPTER EIGHT

RELIGIOUS PLURALISM FROM THE PERSPECTIVE OF CENTRAL AND EASTERN EUROPE

Elżbieta Osewska

Introduction

After the Second World War, Europe was divided into three large regions comprising of western, central and eastern Europe. A 'powerful iron curtain' changed the map of Europe by severing cultural and economic contacts between eastern and western areas thus contributing substantially to the gradual growth of a new differentiation between two parts of the continent. The notion of 'Europe' became limited to the territory outside of the Soviet Union. Consequently the term Eastern European became associated with the distinctive culture and socio-political realities of those eastern countries within the Soviet Union, usually referred to as: the Czech Republic, Slovakia, Hungary, Slovenia, Poland, Estonia, Latvia, Lithuania, Belarus, Ukraine, Russia, Romania, Bulgaria, Macedonia, Albania, Yugoslavia, Bosnia and Herzegovina, Croatia and Moldavia. However it is important to avoid over-generalizations as the reality of the situation was intricate and multifaceted.[1]

The Central and Eastern European cultural and religious map is complex and highly diversified, yet it is often misunderstood by some people in Western Europe who perceive social, economic, political, cultural and religious processes in Eastern Europe on the basis of popular perception and limited experience. Indeed in the contemporary era where many formerly Eastern European countries are now members of the expanded European Union, there is an opportunity to acknowledge and dispel stereotypes and misunder-standings and to help people in both East and West to have a more realistic and accurate interpretation of what is happening in the whole of Europe. This chapter explores the topic of religious pluralism from the perspective of Central and Eastern Europe, with particular emphasis on the situation in Poland.

Poland in a European Context

In terms of religious and cultural traditions, Poland is situated in the middle of Europe as it lies between West and East (between Roman Catholicism and Orthodoxy, Christianity and Islam, Latin and Cyrillic script) and has preserved its specific character,[2] due to its previous links with Latin culture. In one sense one can argue that Poland belongs to Central Europe as distinct from Eastern Europe. Poland's eastern frontiers mark a line where western and central European cultural and religious areas met. In the past Polish intellectuals, artists and Church leaders created an ideological image of Poland as the protector of Christianity's western European Latin culture from the barbarians and pagans. Polish military victories over the Turks and Russians (later Bolsheviks) were interpreted in this context as acts in defence of high western civilisation, and formed part of the Polish national mythology and symbolism. According to this Polish mentality, Catholicism coincides entirely with Polishness. Poland's history testifies to the fact that religious and national identity go hand in hand.[3] It appears as though Poland's political enemies always belonged to other religions or Christian denominations. During the time of the communist regime, the Catholic Church became the defender of Polishness as it supported the spiritual strength of the nation and created an original 'theology of nation' which resulted in the sacralisation of the term and its values.[4] These convictions were especially responsible for a strong ideological protection against sovietisation, recognisable in very high rates of attendance at weekly mass, in widespread parish catechesis, pilgrimages, official religious ceremonies and high levels of vocations to the priesthood and religious life. This may also explain Polish people's expectation that religious values should be recognised in a European Constitution. One could argue that to a certain extent Poland remained autonomous, even under the control of the Soviet Union, due to five factors. These are: the independence of the Roman Catholic Church; the existence and domination of private ownership in agriculture; the link with Western European culture and science; a strong Christian moral value system; and Polish people's insistence on the independence of major areas of public life.[5]

Compared with the pre-war situation in Poland where minority groups composed 35 per cent of the overall population in 1939, in contemporary Poland they form a much smaller group where minorities are currently estimated to compose 1 per cent to 2 per cent of the total population. This situation results from the impact of the Second World War on Poland and the post-war resettlement of the population undertaken by the Allied leaders at Potsdam (1945). Relative to its pre-war composition, the population in contemporary Poland is highly homogeneous. It must be noted that in Poland the specific character of ethnic identity is mostly attributed to religious affiliation. The largest ethnic and religious minority groups in Poland are

German, Ukrainian, Belarussian, Russian and Lithuanian. In general one can say that German people living in contemporary Poland mainly belong to various Protestant denominations which form a mosaic of diversified religious groups from historical Protestant Churches to new religious movements based on evangelical interpretations of the Bible. The presence of the Orthodox Church and the Greek Catholic Church (Byzantine–Ukrainian Church) is clearly visible in Poland. The Greek Catholic Church was formed in 1596 as a result of the Brześć Union with the Roman Catholic Church, and for a long time afterwards was the subject of hostile treatment by the Orthodox Church. In 1946 the Byzantine–Ukrainian Church, in former Polish territories, was incorporated into the Soviet Union and was liquidated by the Soviets. However it was able to survive in the territory of Poland, where the Church founded a seminary in Lublin. The peaceful coexistence of so-called 'Unit' Churches and the Roman Catholic Church is strongly supported by both Churches however in some areas national conflicts still exists. The Orthodox Church has the largest number of members in the eastern part of Poland, especially in the Bialystok region. In several villages with large Russian populations one may observe members of the Orthodox Church keeping norms and rites, known as 'Starowiercy', which predate the reform of this Church. Most Poles positively accept the coexistence of various Christian denominations in Poland.[6]

The fact that Roman Catholic Poland rejoined western Europe at a time when western Europe is becoming more secularised and is moving away from its Christian identity has created a perplexing situation for Polish Catholics and secular Europeans alike. Anticipating the threat of secularization, some Polish Catholics have adopted a negative attitude toward European integration. By contrast, some members of the Polish Episcopate have embraced European integration as a great apostolic assignment for evangelizing and restoring Europe for Jesus Christ. This impetus for restoration has resonated with the Polish mentality and the ancient tradition of seeing Poland as a protector of Christianity.[7]

New Situation – the Homogeneous Balance Shaken
As previously noted the central and eastern European religious map is incredibly complex and is based on specific historical, geographical, social, economic and cultural factors. 'Catholics', 'Orthodox', 'Protestants', 'Jews' and other religious groups are sometimes associated with a cluster of stereotypical traits and prejudicial images. Likewise a superficial reading of the religious map of Central and Eastern Europe might erroneously perceive Islam, Hinduism and Buddhism as religions which do not belong to this European geographical, political, cultural and religious territory.

A survey of the statistical data from February 2009 for Poland shows that 94.7 per cent of Poles (from a total population of 38 million) identify themselves as Roman Catholics. A further 0.4 per cent self-describe as Orthodox, 0.4 per cent Protestant, 0.4 per cent other denominations and 1.2 per cent as Christians. Furthermore 2.1 per cent self-describe as being 'non-religious' while 0.4 per cent are unsure and 0.4 per cent do not want to identify their religion.[8] Other sources such as the *European Values Survey* data for Poland show that 94 per cent of Poles are members of a religion, 4.4 per cent do not identify themselves with any religion, 0.8 per cent are unsure and 0.8 per cent provide no response. Furthermore this survey reports of those who are members of a religious tradition, 91.2 per cent belong to the Roman Catholic Church, 0.7 per cent to the Orthodox Church, 0.3 per cent to Protestant Churches, 0.1 per cent to the Greek Catholic Church, 0.2 per cent to Old Catholic, 0.4 per cent to Jehovah's Witnesses, 0.1 per cent to Islam, 0.1 per cent to Buddhism and 0.6 per cent have given no response. In Poland the pluralisation of the religious and social landscape takes place very slowly.[9] While there has been an increase in the number of new religious movements and sects in Poland, this has not made a significant impact on the overall percentage of Catholics in the country. However the religious evolution reveals underlying shifts in the perception and reception of religious traditions and norms especially in urban areas, where there is evidence of people leaving the Catholic Church. With regard to religious practice the situation in Poland reveals far higher rates of religious practice than in Western Europe. However, when people in Poland widely self-describe as being members of the Roman Catholic Church, it must be noted that there are diverse understandings of membership operative in society. These range from full active membership, through to partial or cultural membership. People's personal statement of membership is not always reflected in their practices, attitudes and lifestyle, which in turn does not always conform to the Catholic Church's requirements for members.[10]

One of the consequences of the EU policy to attract migrant workers from Central and Eastern European countries has been the destabilizing of Poland's population. Between 2004 and 2011, out of Poland's total population of 38 million, almost 2.2 million emigrated, mainly to work and live in old EU member states.[11] Polish people living in Western European countries consequently bring their own cultural and religious identity to the centre of public debate about European society.[12] Of course central and eastern European migrants return to their countries of origin with new cultural and religious rites, symbols, norms and values. Due to these migration processes Polish people have developed a strong sense of respect, community and hospitality[13] and have also developed a gradual sense of western European pragmatism and individualisation.

Therefore any sense of traditional Polish religious homogeneity is being dissolved. Polish people and central Europeans currently have to deal with a different way of imagining cultural and religious reality, which brings into play a conflict between the concern of protecting their cultural, political and religious boundaries, while simultaneously opening up others to enable the emergence of a global network of communication and consumption, independently of ethnic, cultural and religious origin.

In general one can say that the relationships among different belief systems and religious communities may be friendly, tolerant, indifferent or aggressive. In Europe the social, cultural and religious balance has often been deconstructed and reconstructed. By and large, the main cultural, religious and political divisions of Europe remain relatively stable. In this context one's first concern might not be to stimulate interaction between different groups in a pluralistic society. It is more important, while interacting, to identify the kinds of boundaries (historical, linguistic, economic, political, ideological, juridical, sociological) and most especially the mental ones, which impede human solidarity. Identifying and confronting internalised boundaries is an ongoing challenge for a new Europe. It takes intensive work to establish a psychological and spiritual mindset which is open to integrating the concerns of all Europeans and overcoming the 'mental' boundaries which maintain people's indifference.[14]

Religious plurality is a challenge which evokes a variety of reactions. Differences can either be ignored, rejected or tolerated. People can show an open attitude responding to hospitality, or they can opt for a conforming adaptation to an alien situation. People can also choose to work toward transcending 'mental' boundaries. Subsequently the issue of 'tolerance' has become a core issue in Europe, as the structure of Europe changed in a radical way. In a Christian perspective 'tolerance' should be established in peace and love, so it leads to Christian *'agapè'*, a genuine universal love.[15]

In central and eastern Europe the transition from a type of communist society to a capitalist one is perceived as highly problematic.[16] People are still living in a time of transition, where, in one sense, the old system is still present and very influential. Both communism and capitalism seem to coexist, although, in many ways, they could be described as contradictory.[17] In Poland, in the post-communist era, the process of secularisation is not as evident as it is in Western Europe and in some places it is even possible to observe a growing interest in religion.[18] The processes of secularisation, individualisation and indifferentism are not as explicit in Poland as they are in the old Europe. People still follow closely the Catholic Church's teachings, most obviously in relation to observable religious practice, however it is much more difficult to evaluate the impact of Church teaching on their ethical, social or political behaviour. The evolution of Poland's religious landscape appears to reflect a tension between living in a modern European society and adhering to the Christian tradition. Polish people do not appear to 'believe without belonging' as they opt instead for 'belonging'.[19]

For a long time, the Roman Catholic Church in Poland had moral authority over the political government. In recent years the Church had to find a new place in the political arena for achieving the well-being of the faithful. Indeed the Christian Churches in central and eastern Europe are currently facing a direct confrontation between the western tradition (focused on the separation between State and Church) and eastern tradition (with its interest in the integration of the political and the religious powers). According to the Polish sociologist, Janusz Mariański, the Roman Catholic Church in Poland along with other churches and faith communities, may play an important role in instilling the vital value of coexistence, by searching for answers to fundamental questions about the meaning of life, through promoting an understanding of the ethnicity, culture and identity of people and through offering society principles that contribute to the creation of a spiritual foundation or what one might term the humanisation of society. Among the values, which the churches want to protect in this part of Europe are: the dignity of the human person; the sacredness of human life; the marriage-based family; legal protection of individuals and groups; co-operation of all for the benefit of the common good; the right to education; work understood as a personal and social good; political power conceived as service and subordinated to reason; law and human rights; and a vision of social and community relations based on the ethics of solidarity.[20]

Today, inside the different countries of central and eastern Europe different religions legally coexist. However religious plurality has two dimensions. On the one hand, plurality emerges inside every religion as a process of the individualisation of the religious orientation. Conflicting relationships between different religions or denominations result from the multiple interests involved, yet it is possible to observe the shift from doctrinal and formal perceptions of religion to more personal and individual understandings of inter-religious relationships.[21]

In the twenty-first century, in Central and Eastern Europe many Churches are struggling not alone with external problems such as atheism, irreligion, non-belief, denial of the social and ethical role of religion, denial of the authority of Christianity, but also with internal issues such as religious passivity, apathy and indifference among Christians. Diversity has become one of the core conditions of contemporary society.[22] While European churches have generally developed a consensus with regard to a common viewpoint and pastoral policy in the changing context,[23] a tension still remains.

According to Anita Miszalska in times of normative chaos and diversity, religious ties assume ever greater significance and they promote various forms of engagement in civic activity. In recent years in Polish society religion has become a foundation upon which community ties are built.[24] From this perspective Catholic Church and minority religious groups in Central and Eastern Europe may offer a mutual support for ethical praxis.[25]

Pastoral Conclusions and Implications for Religious Education/Learning

For many years ecumenical and inter-religious relations in the countries of central and eastern Europe have suffered from the same restrictions and political pressures that were imposed by the communist governments. In the Czech Republic, Slovakia, Poland and Hungary, Estonia and Romania, as well as Serbia, the ecumenical movement is growing whereas in some Orthodox countries, there are no formal contemporary structures for ecumenical cooperation. This illustrates how difficult it is to establish and sustain relationships between majority and minority churches. In practice, both majority and minority churches are primarily concerned with augmenting their own structure and profile. In Poland, in previous decades, Karol Wojtyła acted as a strong advocate for ecumenism and once he was elected Pope he continued in his ecumenical work. His appeal for tolerance reminded Poles of the rights of non-Catholics in society:

> We Poles, remaining Catholic in an overwhelming majority and finding in Catholicism, in the Catholic Church, the foundation for a spiritual defence ... preserving in our Catholicism, in the Catholic Church, a sort of foundation of inner strength, of our identity and of our spiritual resistance, thanks to which the nation endured – at the same time we respect the convictions of others.[26]

In Poland as a predominantly Catholic country, a new situation calls firstly for an awareness of diversity and plurality, then for overcoming various types of boundaries, especially mental ones so that Polish people may engage in ecumenical and inter-religious dialogue. Respectful dialogue does not require that differences be ignored or played down. The first requirement is that humans seek to understand clearly the positions being outlined. This helps avoid the problem where differences are created through inaccurate perceptions of what is said. Clarification of intended meaning should therefore be the first priority for both speakers and respondents. Confrontation with a changing social environment and the need for further mutual adjustments, bring to light the nature of ecumenical and inter-religious dialogue: to recognise its complexity, to understand its processes, to become conscious of the risk of the failure of dialogue.

In this perspective the Pontifical Council for Promoting Christian Unity reminds us that:

> Dialogue is at the heart of ecumenical cooperation and accompanies all forms of it. Dialogue involves both listening and replying, seeking both to understand and to be understood. It is a readiness to put questions and to be questioned. It is to be forthcoming about oneself and trustful of what others say about themselves. The parties in dialogue must be ready to clarify their ideas further, and modify their personal views and ways of living and acting, allowing themselves to be guided in this by authentic love and truth. Reciprocity and mutual commitment are essential elements in dialogue, as is also a sense that the partners are together on an equal footing. Ecumenical dialogue allows members of different Churches

and ecclesial Communities to get to know one another, to identify matters of faith and practice which they share and points on which they differ. They seek to understand the roots of such differences and assess to what extent they constitute a real obstacle to a common faith. When differences are recognised as being a real barrier to communion, they try to find ways to overcome them in the light of those points of faith which they already hold in common.[27]

Growing religious pluralism in central and eastern Europe requires a dialogue with a specific approach, based upon a personalistic norm[28] and deeper understanding of personal faith tradition. Dialogue occurs at the boundary of different religious and cultural identities and geo-political territories. Only the creation of some safe intermediary space for dialogue can bring about successful inter-religious understanding.[29] Authentic dialogue respects the dignity common to all human beings despite race, ethnicity, class, origin, status, education or wealth, and it promotes the true freedom of people.

Dialogue should be relevant to the lives of people in central and eastern Europe, who are still struggling to survive in a time of economic crisis and lack of family policy.[30] In their daily life many people try to achieve some form of pragmatic mutual understanding. They acknowledge that they have to live and work together even though they may not see any benefit in deepening a sense of the otherness or subjectivity of the other person. At a time of financial crisis, unemployment, and poverty religions should help individuals and religious communities to find meaning in life as well as ultimate security. Religious education should not be just a transmission of practice and belief or pure socialisation because in the present context it needs to help young people to identify with their faith with passion, creativity and integrity. Christian Religious Education has a responsibility to maintain the integrity of the Christian faith developed over two thousand years of Christian tradition. Secondly, it seeks to help pupils to learn how to think critically about contemporary spiritual and moral issues and to interpret them wisely. In relation to ecumenical or inter-religious dialogue, religious education should forsake a more typical 'formal' (comparative or doctrinal) approach in favour of cultivating an overall climate of respect, love, dialogue and responsibility.

Religious education in Poland is concerned with cultivating knowledge about and formation in the Christian faith, so its aim is still catechetical.[32] Yet one must ask if the values, criteria and norms presented during religious education lessons, help pupils to find life and grow as people in a new pluralistic society? Most religious education teachers in Poland (both in state and private schools) work according to a 'committed Catholic model', while some try to follow an open and constructive 'cooperative' approach with pupils. It is important to remember however, that Religious education works in tandem with the home, and that students are also shaped by their local communities,[33] and by the media, powerful agents in developing young people's attitudes.

Nonetheless, religious education in the context of religious pluralism requires a maturity of vision and should prepare young generations to understand the changing influence of religion on societies and events in society. According to Herman Lombaerts a wise interpretation acknowledges various influences at work and resists the temptation to oversimplify; it accepts failures along with successes; it candidly asks questions and does not eliminate any embarrassing answers; it accepts both strengths and weaknesses. Also it attempts to extend the community's capacity to look carefully at history and interpret the influence of various factors.[34] Religious dialogue connected with religious education may be life changing, but only on condition that people are encouraged to question, search and redefine themselves in the light of their own learning.

Religious education outlines long-term goals to be set for children and young people in a particular society, in a particular time and context. In the twenty-first century, after succession into the European Union, religious education in central and eastern Europe needs to be an interactive process, where learners, together with teachers, are not only learning about the Christian heritage, but also develop a sense of identity, belonging, respect, responsibility and love preparing them for life in a plural society.

NOTES

1. See G. Węcławowicz, *Contemporary Poland: Space and Society* (London: UCL Press, 1996), pp. 7–13; E. Osewska, 'To Educate in a Diversified Europe', in *The Person and the Challenges* 1 (2011), pp. 72–73.

2. See J. Kłoczowski, *A History of Polish Christianity* (Cambridge: Cambridge University Press, 2000).

3. On the history of Poland see N. Davies, *Heart of Europe: A Short History of Poland* (Oxford: Oxford University Press, 1986); J. Kłoczowski, *A History of Polish Christianity* (Cambridge: Cambridge University Press, 2000); Z. Zieliński, *Kościół w Polsce 1944–2002* (Radom: POLWEN 2003).

4. See E. Osewska, 'To Educate in a Diversified Europe', *The Person and the Challenges* 1 (2011), pp. 72–73.

5. See H. Lombaerts and E. Osewska, 'Historical and Geo-Political Reality of a United Europe', in *Catholic Education, European and Maltese Perspectives: Church School's Response to Future Challenges*, ed. by S. Gatt, H. Lombaerts, E. Osewska, and A. Scerri (Floriana: Secretariat for Catholic Education, 2004), pp. 27–43; E. Osewska, 'Le pèlegrinage à Czestochowa: Lieu d'éducation dans la foi', *Lumen Vitae Revue* (2007), pp. 247–265.

6. See G. Węcławowicz, *Contemporary Poland: Space and Society* (London: UCL Press, 1996), pp. 152–156.

7. J. Casanova, 'Religion, European Secular Identities and European Integration', in *Religion in an Expanding Europe*, ed. by T. Byrnes and P. Katzenstein (Cambridge: Cambridge University Press, 2006), pp. 65–71.

8. Centrum badania opinii społecznej, *Wiara i religijność Polaków dwadzieścia lat po rozpocz-ęciu przemian ustrojowych* <http://www.cbos.pl/SPISKOM.POL/2009/K_034_09.PDF> [accessed 6 Nov. 2012].

9. See J. Mariański, *Katolicyzm polski: Ciągłość i zmiana. Studium socjologiczne* (Kraków: WAM, 2011), p. 24.

10. Mariański, p. 32. See also I. Borowik, T. Doktór, *Pluralizm religijny i moralny w Polsce: raport z badań* (Kraków: NOMOS, 2001); *Od Kościoła ludu do Kościoła wyboru: religia a przemiany społeczne w Polsce*, ed. by I. Borowik and W. Zdaniewicz (Kraków: NOMOS, 1996); I. Borowik, *Procesy instytucjonalizacji i prywatyzacji religii w powojennej Polsce* (Kraków: Wydawnictwo Uniwersytet Jagielloński, 1997); *Kościół i religijność Polaków 1945–1999*, ed. by W. Zdaniewicz and T. Zembrzuski (Warszawa: Pallotinum, 2000).

11. Główny Urząd Statystyczny, *Informacja o rozmiarach i kierunkach emigracji z Polski w latach 2004–2011* <http://www.stat.gov.pl/cps/rde/xbcr/gus/lud_infor_o_rozm_i_kierunk_emigra_z_polski_w_latach_2004_2010.pdf> [accessed 9 Nov. 2012).

12. See *Polish–Irish Encounters in the Old and New Europe*, ed. by S. Egger and J. McDonagh (Bern: Peter Lang, 2011).

13. See A. Zamoyski, *The Polish Way: A Thousand-Year History of the Poles and Their Culture* (New York: Hippocrene Books, 1994).

14. E. Osewska, 'To Educate in a Diversified Europe', *The Person and the Challenges* 1 (2011), pp. 77–78.

15. See J. Tischner, *The Spirit of Solidarity* (San Francisco: Harper & Row, 1984); E. Osewska, J. Stala, 'Ethical Need for Authentic Fraternity Rooted in the Bible', in *Biblia a Etika: Etické Dimenzie Správania*, ed. by D. Hanesová (Banská Bystrica: Univerzity Mateja Bela, 2011), pp. 134–139.

16. I. Wallerstein, *Historical Capitalism with Capitalist Civilization* (London/New York: Verso, 1995), pp. 95–109.

17. H. Lombaerts, 'Education in European Perspective', *Horyzonty Wychowania* 2 (2002), pp. 155-156.

18. See G. Davie, *Europe, the Exceptional Case: Parameters of Faith in the Modern World* (London: Longman and Todd 2002); *Religion in Contemporary Europe*, ed. by J. Fulton and P. Gee (Lewiston/Queenston/Lampeter: Edwin Mellen Press, 1994).

19. See A. Zwoliński, *Katolik i polityka* (Kraków: WAM, 1999); J. Mariański, *Katolicyzm polski: Ciągłość i zmiana. Studium socjologiczne* (Kraków: WAM, 2011).

20. See J. Mariański, 'The Roman Catholic Church in Poland and Civil Society: Contradiction or Complementarity?' *Religious Studies and Theology* 27/1 (2008), pp. 26–27; J. Mariański, *Religijność społeczeństwa polskiego w perspektywie europejskiej: Próba syntezy socjologicznej* (Kraków: Nomos, 2004).

21. E. Osewska, 'L'educazione oggi in un'Europa diversificata', in *Europa, scuola, religioni: Monoteismi e confessioni cristiane per una nuova cittadinanza europea*, ed. by F. Pajer (Torino: SEI, 2005), pp. 47–64.

22. See D. Pollack, *Religiousness Inside and Outside the Church in Selected Post-Communist Countries of Central and Eastern Europe, Social Compass* 50 (2003), pp. 321–334; H. Lombaerts, 'The Impact of the Status of Religion in Contemporary Society upon Interreligious Learning', in *Interreligious Learning*, ed. by D. Pollefeyet (Leuven: Leuven University Press, 2007), pp. 70–76.

23. World Council of Churches, *Christian and Education in Multi-Faith Milieu*, Salford, 1991.

24. A. Miszalska, *Moralność a demokracja – uwagi o stylu moralnym współczesnego społeczeństwa polskiego*, in *Kondycja moralna społeczeństwa polskiego*, ed. by J. Mariański (Kraków: WAM, PAN, 2002), pp. 163–187.

25. See J. Tischner, *The Spirit of Solidarity* (San Francisco: Harper & Row, 1984).

26. K. Wojtyła, *Poszanowanie wolności religijnej* (Kraków, 25 Jan. 1976), in K. Wojtyła, *Kazania, 1962–1978* (Kraków: Znak, 1979), p. 398.

27. Pontifical Council for Promoting Christian Unity, *Directory for the Application of Principles and Norms on Ecumenism*, p. 172.

28. See K. Wojtyła, *Love and Responsibility* (San Franciso: Ignatius Press 1993).

29. H. Lombaerts, 'The Impact of the Status of Religion in Contemporary Society upon Interreligious Learning', pp. 81–86.

30. See E. Osewska, *Modele komunikacji interpersonalnej i ich znaczenie dla katechezy*, in *Wybrane zagadnienia z katechetyki*, ed. by J. Stala (Tarnów: Biblos, 2003), pp. 111–142; E. Osewska, *Możliwości i ograniczenia polityki rodzinnej w krajach Unii Europejskiej*, in *Rodzina jako środowisko rozwoju człowieka*, ed. by W. Piotrowski (Tarnów: Biblos, 2004), pp. 89–119; E. Osewska, *Uwarunkowania wychowania religijnego w rodzinie*, in *W kręgu rodziny*, ed. by E. Osewska and J. Stala (Poznań: Księgarnia Sw Wojciecha, 2003), pp. 13–21.

31. H. Lombaerts, 'The Impact of the Status of Religion in Contemporary Society upon Interreligious Learning', pp. 81–86.

32. See Konferencja Episkopatu Polski, *Dyrektorium katechetyczne Kościoła katolickiego w Polsce* (Kraków: WAM); Konferencja Episkopatu Polski, *Podstawa programowa Kościoła katolickiego w Polsce* (Kraków: WAM, 2001); Komisja Wychowania Katolickiego Konferencji Episkopatu Polski, *Program nauczania religii* (Kraków: WAM, 2001).

33. See J. Stala and E. Osewska, *Anders erziehen in Polen: Der Erziehungs und Bildungsbegriff im Kontext eines sich ständig verändernden Europas des XXI Jahrhunderts* (Tarnów: Polihymnia, 2009); H. Lombaerts and E. Osewska, 'The Modern Christian Family as a First Setting for Religious and Moral Education?' in *Religious Education/Catechesis in the Family: A European Perspective*, ed. by E. Osewska and J. Stala (Warszawa: UKSW, 2010), pp. 11–25; J. Stala, *Familienkatechese in Polen um die Jahrhundertwende. Probleme und Herausforderungen* (Tarnów: Biblos, 2008); J. Stala and E. Osewska, *Sociological Aspects of Family Religious Education in Poland*, in *Religious Education/Catechesis in the Family: A European Perspective*, ed. by E. Osewska and J. Stala (Warszawa: UKSW, 2010), pp. 167–177.

34. See H. Lombaerts, 'The Impact of the Status of Religion in Contemporary Society upon Interreligious Learning', pp. 54–86; H. Lombaerts and D. Pollefeyet, 'The Emergence of Hermeneutics in Religious Education Theories: An Overview', in *Hermeneutics and Religious Education*, eds. H. Lombaerts, and D. Pollefeyet (Leuven: Leuven University Press, 2004), pp. 47–49.

SECTION III: PLURALISM AND RELIGIOUS EDUCATION
IN IRISH SCHOOLS

CHAPTER NINE

PLURALISM, DIALOGUE AND RELIGIOUS EDUCATION IN *SHARE THE GOOD NEWS: NATIONAL DIRECTORY FOR CATECHESIS IN IRELAND*

Gareth Byrne

Share the Good News: National Directory for Catechesis in Ireland (SGN) is the landmark document issued by the Irish Episcopal Conference in December 2010 and launched on 5 January 2011. A National Directory for Catechesis seeks to set out the vision, organisation and planning associated with evangelisation, catechesis and religious education from the perspective of the Catholic Church at national level. Its purpose is transparent. The Directory sets down a framework for the presentation of and engagement with the Good News of Jesus Christ. It seeks to be a catalyst for renewal in faith of adult Catholics. It aims to ensure that they can share their faith with coming generations. It hopes to encourage members of the Catholic Church to enter into conversation with each other and with their neighbours concerning the love of God they have come to know in Jesus Christ and in each other. It acknowledges that all are invited to fulfilment in God's love: 'God offers salvation to all. God calls us to become, together, one family, working in common purpose, in communion with God and with one another' (SGN 26).

The introduction to *Share the Good News* sets itself a respectful but demanding programme of dialogue. The Irish bishops believe this document can be an instrument contributing to peace, reconciliation and new hope in Ireland; a support for concerned ecumenical dialogue; an invitation to those of other world religions to enter into an exchange of ideas about life lived in God's presence; and a prompt for interaction between members of the Church and those who do not profess belief in God, such that all are enriched and learn together on the journey of life (SGN 6).

The Irish Context Today
It has been said that *Share the Good News* is current and practical in its outlook.[1] The Directory recognises that while many people in Ireland today continue to acknowledge their Catholic faith, they are increasingly circumspect when it

comes to naming and expressing the correlation between religion and daily life.[2] The revelations concerning child sexual abuse, particularly by clergy and religious, and the lack of an appropriate response over decades, has had a devastating effect on the Catholic Church in Ireland, on victims in the first place and in turn on the whole Church (SGN 11). The National Directory for Catechesis recognises that religious practice is fast declining, especially among young Catholics (SGN 8). Contemporary culture and the challenge it presents for Christian commitment are addressed in the document, taking life as it is lived in Ireland today as the starting point. Building on a rich Christian tradition, Ireland's engagement with the wider world, and its promise and potential into the future are examined. Themes grappled with include: the ups and downs of economic realities; overcoming social exclusion; the need for ecological awareness; the significance of the sciences and technology; and the contribution of diversity, globalisation, and communications technology to our world. Committed dialogue with all these issues is recommended, if the power for good that religious faith can be, for the individual and for society, is to be recognised and impact positively on coming generations (SGN 9–20).

Church and State

As well as understanding the culture we live within and seek to shape, the Directory sees the contribution of religion to the public square, and the dialogue between Church and State, as particularly significant. Faith and life are of one piece, it suggests, and both the richer for the conversation between them when it is open, honourable and compassionate (SGN 21).

In Ireland today, as elsewhere, it is clear that the plurality of cultures and religious affiliations that now exists, necessitates a keen understanding of the place of religion in the modern secular state. Both religion and the State should be recognised and respected. The Christian community should engage in real dialogue with modern, and today postmodern, society, and should never, *Share the Good News* suggests, become closed in on itself. The Church should constantly seek to contribute to the cultural and moral growth of society, 'entering into ongoing and mutually beneficial conversation with the State' (SGN 21). As Pope Benedict has put it:

> The world of reason and the world of faith – the world of secular rationality and the world of religious belief – need one another and should not be afraid to enter into a profound dialogue, for the good of civilisation. Religion, in other words, is not a problem for legislators to solve, but a vital contributor to the national conversation.[3]

A sustained discussion between faith and culture can only take place if the changing context is acknowledged, if analysis of social and cultural developments is taken seriously, and if the reality in which people live their lives continues to be newly discovered and engaged with enthusiastically:

Openness to dialogue with all, based on the ideals of human dignity, human good, human rights, justice and respect, is an important starting point for any discussion (SGN 24).

Dialogue and Proclamation

Into the dialogue of life the Christian carries Christ, witnessing to the power of his love and to the experience of being loved by him. This is wholly understandable and appropriate. While encouraging others to speak their truth, the Church exists in order to evangelise, that is 'to proclaim in words and action the Gospel, the Good News revealed to us in Jesus Christ, through the grace of the Holy Spirit, that we are loved by God for all eternity' (SGN 25).

In the past, evangelisation was often associated with the mission of the Church in the West to lands well beyond Europe, contributed to energetically by the Irish Church. *Share the Good News*, as its name suggests sees the person and message of Jesus Christ as good news indeed. In Ireland, today as always, Christians bear witness to each other of God's love for them. In ordinary ways, they lead each other into an ever deeper, though often unspoken, understanding of the hope that is theirs in Jesus Christ. The meaning of the Gospel is brought fully alive in the dialogue, whether formal or informal, that takes place first of all at home and within the local parish community, then perhaps between people of different Christian traditions, and eventually with people of other religions and world views (SGN 30).

Today, in each of these contexts, dialogue and proclamation of the Gospel go hand in hand, entered into with a humble spirit and with a deep reverence for people and communities.[4] To proclaim the Gospel is not in any way to disrespect the other. Rather it involves dialogue, careful and patient listening and the willingness to enter into honest and open conversation, 'always taking the person as one's starting point and always coming back to the relationships of people among themselves and with God'.[5] The message of Christ's love in all its richness is a gift to be carried lightly but wholeheartedly. Without doubt, the Directory argues, this love has the power to call a person to conversion, but it is the Spirit of Christ, the Spirit of Love and Freedom, that will open the eyes, the mind, the heart: 'Only appropriate processes should, of course, be employed, so that the Gospel is always freely given and freely received (SGN 31).'

The dialogue envisaged in *Share the Good News*, is, in the first place, internal to the local Christian community, seeking through catechesis to deepen the Christian faith of those preparing for or already initiated into the faith (SGN 34–37). This conversation focused on faith can also, at a particular moment, become ecumenical (SGN 62) and/or inter-religious (SGN 65–67) reaching out to those of other denominations and faiths. It must also understand the challenge of inculturation (SGN 63–64), opening up an engagement with the culture of a particular time and place, and with people professing a variety of diverse world views. On the one hand, culture in Europe and further afield has been shaped over twenty centuries by the Christian tradition. On the other hand, Christians today, as always, are shaped by the culture within which they live as well as by the Gospel. Inculturation is a two-way process. Christians bring Christ with them into everyday life and everyday life helps put them in touch with, and keeps them close to, the truth he offers them. For the Christian, life and faith can never be separated: 'The truth of life today and the truth we come to know in the Gospel disclose each other, inform each other, build upon each other (SGN 63).'

Pluralism, Secularism and Schools
Share the Good News clarifies the important distinction between secularism and pluralism, something which while foundational to the question under discussion, is often blurred in daily discourse. While we all use the term 'secular' to describe what is of this world and must be engaged with, by 'secularism' is meant a radical attempt to exclude God and religion from culture and from public life, 'a profound break not only with Christianity but, generally, with the religious and moral traditions of humanity' (SGN 21). Secularism cannot be seen as a neutral stance but is rather a philosophy that strongly argues a position against other philosophical understandings and in particular against any perceptible demonstration of religion or discussion of religious faith in the public domain. 'Pluralism' however, properly understood, empathises with the variety of world views that are manifest in modern societies and upholds their right to contribute to debate: 'Pluralism [...] at its best upholds positive respect for and interest in the quest for truth engaged in by individuals, by faith communities and other groups in society' (SGN 21). Terrence Merrigan in his chapter in this volume concludes that pluralism is often misunderstood and misused in modern European society to silence religion and prevent it contributing to public discourse. In fact, a truly pluralist society must continually seek to protect itself from two undermining trends: allowing itself to become a cover for secularism dressed up as something neutral and objective; and a tendency toward relativism, refusing to judge as to what it right and true and just.

It is apparent from the National Directory for Catechesis and other recent documents that the Catholic Church in Ireland accepts that, given the plurality of religious and other beliefs that exist in Ireland today, there should be greater choice and diversity within the national education system.[6]

Acknowledging this reality, the Church at the same time stands over its contribution to education and the positive impact of the distinct ethos, discussed in the next section of this article, under which Catholic schools operate. Clearly, today, the Catholic Church in Ireland does not see a need for all schools to be Catholic schools. It does expect, however, that Catholic schools, and faith schools generally, be treated equally with other schools in a society that seeks to be genuinely pluralist. This means that they would continue to be supported by the State as one of the significant options available to parents/guardians for their children – indeed the option persistently chosen by the majority of parents in the Republic of Ireland:

> The Church continues to be involved in education as it forms a central part of its mission and because there are parents who wish to have their children educated in a context that respects both faith and reason. We hope that those educated in such a context will be able to make a dynamic contribution to our democratic society, to the life of the Church and to the dialogue of faith and culture.[7]

The Catholic Education Ethos

The Catholic understanding of education is based on the person's ultimate dignity as an individual and directed always toward their growth as a person.[8] This understanding is not unique to Catholic education but it is central to it. More precisely, as will be clear from the earlier part of this presentation, the Catholic vision of education supports the individual's search for meaning in the context of Jesus Christ's demonstration of God's all-embracing loving kindness. Autonomy, independence and self-sufficiency are cherished. They are balanced by a focus on 'relationality, interdependence and transcendence' (SGN 28). The suggestion that other kinds of schools, free from religious interest, are by definition somehow more open, free and respectful is not coherent. Each school must be able to justify its ethos and the way in which its characteristic spirit contributes to the experience of pupils, staff, parents and other stakeholders. A Catholic education ethos understands itself as a humanising and caring activity, seeking to open the person to freedom and completion, and to spiritual and moral responsibility, lived respectfully with Christ in the world and with its peoples, celebrating all of life in a spirit of justice, generosity and gratitude (SGN 147–148).

The Catholic school, then, endeavours to be a good school and to add value by bringing Christ, his love, his teaching, his message, alive, day-by-day, in the school and beyond. This added value is what is distinctive about a Catholic education. It understands all of life as a theatre within which we are introduced by Christ to the gifts which speak to us of God's generosity and care for us and of our responsibility to live ethically for the good of all. It suggests a way of life rooted in love of God and love of neighbour:

- Catholic education is inspired by Jesus Christ. It is person-centred, seeking to develop the full potential of each person
- Catholic education proposes a sacramental view of reality, helping pupils to see God 'in the bits and pieces of everyday life'
- Catholic education takes place in open, happy, stimulating and mutually respectful communities

- Catholic education values intellectual and practical reason, promoting dialogue and understanding between faith, tradition, culture and heritage
- Catholic education values tolerance and inclusiveness. Catholic schools welcome pupils of other traditions, faiths and none, seeing diversity as offering opportunities for deeper understanding among people holding diverse convictions
- Catholic education seeks to enable pupils to act with integrity and justice, in pursuit of the common good in an imperfect world, and to act as stewards of creation.[9]

Religious Education in a Pluralist Society

Religious education has a significant part to play in the Catholic school (SGN 152). In fact, it has a vital role to play in all schools in a society which celebrates diversity. How we define religious education in schools in Ireland in the future may well differ according to patronage model. There will undoubtedly, however, continue to be a need in society, not only for the individual and the community to understand religion but, as a committed believer or otherwise, for constructive engagement with religion, religions and other world views. Anything less leaves the coming generations open, at a minimum, to ignorance and misinformation. In a post-9/11 world this would be remiss. There are other risks too: a reduced amount of reference points for the fullest possible discourse on beauty, truth, justice and love; a diminished basis upon which to conjure deeply with the questions of meaning put before us in life; and a possible lack of awareness and respect for the lived response of so many others to life and all its gifts. The first 'Mutual Ground' conference held at Mater Dei Institute of Education in October 2011 (and reproduced in Chapters 1–4 of this volume), reaffirmed the great hunger among those in the field of religious education, and in education generally in Ireland, for discussion of the importance of good religious education and how it can help promote the growth of individuals, of the local community and of society itself. The 'mutual ground' project allows all, whether religious or not, to support the need for an engaged, generous, reflective, and active religious education in our schools. It does not seek to impose one definition of religious education on our efforts, but supports those efforts while allowing for a diversity of approaches. It suggests a ground that all can hold in common while understanding that different contexts and circumstances will necessitate a varied approach according to the desires and needs of participants. Following on from and developing the tradition of including religious, spiritual and moral education in schooling in Ireland over the centuries, we have an opportunity to define again for our time what we mean by an holistic approach to education, taking all of life as our subject matter and helping young people to be informed, confident, involved and respectful of others and their commitments.

The Catholic school is a place where dialogue and respect are encouraged. *Share the Good News* is very clear in its expectation that the Catholic school is open to pupils from all cultural and religious backgrounds (SGN 148). It does not restrict the gift of Catholic education to Catholic pupils. Schools are an outreach of a local community and the Catholic school is an outreach of the local Catholic community. It has a duty of care, in the first place, to the Catholic children of the locality and to their parents. In the Catholic primary school the religious education and formation of Catholic children in support of parents, guardians and the local parish or parishes is without doubt a prime concern (SGN 99–103). In the Catholic second-level school the personal search for meaning and identity among Catholic young people, a growing facility for critical reflection on their part, and a deepening commitment to love of God and service of neighbour, are instinctive (SGN 107–111).

In embracing young people from beyond the Catholic community the Catholic school treats them with the greatest honour. It respects the faith and beliefs of all young people under its care. The right of parents to withdraw their children from denominational religious education and formation has always been respected. Clearly, young people should not in any way be subjected to proselytising or indoctrination (SGN 101). This is a self-evident principle in the Catholic and other school sectors. Indoctrinating young people with a secularist world view would be equally unacceptable. The Catholic school seeks to be 'utterly respectful of everyone's belief system' (SGN 148), offering everyone an invitation to understand, engage with and honour the characteristic spirit of the school, appropriately, without, in any way, imposing on the conscience of pupils.

It should be noted that *Share the Good News* differentiates between catechesis, bringing young people and adults to a mature Christian faith, an activity that properly takes place within a community living out its Christian faith (SGN 34–35), and religious education which while contributing to the faith formation of Catholic pupils, can be defined in ways that allows for a broader mix of participants. The Irish Catholic Bishops' Conference advocates an approach to religious education, in whatever way it is defined in different circumstances, that always respects the religious life and tradition of the young person (and teacher) involved. It should support the Catholic young person in their faith, while helping them enter into dialogue with other young people on their journey too:

> Religious education wherever it takes place, should be carried out in a way that supports the faith life of the Catholic student, strengthening the harmony between what is known, who one is becoming and how one lives one's life (SGN 38).

Not all Catholic pupils will attend Catholic schools. This will particularly be the case when there is a wider diversity of patronage options for parents.

Following the argument that is being made here, they too, along with other pupils, should, normally, be given the opportunity to participate in an appropriate form of religious education. The National Directory for Catechesis expects that the religion of young Catholics will be acknowledged and suitably supported in all schools in a pluralist society (SGN 39). In addition, Catholic parents, whose children attend schools other than Catholic schools, are asked, with the support of the parish, to ensure that additional faith formation takes place in an appropriate catechetical space, beyond the school day (SGN 103). This is not an extra burden placed on them but is indicated as part of what all Catholic parents seek for their children in one way or another.[10]

Home, Parish and School Working Together

Faith development, through all the stages and transitions of life, in a variety of contexts, and for a variety of Christians on their particular journey, is at the heart of *Share the Good News*. The National Directory for Catechesis, celebrating the contribution of schools, moves the Church beyond any dependence on the school alone and its teachers for the faith development of young people. This is a community effort, undertaken together by all the members of the Church, locally and universally, walking with Jesus Christ and encouraged by his Holy Spirit. It is the work of home, parish and school, undertaken conscious of the need for dialogue with the beliefs and hopes of others. Religious education in schools plays a crucial role. It opens Catholic children, and others, to know and understand their own faith and the beliefs of others in a context today of diversity and plurality. Religious education prepares young people for life and at its best sends them back home, and to their faith community and/or to other communities of commitment, prepared for conversations about life and faith, about meaning and identity and relationship, about justice, truth and love.

Conclusion

In concluding this overview of the contribution of *Share the Good News* to the debate on pluralism, dialogue and religious education, it can be said that it strongly supports the place of religious education in the school curriculum, not just the study of religion, but engagement, in an age-appropriate manner, with how religion and belief effect life, deepen the experience of a person, and can lead them to encounter more fully themselves, the other, the world in all its richness, and ultimate meaning however this is conceived. The inference, however, is that we need to commit ourselves to carefully defining religious education, especially, when it is suggested that there may be a plurality of forms of religious education to be discovered in a pluralist society.

NOTES

1. Donal Murray, 'Teaching the Faith and Sharing the Gospel', *The Furrow*, 63/5 (2012), pp. 259–273.

2. Gareth Byrne, 'Communicating Faith in Ireland: From Commitment, through Questioning to New Beginnings', in *Communicating Faith*, ed. by John Sullivan (Washington DC: Catholic University of America Press, 2011), pp. 261–276.

3. Benedict XVI, *Address of His Holiness Benedict XVI*, Westminster Hall, 17 Sept. 2010 <http://www.vatican.va> [accessed 12 Sept. 2012].

4. Pontifical Council for Inter-Religious Dialogue, *Dialogue and Proclamation* (1991) <http://www.vatican.va> [accessed 12 Sept. 2012].

5. Paul VI, *Evangelii nuntiandi* 20 (1975) <http://www.vatican.va> [accessed 12 Sept. 2012].

6. See Irish Catholic Bishops' Conference, *Catholic Primary Schools: A Policy for Provision into the Future* (2007), 5 <http://www.catholicbishops.ie> [accessed 14 Sept. 2012]; SGN 103.

7. Catholic Schools Partnership, *Catholic Primary Schools: Looking to the Future*, p. 25 <http://www.catholicbishops.ie> [accessed 14 Sept. 2012].

8. The Congregation for Catholic Education, *The Catholic School* (1977), 29 <http://www.vatican.va> [accessed 12 Sept. 2012]; SGN 28.

9. See Irish Catholic Bishops' Conference, *Vision '08: A Vision for Catholic Education in Ireland* (2008) <http://www.catholicbishops.ie> [accessed 14 Sept. 2012]; SGN 101.

10. Gareth Byrne, 'Children's Religious Education: Challenge and Gift,' *Nurturing Children's Religious Imagination: The Challenge of Primary Religious Education Today*, ed. by Raymond Topley and Gareth Byrne (Dublin: Veritas, 2004), pp. 237–251.

CHAPTER TEN

RELIGIOUS PLURALISM AND EDUCATIONAL PRACTICE IN NORTHERN IRELAND

Niall Coll

While debate about how best to include learning about different world religions in the school curriculum has moved centre stage in religious education circles in much of Europe, Northern Ireland's unique context means in the first instance that talk of religious pluralism refers to promoting more mutual knowledge and understanding between its different Christian traditions. Religion has, of course, been an important ingredient in the history of conflict in Ireland.[1] This is particularly so in the north where the arrival and settlement of Protestants (mostly Scottish Presbyterians) in the seventeenth-century sowed the seeds of bitter divisions in ethnic, political, economic and religious matters. Following independence for the south from the UK and partition, the new Northern Ireland state's Unionist government exercised power unfairly over the Catholic nationalist minority leading to the emergence in the 1960s of the Civil Rights Association to protest against injustices. Michael Hurley explains that 'Behind this discrimination lay a deep-seated fear of Rome.'[2] Protestants have a long history of fearing and attempting to subjugate the native population and their faith.[3] Their philosophy of 'No Surrender' meant that Catholic grievances were never addressed following the establishment of the northern state. The Provisional IRA emerged in December 1969 and by 1971 had acquired an offensive capacity. Simultaneously, different forms of Unionism and Loyalism coalesced in the Ulster Defence Association, formed in December 1971.[4] The gun had reappeared with a vengeance in Irish politics. By the time of the 1994 ceasefire, over 3,700 people had lost their lives in 'The Troubles'. Talk of religious pluralism, not least in an intra-Christian context, its importance, and sensitivities around it, are thus of particular importance in Northern Ireland.

The Importance of Religious Voices in Promoting Peace
In the face of common assumptions internationally that the Northern Ireland conflict is predominantly, even completely, a religious one, it needs to be

acknowledged that religious voices have also been to the fore in promoting peace and greater reconciliation.[5] In the wake of the Second Vatican Council (1962–65) considerable ecumenical progress was made at an unofficial level. The outbreak of violence 'spurred or shamed' the Catholic and Protestant Churches into making official contact for the first time.[6] Against the background of escalating violence the leaders of the four main churches in Ireland, Catholic, Presbyterian, Church of Ireland and Methodist, formed a working group to calm fears and promote peace. 'The churches were more ready than the political parties to stretch out hands of friendship.'[7] Arguably one of the most important Church initiatives during the Troubles was the work of the Redemptorist Peace Ministry among Republicans, associated especially with Fr Alex Reid.[8] It facilitated a *tearmann* – a safe place where republicans and representatives of moderate nationalists and the Irish government could meet. This laid the basis for the ceasefires and the subsequent Good Friday Agreement of 1998 giving rise to a dramatically changed Northern Ireland with its power-sharing Executive and the hope that it will consolidate the peace that the north has enjoyed over the last decade. (Fr Reid and the former Methodist President, Dr Harold Good, were the two witnesses to IRA decommissioning of arms in 2005.) That the Churches have played an important role in promoting peace during the Troubles is generally accepted. Many wonder, however, whether the existence of separate schools for Protestants and Catholics have contributed to community divisions and violence in the past and even in the present.[9]

Educational Provision in Northern Ireland
The emergence of denominational education in Ireland is in no small measure the legacy of the strong animosities and fear of proselytism which were such a feature of nineteenth-century life. Following partition the Protestant Churches in the north were able to transfer their schools into a state-controlled system confident that their Protestant ethos and character were secure. Meanwhile the Catholic bishops were conscious of the need to secure and defend Catholic interests, especially in relation to the Church's role in education.[10] These historical points are helpful in explaining the basic structure of schooling in Northern Ireland today. We note some relevant statistics:

- There are 1,591 schools and preschool education centres, 524 of which are Catholic maintained
- About 51 per cent of students at all levels attend a Catholic maintained school
- Integrated schools which explicitly cater for pupils from Catholic, Protestant and other faith backgrounds account for 6.7 per cent of the whole school population
- 91 per cent of Protestant primary children attend controlled (or state) schools and 88 per cent of Catholic primary pupils attend Catholic maintained primaries.[11]

Aidan Donaldson has rightly noted that 'In a divided society such as Northern Ireland, it is only natural and correct that the role of education should be closely scrutinised and monitored to assess how effective schools are in promoting tolerance, mutual understanding and the common good.' He alludes to the fact that notable academics like Roy Foster and Richard Dawkins have entered the fray to agree with those who argue that if Northern Ireland is to become a pluralist, accommodating and tolerant society at peace with itself, then it must promote integrated schooling. 'The (not always) unspoken corollary is that faith-based schools – specifically Catholic schools in the context of Northern Ireland – are in some way inferior, backward, and even dangerous insofar as they ... contribute to division and the continuation of sectarian attitudes.'[12]

The Catholic bishops, among others, reject such claims and point to Catholic education's commitment to the work of reconciliation and social justice, as well as to the high quality of educational outcomes, both formal and informal.[13]

In its important long-term policy document, *A Shared Future*, the Northern Ireland government acknowledges that 'The exercise of parental choice is central and both integrated and denominational schools have important roles to play in preparing children for their role as adults in a shared society.' But it goes on to add the qualification that 'There is a balance to be struck, however, between the exercise of this choice and the significant additional costs ...'[14] The current Minister for Education, Sinn Féin's John O'Dowd, acknowledges that parents have the right to express a preference for schools that reflect a religious, or integrated, ethos. He adds that his department operates a community relations, equality and diversity policy which seeks to ensure that children and young people develop self-respect and respect for others by building relationships with those of different backgrounds and traditions.[15] Significantly, opposition to the existence of Catholic schools has been voiced loudly recently by the Democratic Unionist First Minister, Peter Robinson, when he criticized 'a benign form of apartheid' and called for an end to Government funding of Catholic schools as part of a push toward an integrated education system.[16]

Speaking for the Catholic sector, Bishop Donal McKeown argues that access to faith based education is a key characteristic of a modern pluralist society, that Catholic schools thrive in the most modern and advanced societies and that they tend to provide good value for the public money that they receive. He goes on to assert that the real sign of maturity in Northern Ireland will not be when everyone goes to a secular school, but, rather, 'when diversity of provision is seen as an enrichment for society and not as a threat to its stability'.[17] Similar sentiments are expressed by Philip Barnes, who, writing from a Northern Ireland Protestant faith perspective, and as one who is also well acquainted with religious education in schools in England and Wales, affirms the contribution of faith schools to the realization of legitimate and progressive educational values including the cultivation of tolerance, moral integrity and civic virtue.[18]

Religious Education in Northern Ireland

Religious education has evolved differently in controlled state schools and maintained Catholic schools in Northern Ireland. In state schools as society became more secular in the 1960s it became less about Christian nurture, as it had been hitherto, and had to be justified more and more on strictly educational grounds.[19] Catholic schools, while, of course, committed to academic attainment, also emphasise explicitly the importance of promoting the religious and spiritual development of pupils, work that is all the more important in an increasingly secularised society. Schools are to be faith communities assisting parents and parishes in fostering personal faith development. The influential vision document for Catholic education in Northern Ireland, *Life to the Full*, describes the Catholic school as 'a vital instrument in the Church's mission' called to help nurture each person's spiritual and personal development – pupils and staff alike. 'Inspired by the teaching of Christ the school's ethos seeks to promote a more just and humane world.'[20]

This involves the challenge of promoting inclusiveness, a theme which is regarded as a top priority in wider society today. It is emphasised that Catholic schools are not just for Catholics: 'All schools should be welcoming and fair to pupils and staff from other traditions, and ensure that relationships with them reflect justice and promote self esteem.' Catholic schools are to be open to children of all traditions whose parents accept the mission statement and aims of the school. Indeed, the presence of these children enriches the education experience offered by the school and is a practical expression of the commitment to promote broader participation and inclusivity.[21]

The Religious Education Curriculum in Northern Ireland

One of the avowed aims of the Northern Ireland Curriculum is to contribute to the spiritual development of pupils. It requires that all schools should offer a broadly based curriculum which 'promotes the spiritual, emotional, moral, cultural, intellectual and physical development of pupils at the school and thereby of society ...'[22] The most important piece of legislation in education over the last two decades has been the Education Reform Order of 1989, the main aim of which was to provide for a new statutory curriculum.[23] Because religious education was excluded from the seven compulsory areas of study it was perceived by the Churches that the role of religion was being marginalized in schools. In an attempt to address the situation, and surely aware of the importance of promoting better levels of religious knowledge and mutual understanding among pupils and students in a divided society, the then Minister of Education invited the Churches to work together to develop their own syllabus of Religious Education which would be mandatory in schools. (Religious Education is now a compulsory element of the Northern Ireland curriculum for all government funded schools.) The Programme of Study, first implemented in 1993, was agreed by the four main Christian denominations and was a considerable ecumenical achievement, and one welcomed by the government.[24] It is mostly Christian in character with its three main 'Learning Objectives': i) The Revelation of God, ii) The Christian Church and iii) Morality.[25] One of the key characteristics of the programme is its emphasis on developing pupils' knowledge of the Bible. Whatever divides Catholics and Protestants in terms of history and belief in Northern Ireland, a good grounding in Scripture, even in a more secular society, should hopefully be an important motive and resource in nudging both traditions toward genuine reconciliation. Thus schools have an important role to play in developing greater recognition of a shared religious culture which honours those words that call us to 'love your enemy', to 'turn the other cheek', to act like the Good Samaritan, in the hope that they can be important in shaping that shared future which government and wider society, for the most part, seek. Another aspect that merits particular mention is the extent to which the Key Stage 3 programme seeks to facilitate learning about what all Christians hold in common in terms of their key beliefs and religious practices before turning to a study of the main distinctive characteristics of each of the four main Christian traditions in Ireland.

The Religious Education Programme of Study's emphasis on Christianity has been criticized in some quarters for being overly-conservative and exclusive of the other world faiths, especially in wake of the in-migration of some peoples of different religions and cultures during the last two decades. (The 2011 Northern Ireland Census recorded that 0.8 per cent of people described themselves as being of 'other religions and philosophies'.) In *A Shared Future* the government has spoken of the importance of 'Developing opportunities for shared inter-cultural education at all levels'.[27] Thus in 2007 a Revised Core Syllabus, approved by the four Churches, was introduced and the Key Stage 3 Programme (pupils aged 11 to 14) was amended to include the study of two other world religions. This development served to underline and confirm the already well-established practice in Catholic schools of studying world religions as evidenced by the *Fully Alive* programme which is followed in most schools.

Multi-Faith or Inter-Religious Education?
One of the most pressing questions which religious educationalists in Northern Ireland face is to identify which approach or methodology they will use in teaching world religions. Opinions vary: is it best to adopt the multi-faith, phenomenological approach favoured in post-confessional England with its

preference for neutrality and underplaying, if not actually excluding, the place of Religious education in fostering (personal) religious faith?[28]

Dermot Lane, one of Ireland's leading Catholic religious educationalists, and with an eye to how Catholic education in particular, both north and south, should respond to changes in society and school curriculum, advocates what he terms inter-religious education. He is keenly aware that the Second Vatican Council (1962–65) taught that Christians should seek out 'the spiritual and moral truths' found in other religions, noting that they 'often reflect a ray of that truth which enlightens all'.[29] Indeed *The National Directory for Catechesis in Ireland*, conscious of our globalised culture and the greater diversity of people now living on the island of Ireland, has acknowledged the ever-growing importance of authentic inter-religious dialogue: 'We seek to learn more and more about the ways God works in the world, receiving from and giving to those of other religions.' Furthermore it says: 'We engage also with those who do not have a religious commitment that, through inter-religious dialogue, we may learn together something of the truth that seeks to transform us all.' It recommends that while catechesis and all faith development at the parish or school level should always take place in an environment that is genuinely supportive of the participants' own Christian faith, it can also 'usefully embrace learning about a variety of religions and their truth claims. We should be able to honour people of different religious convictions, and reverence their commitment, without in any way succumbing to relativism'.[30]

In promoting this inter-religious approach, religious education would aim to go beyond simply communicating detached information about other religions – the so-called phenomenological approach – and seek, rather, to promote an authentic encounter of mutual understanding of the other with a view to opening up the possibility of deepening one's own faith and the faith of the other. As Lane puts it, the better that one is grounded in one's own religious tradition then the more enriching such encounter will be.[31]

Returning to the Northern Ireland context in particular, some feel that the school curriculum here should reflect the phenomenological approach and argue that the cause of equality requires a new syllabus, much less Christian and more multi-faith in character.[32] Philip Barnes opposes this view arguing that there is no empirical evidence to substantiate a connection between multi-faith religious education and favourable attitudes toward members of minority religions and culture. But he also concedes, however, that there is similarly no empirical evidence demonstrating the absence of such a connection.[33] Elsewhere he wonders, provocatively, if clamour to introduce a multi-faith, phenomenological approach in Northern Ireland should be viewed as 'as an attempt to further the process of secularization in education by reducing the influence of Christianity in schools'.[34]

Conclusion

In a post-conflict Northern Ireland there needs to be a greater acknowledgement of the importance of fostering good religious education in what is still a divided society. Deepening knowledge and sympathy (hopefully) between pupils and students from both Protestant and Catholic backgrounds on their respective Christian traditions is essential work. This task is arguably all the more important in our increasingly secularised society to guard against a sectarian secularism between unionist and nationalist which might be all the more bitter since it would be unable to recognise and be challenged by the gospel call to love one's neighbour. There also needs to be a deeper reflection on how best to integrate teaching about other world religions into the curriculum. This work is all the more necessary in our globalised and more religiously pluralized society. How to do this in a way that is both true to the pupils' own religious traditions and open to the other will be an important priority in the years ahead.

NOTES

1. Oliver P. Rafferty, 'The Catholic Church and the Nationalist Community in Northern Ireland', *Éire-Ireland*, 43 (2008), p. 99.

2. Michael Hurley, 'Northern Ireland and the Post-Vatican II Ecumenical Journey', in *Christianity in Ireland; Revisiting the Story*, ed. by Dáire Keogh and Brendan Bradshaw (Dublin: The Columba Press, 2002), p. 262.

3. John D. Brewer and Gareth I. Higgins, *Anti-Catholicism in Northern Ireland, 1600–1998: The Mote and the Beam* (Houndmills, Basingstoke: Macmillian Press, 1998), p. 12.

4. Alvin Jackson, *Ireland 1798–1998* (Oxford: Wiley–Blackwell, 1999), pp. 374–75.

5. Former Irish President Mary McAleese has spoken of the key role that the Christian Churches have played there as constant persuaders for peace and healthy cross-community relationships. See Greg Ryan, 'Church Can Nurture Seeds of Peace, says McAleese', *Church Times*, 23 May 2008.

6. Hurley, p. 265.

7. Eric Gallagher and Stanley Worrall, *Christianity in Ulster, 1968–1980* (Oxford: Oxford University Press, 1982), p. 38.

8. Kevin Rafter, 'Priests and Peace: The Role of Redemptorist Order in the Northern Ireland Peace Process', *Estudios Irlandeses*, 28 (2003), p. 172.

9. Tony Gallagher, 'Faith Schools in Northern Ireland: A Review of Research' in *Faith Schools: Consensus or Conflict*, ed. by Roy Gardner, Jo Cairns and Denis Lawton (London: Routledge, 2005), p. 156.

10. See Michael McGrath, *The Catholic Church and Catholic Schools in Northern Ireland: The Price of Faith* (Dublin: Irish Academic Press, 2000), p. 2.

11. <http://www.deni.gov.uk/enrolments_in_schools_1112_-_february_release_-_final_revised 2-2.pdf> and Kathryn Torney <http://www.thedetail.tv/issues/150/religioninschools/how-integrated-are-schools-where-you-live> [accessed 25 Nov. 2012]. Her figures are for the academic year 2011/12.

12. Aidan Donaldson, 'Catholic Education at the Crossroads: Issues Facing Catholic Schools in Northern Ireland' in *International Handbook of Catholic Education: Challenges for School*

Systems in the 21st Century, Part One, ed. by Gerald R. Grace and Joseph O'Keefe (Dordrecht, The Netherlands, 2007), p. 231.

13. The Catholic Bishops of Northern Ireland, *Building Peace Shaping the Future* (Armagh, 2001), pp. 4–6.

14. *A Shared Future: Policy and Strategic Framework for Good Relations in Northern Ireland*, Section 2.4.5, published Monday 21 Mar. 2005 <http://www.ofmdfmni.gov.uk/asharedfuture policy2005.pdf> [accessed 25 Nov. 2012].

15. See Kathryn Torney, *The Irish Times*, 23 Nov. 2012.

16. *Belfast Telegraph*, 16 Oct. 2010.

17. Address by Bishop Donal McKeown at the launch of Northern Ireland Catholic Schools Week 2011) <http://www.catholicbishops.ie/2011/01/24/address-by-bishop-donal-mc-keown-at-northern-ireland-launch-of-catholic-schools-week-2011/> [accessed 25 Nov. 2012].

18. L. Philip Barnes, 'Religion, Education and Conflict in Northern Ireland', *Journal of Beliefs and Values*, 26 (2005), p. 125.

19. Barnes, 2005, p. 128.

20. Council for Catholic Maintained Schools (CCMS), *Life to the Full: A Vision for Catholic Education* (Hollywood, Co. Down, 1996), pp. 7–9.

21. The Catholic Bishops of Northern Ireland, 2001, pp. 8–9.

22. <http://www.deni.gov.uk/index/schools-and-infrastructure-2/schools-management/79-school_governors_pg/schools_79_governor-roles-and-responsibilities_pg/schools_79_cha pter-7-revised-curriculum_pg.htm> [accessed 15 Dec. 2012].

23. Barnes, 2005, p. 129.

24. David Armstrong, 'Religious Education in the United Kingdom and Ireland – Northern Ireland' in *Debates in Religious Education Teaching*, ed. by L. Philip Barnes (Routledge, 2011), p. 33.

25. See Sharon Haughey, 'Catholic Religious Education in Northern Ireland' in *Exploring Religious Education: Catholic Religious Education in an Intercultural Europe*, ed. by Patricia Kieran and Anne Hession (Dublin: Veritas, 2008), p. 179.

26. See, for example, Norman Richardson, 'Religious Education in Northern Ireland' (2011) <http://www.mmiweb.org.uk/eftre/reeurope/northern_ireland_2011.html> [accessed 25 Nov. 2012].

27. *A Shared Future*, 2.4.5.

28. L. Philip Barnes, 'Impact N. 17: Religious Education: Taking Religious Difference seriously' (Philosophy of Education Society of Great Britain, 2008), p. 22 <https://www.philosophy-of-education.org/Pdfs/17_barnes_impact_text.pdf> [accessed 25 Nov. 2012].

29. Dermot Lane 'Nostra Aetate and Religious Education' in Kieran and Hession, 2008, p. 93. See also his *Stepping Stones to Other Religions: A Christian Theology of Inter-Religious Dialogue* (Dublin: Veritas, 2011), pp. 62–95.

30. Irish Episcopal Conference, *Share the Good: National Directory for Catechesis in Ireland* (Dublin: Veritas, 2010), 65, 67.

31. Lane, pp. 93–94.

32. Philip Barnes regards the Equality Commission of Northern Ireland as representative of this view. See Barnes (2005), p. 130.

33. Barnes, 2008, p. 22.

34. Barnes, 2005, p. 131.

Chapter Eleven

Inter-religious Education and the Future of Religious Education in Catholic Primary Schools

Anne Hession

Children start learning about world religions in preschool. This learning may be largely incidental learning which arises from the children's own background and experience. It may perhaps come from a contribution to the morning 'news time'. For example, Atif, a little boy in my child's preschool class, told her all about his family's celebration of Eid. Likewise my child who is a member of another world religion, Christianity, told him all about her trip to her cousin's christening. Children's incidental learning about religions, through discussion of something brought into the classroom, or seen on television, or encountered in a story, will remain important right through the primary school. However, it is now recognised that Christian religious education at every level should include inter-religious education which enhances students' capacity to engage with people of other religious faiths and beliefs. The Pontifical Council for Inter-religious Dialogue expressed it well when it stated:

> The Christian who meets other believers is not involved in an activity which is marginal to his or her faith. Rather is it something which arises from the demands of that faith. It flows from faith and should be nourished by faith.[1]

This chapter explores the question of how teachers might organise systematic inter-religious learning in the context of the formal religious education curriculum in the Catholic primary school. The question of why Catholic teachers should consider this an integral part of Christian religious education is examined and the goals of such learning in the context of the primary religious education curriculum are proposed. Three theological and three philosophical principles are proposed as a guide for Catholic teachers to enable them to decide on matters such as: how to approach inter-religious learning with young children; the knowledge, skills and attitudes to be fostered; and the kinds of educational experiences that might be offered in the primary school.

Why Inter-religious Learning?

Before developing an approach to inter-religious learning, the question of why it might be included in a Catholic primary religious education curriculum needs to be addressed. Teachers might legitimately ask whether this aspect of Christian religious education should be left to secondary school, given the crowded nature of the primary school curriculum. The concern might also be raised that education about other religions might undermine young children's capacity to engage with their own. Might it not be better to have an exclusive focus on children's own religious faith at primary level, precisely so that they will be able to embrace the challenge of religious and ethical diversity with confidence as adolescents and adults? Might young children be confused by introducing them too early to alternative world views? The statements above express fears which are understandable. These fears may be particularly heightened because of a general lack of clarity about the legitimate goals of religious education (as distinct from catechesis) in faith-based schools.[2] However, the goal of education is to help children adapt to their environment and to live their lives with meaning and purpose in contemporary society. In Europe today, most children are growing up in a religiously plural social environment, and Catholic educators who wish to take this reality seriously simply cannot ignore the challenge to help children develop strong, meaningful and purposeful religious identities in a context where there are many other religious and non-religious world views and ways of life.

The Goal of Catholic Religious Education and Inter-religious Learning

The goal of a Catholic primary religious education curriculum is Christian identity, in the sense that Catholic religious education intends to enhance the learner's understanding of the Christian tradition and how to embody that tradition in the contemporary world.[3] Therefore one of the purposes of Catholic primary religious education and formation is to show children how to develop Christian identity authentically in a religiously plural and diverse world. This means helping students to develop a mature understanding of their own religious faith, which includes developing an attitude of 'sympathy' and of 'dialogue' toward people of other faiths and world views. Catholic children need to learn who they are as Christians in the context of other traditions rather than over and against them. The educational challenge is to enhance understanding of oneself as a Christian through increasing knowledge of the other.[4]

The pluralistic context of children's development today requires competencies in religion that go beyond the goals of religious nurture or catechesis. Of course children need to be formed as members of the Church, but they also need to be prepared for religious life in the world and for conversations on matters of religion and belief that occur outside of the Church, in the public square. In other words, children now need to be able to speak two languages: the 'in-house' language of their own religion, and the public language required to converse meaningfully with people of other religions and beliefs. In primary school, children can lay the foundations for understanding the place of religious and philosophical beliefs and practices in human life by learning to appreciate their importance in the lives of people in their own families, schools and communities. They can be taught how to express their own faith in the presence of others and how to respect the expression of faith and/or belief on the part of others. They can develop an understanding of how religious beliefs can lead to ethical behaviour and of how people of belief can work together to create a better world.

Three Theological Principles for Inter-religious Learning

A pedagogy of inter-religious learning for the Catholic primary school will be deeply and firmly rooted in Catholic faith. The fundamental principles, or doctrinal foundations, for the relationship of Catholics toward other religions, were laid down by the Second Vatican Council.[5] The general educational goal that emerges from this teaching lies in the mandate to encounter and come into dialogue with people of other religions.[6] Sottocornola has already outlined two fundamental principles of education for inter-religious dialogue drawn from the Church's teaching at Vatican II.[7] These two principles will be examined here in the context of primary religious education. Another principle is added which emphasises the importance of the relational and ethical aspects of the encounter with difference. These three principles will imbue the contents and inspire the methodology of Catholic primary inter-religious education.

I) For Christians there is an ethical imperative to respond to the Other. Children should be taught that the way in which Christians experience God involves an encounter with the self and with others (including people of other religions and beliefs).[8] Therefore, their faith calls them to profound respect for and dialogue with people of other religions and beliefs. The parable of the Good Samaritan teaches that 'loving one's neighbour' means being a neighbour to people of other religious faiths. Hence, learning *about* and *from* people of other religions and beliefs is obeying the ethical command to love one's neighbour. As James Michael Lee suggests, 'If we are to teach learners to engage in religiously pluralistic activities, we should teach them how to love other religious traditions and their adherents rather than simply to know them.'[9] Indeed, it could be argued that the main goal of inter-religious learning at primary level is the development of awareness, together with positive attitudes, relationships and values. In other words, primary inter-religious learning should establish the basis for appropriate *relationships* with religious others. At secondary and third level the concern with faithful understanding of other religions and even critical reflection on those religions will have more importance. Yet at any level, inter-religious education is not simply a matter of learning information, but of forming the dispositions, attitudes, and character that enable one both to understand and respond ethically to others in a multi-religious world.

II) The right of all human beings to religious freedom was declared by the Second Vatican Council in its document entitled, *Dignitatis humanae* (Of the Dignity of the Human Person, 1965). At the heart of this document lies the principle that a person's response to God in faith must be free and can never be coerced. Christians who take their own religious freedom seriously are called to an even more conscientious respect for the religious freedom of others. The implications for inter-religious education are many. First, Catholics are called by God to respect the beliefs of others, to respect religious freedom, and to honour differences. As Sottocornola explains:

> Children, from a very early age, and young people, should be taught that since human beings cannot be forced into believing one thing or the other, or to belonging to one religion or the other, but have to respond freely to the innermost longing of their heart towards truth, there is bound to be a plurality of responses, a variety of religious expressions, and that these must be respected, no matter how wrong they may appear to us, as long as they do not infringe on other people's equal right to freedom in their own search for truth and happiness.[10]

Second, while Catholics are called to witness to their faith in Christ in word and deed this must be done in a manner that respects the religious faiths of others.[11] Third, Children need to be taught not only that the Church reproves discrimination against people on the basis of race, colour or religion (what Hobson and Edwards term 'negative tolerance'), rather Catholics are called to go even further in extending 'respect and love' to those who think or act differently than they do in religious matters.[12]

III) Catholics are called to have *a positive attitude to other religions which have to be looked at with true, genuine 'sympathy'.*[13] The Church at the Second Vatican Council adopted a positive, sympathetic, attitude toward the other religions. Thus while Catholics will always judge the compatibility of the beliefs espoused by adherents of other religions with the tenets of their own, the Church calls them to an attitude, by which they look for the positive aspects of other religions and 'acknowledge ... the spiritual and moral truths' to be found in them.[14]

The approach to other faiths adopted by the Council puts forward a vision of how other faiths *relate* to the Church.[15] For example, the longest article in *Nostra aetate*, article four, addresses the relationship between the Church and Judaism. Similarly, article three urges mutual understanding between Muslims and Christians because of their common links to the faith of Abraham. The pedagogical approach that most accurately reflects this theological position is that 'we must give priority and pre-eminence to Catholicism and seek to show the place and value of the other religions in relation to it.'[16] In other words, Catholic teachers will not simply present all religions as the same or as equally valid but will reflect the reality of Christianity's relationship to other world religions as it is spelt out in the documents of Vatican II, whereby some are considered to be closer to us than others.[17]

The first step toward inter-religious awareness in the primary school is to make the connection between Christianity and Judaism. The teaching of Judaism should receive special attention because of the close connections between it and Christianity. This awareness could be built upon through the exploration of the other great monotheistic faith – Islam. The intention is to show the value and place of these two Abrahamic religions in relation to Christianity. Children who have examined these two religions with appropriate sensitivity and respect at primary level will have laid the foundations for the study of other world religions at secondary school level. It is not what children have come to know about Judaism or Islam but their skills and attitudes in engaging respectfully with the texts, practices, and adherents of these religions that will provide them with a sense of how to proceed when they engage with other religions further in secondary school and beyond.

Philosophical Principles for Inter-religious Learning

(a) The first philosophical principle takes seriously *the right of children to be educated in their own religion.*[18] Many writers support the idea that children need to begin with a 'primary culture'.[19] Michael Polanyi calls it our 'fiduciary framework' which is the framework of beliefs and presuppositions we have come to hold as a result of our upbringing. This is understood as essential to becoming an individual, and as a foundation for growth toward autonomy. Intelligent religious living in contemporary liberal democracies requires that nurture or formation in a particular religion be combined with a form of critical religious education which preserves the child's autonomy.[20] A strong formation in one world view lays a necessary foundation for genuine respect for and appreciation of the world view of others. One implication of this principle is that children will neither be invited to compare religions directly, nor to make judgements about the validity of their truth claims in primary school. As Hobson and Edwards affirm:

> For primary students in religious education (as in moral education) there is a need for students to appropriate their home religion first and to develop some awareness of other religions before they can begin to subject it to closer scrutiny. This would imply the teaching approach would be predominantly descriptive.[21]

(b) In the Catholic primary school, *the learning process is understood as interpretation, not as a 'neutral' or 'objective' model.* There is no such thing as a neutral observer of religions and there is no such thing as a neutral objective study of religion. Contemporary theories of understanding and interpretation highlight that our understanding is inevitably shaped and limited by the prejudgements or expectations we bring to that which we wish to understand. Children's understandings will always be shaped by their location and experience, which may be quite different from the location and experience they seek to understand. Therefore, Catholic children will begin the task of interpretation and understanding of the religious other by responding from their distinctive religious location as Christians.[22] One implication of this understanding is that educators foster the awareness in children that inter-religious learning is not a simple task. Rather it requires sustained, respectful and careful effort on our part. As Berling notes:

> The first principle in that effort is recognizing and acknowledging difference as difference, not reducing another person, culture, or religion to a variation of what the interpreter knows based on his own 'form of life'. This principle cannot be overemphasized, since in the interests of making other religions accessible, authors and teachers all too often present them as simply variations on the familiar ... a genuine encounter with another religion should cause some discomfort, some loss of 'inward ease'.[23]

Taking this principle seriously requires that systematic teaching be preferred to thematic teaching in the Catholic primary school. In thematic teaching, religious faiths are taught by comparisons or by isolated treatment of festivals, rites of passage, worship, writings or key figures. There is a danger in this approach that the impression is given that religion centres on communal experiences facilitated by participation in religious rites and practices, thereby minimising the doctrinal element in religion.[24] In systematic teaching, the teaching of other faiths focuses on one faith at a time. It starts from the religions' own understanding of itself and an understanding of what it is to be a member of that particular faith community. The unique nature of that particular religious commitment is respected. There is some research data to support the idea that a positive attitude to religion is more likely to result from systematic teaching than from thematic or mixed teaching. While there is a need for more research in this regard, a systematic method of teaching may have to be preferred on educational as well as philosophical grounds.[25]

Related to this is the idea that religion is studied best not through data or lists of doctrines but in the lives of people shaped by a particular religion.[26] The realisation that religions are *lived by people* is an excellent foundation for later study of people's beliefs, the nature of their faith, the significance of their worship, the origins and historical development of the religion and so on. Furthermore, the teaching of other faiths should prioritise the indigenous cultural manifestation of those faiths where possible. For example, Irish Catholic children might be helped to enter imaginatively into the life of an Irish Muslim family, to try to understand what Islam is like in practice, especially as it affects the children of the family. Children would be enabled to look at Islam from the point of view of the child concerned, to try to stand in her shoes, and to realise that it is profoundly important to her.

(c) Catholics take seriously the alternative truth claims of different religions. When religions are studied via phenomenological, sociological or historical approaches, the issue of the truth status of religious statements is not given sufficient treatment. Often such approaches are based on the liberal assumption that the different religions are equal and complementary paths to salvation. Such methodologies do not confront students with the crucial question of the validity of the truth claims of various belief systems.[27] However, it is important to teach children from a young age that all religions and belief systems make significant truth claims, about God, about the human being, about the way the world is structured, about suffering and evil; and that there are often profound and important differences between those claims. A Catholic approach to world religions will reject an instrumentalist or relativist position which denies the fact that each religion claims to be true. True respect for difference demands that Catholic children are encouraged to believe in the exclusive nature of the truth of their particular religious commitment to Jesus Christ; that Christian faith is not lightly correlated with what is manifestly different; and that the difference between Christianity and other religions is faithfully acknowledged.[28]

Educational Outcomes

With these theological and philosophical principles as a guide, some educational outcomes suggest themselves for inter-religious learning at primary level. At junior level (4–8 year olds), children could be taught to identify their own religious identities and the religious and/or cultural identities of others. The religious festivals of all children in the class could be recognised as one very important way of acknowledging the children's significance and valuing their identities. Children could also be invited to listen to and discuss simple stories about children in other faith communities in their own country. They could be taught to identify Christian and other faith communities in their locality and begin to investigate the religious practice of children in indigenous Jewish and Muslim communities (e.g. how they pray).

At senior level (9–12 year olds) children could begin to discuss the importance of religious or philosophical beliefs in the lives of people in their communities. They could research religious faith communities with a significant local presence (Christian/Jewish/Muslim) and investigate ways of respecting and learning about and from people who adhere to other religions or belief systems in their community. They could be invited to investigate how people of other religions and beliefs in their own country practise their beliefs today and to relate these to their own Catholic religious practice. Finally children might be encouraged to engage in ecumenical and inter-faith activities such as identifying ways in which pupils of all beliefs in the school can engage with local community projects based around charity and justice, or inviting outside speakers or parents who are involved in faith-based charitable organisations to share their commitment to creating a better world. A suggested time allocation for juniors is one week of study (two and a half hours) of other faiths per year. Seniors might have two weeks (five hours) set aside for the study of other faiths per year.

Conclusion

Formal inter-religious learning in the Catholic primary school lays the foundations for inter-religious learning in post-primary school and beyond. The goal of such learning is a greater understanding of self and other which enables the development of a rooted and adaptive Christian religious identity capable of healthy inter-religious living in a multi-religious world. Formal inter-religious learning builds on the encounter with difference experienced at home and in the school by inviting children to deepen their awareness and knowledge of difference, to respect the religious faiths and/or beliefs of others, to develop positive attitudes toward people of other faiths, to enter into respectful dialogue with others, and to grow in appreciation of their own religious experience, commitment and beliefs in light of the experiences, commitments and beliefs of others. These kinds of knowledge, skills and attitudes enable Catholic children to develop a more reflexive type of Christian religious identity than previous generations. In this way, inter-religious learning plays an integral part in authentic Christian identity formation in a multi-religious world.

NOTES

1. Pontifical Council for Inter-religious Dialogue, *Letter to Presidents of Bishops' Conferences on the Spirituality of Dialogue*, Vatican City, 3 Mar. 1999, p. 1.

2. For a discussion of some of the issues here, see Richard Rymarz, 'Catechesis and Religious Education in Canadian Catholic Schools', in *Religious Education: The Official Journal of the Religious Education Association*, 106/5 (2011), pp. 537–549.

3. Judith A. Berling, *Understanding Other Religious Worlds* (New York: Maryknoll, 2004), pp. 71–73.

4. Terence J. Lovat, 'Educating about Islam and Learning about Self: An Approach for Our Times', in *Religious Education*, 100/1 (2005), pp. 38–51.

5. For an exploration of the theological foundations for inter-religious dialogue together with a summary of Church documentation dealing with the relationship of the Church to other religions, see Dermot A. Lane, 'Nostra Aetate and Religious Education', in *Exploring Religious Education: Catholic Religious Education in an Intercultural Europe*, ed. by Patricia Kieran and Anne Hession (Dublin: Veritas, 2008), pp. 83–96.

6.   Stefan Altmeyer, 'Competences in Inter-religious Learning', in *International Handbook of Inter-religious Education*, ed. by K. Engebretson, M. de Souza, G. Durka and L. Gearon (Dordrecht: Springer, 2010), pp. 634–635.

7.   Franco Sottocornola, 'Some Notes Regarding Formation to Inter-religious Dialogue', *Religious Education of Boys and Girls*, Concilium 2002/4 (SCM Press: London), pp. 99–100.

8.   Altmeyer, p. 634.

9.   James Michael Lee, 'The Blessings of Religious Pluralism', in *Religious Pluralism and Religious Education*, ed. by N. H. Thompson (Birmingham: Religious Education Press, 1988), p. 71.

10.   Sottocornola, p. 99.

11.   *Dialogue and Proclamation* 59, 82; *Evangelii nuntiandi* 5.

12.   *Nostra aetate* 5; *Gaudium et spes* 28; Peter R. Hobson and John S. Edwards, *Religious Education in a Pluralist Society* (London: Woburn Press, 1999), talk about the notion of positive tolerance, in which children learn not merely to 'put up with' the ideas of others (what may be termed negative tolerance) but to actually welcome diversity and look on this as a valuable stimulus in their own search for meaning.

13.   *Lumen gentium* 16; *Ad gentes* 9, 11; *Nostra aetate* 2.

14.   *Nostra aetate* 2.

15.   *Lumen gentium* 16.

16.   Michael J.G. Cooke, 'Inter-Faith Perspectives: More Questions than Answers', in *Contemporary Catholic Education*, ed. by Michael A. Hayes and Liam Gearon (Herefordshire: Gracewing, 2002), p. 197.

17.   Cooke, p. 199.

18.   Friedrich Schweitzer, 'Children's Right to Religion and Spirituality: Legal, Educational and Practical Perspectives', in *British Journal of Religious Education*, 27/2 (2005), pp. 103–113.

19.   Hobson and Edwards (1999); T. H. McLaughlin, 'Parental Rights and the Upbringing of Children', *Journal of Philosophy of Education*, 18/1 (1984), pp. 79–81; Elmer Thiessen, 'Religious Education and Committed Openness', in *Inspiring Faith in Schools*, ed. by Marius Felderhof, Penny Thompson, and David Torevell (Aldershot, Hampshire: Ashgate, 2007), p. 38; Brenda Watson, *Education and Belief* (Oxford: Blackwell, 1987), pp. 58–9.

20.   Andrew Wright, *Spirituality and Education* (London: RoutledgeFalmer, 2000), chapters 11–12; Gabriel Moran, 'The Aims of Religious Education', in *Reshaping Religious Education* (Louisville, Kentucky: Westminster John Knox Press, 1998), pp. 30–43; Ian MacMullen, 'Education for Autonomy: The Role of Religious Elementary Schools', *Journal of Philosophy of Education*, 38/4 (2004).

21.   Hobson and Edwards, p. 167.

22.   Berling, p. 64.

23.   Berling, p. 66.

24.   Philip Barnes, 'Religious Education and the Misrepresentation of Religion', in *Inspiring Faith in Schools*, p. 82.

25.   Willian K. Kay and D. Linnett Smith, 'Religious Terms and Attitudes in the Classroom (Part 1)', in *British Journal of Religious Education*, 22 (2000), pp. 81–90.

26.   W. Cantwell Smith, *Towards a World Theology: Faith and the Comparative History of Religions* (Maryknoll, NY: Orbis Books, 1989), p. 3; Cooke, p. 197; A. Wright, *Critical Religious Education, Multiculturalism and the Pursuit of Truth* (Cardiff: University of Wales Press, 2007), p. 202.

27.   Hobson and Edwards, p. xiv; L.P. Barnes and W.K. Kay, *Religious Education in England and Wales: Innovations and Reflections* (Leicester, UK: R.T.S.F, 2002), p. 56; Philip Barnes, pp. 75–86.

28.   Michael Barnes, 'Faith, Dialogue and the "Catholic Instinct": Discerning the Significance of Other Faiths', in *Exploring Theology: Making Sense of the Catholic Tradition*, ed. by Anne Hession and Patricia Kieran (Dublin: Veritas, 2007), pp. 289, 292–3.

SECTION IV: RELIGIOUS PLURALISM AND DIVERSITY: CRITICAL PERSPECTIVES

CHAPTER TWELVE

TOWARD CHANGE: EXPLORING TENSIONS IN ETHICAL-RELIGIOUS PEDAGOGY IN IRISH PRIMARY EDUCATION

Jones Irwin

the creation of multiculturality … calls for a certain educational practice. It calls for a new ethics, founded on respect for differences, a unity in differences.[1]

Introduction

The above epigram from Paulo Freire indicates that the attempt to create an authentically 'multicultural' society, a place where different individuals, cultures, ethnicities and religions can coexist harmoniously, is not something we can assume or simply hope to discover without effort. Rather, Freire suggests, 'multiculturality' is a reality which must be *created*. It is not insignificant that Freire immediately connects this creativity to the need for a 'certain educational practice', for it is often in our educational institutions that we see the greatest challenges to, and opportunities for, the fostering of dialogue between diverse cultures and peoples. In this essay, I will explore some of the significant obstacles to the creation of such a Freirean multiculturality within an Irish educational context, as well as important opportunities which can enable change, with a focus on the nature of ethical and religious education at primary school level in Ireland.

The Denominational Context of Irish Primary Schooling

Understanding the nature of such ethical and religious education depends upon an understanding of the peculiarity of the Irish context of primary schooling and the significance of the distinction between denominational and multi-denominational pedagogy. On the one side, a denominational religious ethos aims as a matter of policy to foster in young people of that denomination a commitment to their religion. This involves (at least in Ireland) the teaching of religion as faith formation in school time, preparation for sacraments by the class teacher as well as a foregrounding of the symbolism of the particular religion throughout the school[2]. In multi-denominational education, on the other hand, the truth claims of religion and other belief systems are explored as part of the school's ethos but truth is not associated with a particular view. Students study a comparative religious and ethics programme, where belief systems are critically explored without the assumption of any one faith. Sacramental preparation does not take place in school time and the symbolism of the school must represent a diversity of perspectives.[3]

At the time of writing, 96 per cent of state schools are denominational, with 90 per cent being Catholic and 6 per cent Church or Ireland (Protestant). To put this in historical context, 100 per cent of state primary schools were denominational up until the late 1970s and, even by 2001, only 1 per cent of schools were multi-denominational.[4] There has thus been a 3 per cent change in the last ten years but the Irish situation remains unique in a European, and even global context,[5] where a far more significant number of state primary schools would be either multi-denominational or non-denominational.[6] Increasingly in the Republic of Ireland, there is support and demand for a more diverse approach to primary schooling, where at present a mere 4 per cent of state schools are multi-denominational and where there are no state non-denominational schools. It can be argued, however, that the Third-level Colleges of Education are significantly out of step with this movement for change, insofar as 100 per cent of state Colleges of Education remain denominational, with one Protestant or Church of Ireland in ethos (The Church of Ireland College of Education, Rathmines) and the remainder Catholic, e.g. St Patrick's College, Drumcondra and Mary Immaculate College, Limerick.[7] On all but the most traditionalist of readings, this situation raises very significant issues and problems for both teacher–students and their teacher–educators in the Colleges of Education. The Forum on Patronage and Pluralism[8] made its final recommendations in April 2012 and alongside the significant implications for all schools, these recommendations also have specific things to say about the need for change in Initial Teacher Education in an Irish context. In March 2012, the Minister for Education and Skills, Ruairi Quinn, requested the Higher Education Authority (HEA) to undertake a review of the structure of such Initial Teacher Education (ITE) provision in Ireland. This follows on from the significant changes in the content of ITE programmes developed in the Teaching Council's *Policy on the Continuum of Teacher Education*[9] as well as the decision to extend the three year BEd programme for primary school teachers in Ireland from three to four years, beginning in September 2012.[10]

This is, therefore, a time of significant challenge and transformation in Irish education. Even recent Christian commentators have pointed to a rather specific strain of denominational education in an Irish context, which has tended to abstract a one-dimensional 'managerial' approach to education from a much more complex post-Vatican II Christian hermeneutics. As James Norman observes: 'The Vatican documents suggest that patrons/trustees cannot legislate for an ethos, it is something that can only be facilitated from within the life of the school. The trustees of Irish Catholic schools have adopted a paternalistic understanding of ethos, which can be said to have developed an attitude of compliance among those who work in Catholic schools.'[11] What Norman says of schools might equally be applied to the Third-level context. Amongst students and educators, one can argue that there has been a tradition of 'compliance' with religious authority in Initial Teacher Education. Up until 2011, all students in Third-level Colleges of Education (irrespective of background, ethnicity, and religion) had completed the heavily weighted Religious Education modules, as well as the supposedly 'optional' Certificate in Religious Education.[12] As the Forum report notes, 'Outside the BEd course, the colleges also offer a Certificate in Religious Studies as an optional course. While it is not compulsory, the fact that the Certificate tends to be a requirement for appointment in a denominational school leads the great majority of the students to take the Certificate programme'.[13] It is arguable, in Freire's terms, that this hegemony represents the great 'culture of silence' in Irish education and, returning to our epigram, we can argue that what he calls there a 'new ethics' would seem to be precisely what is required if the Irish education system is to be a place which can genuinely claim to represent 'respect for differences'.

'It Calls For a Certain Educational Practice' – Implementing the Recommendations of the Forum

> Many people believe that their culture is the core of the one life worthy of human beings or that those belonging to supposedly inferior cultures count for little or nothing. I call such beliefs and the conduct they motivate 'chauvinism'.[14]

The significant need for change at the level of Irish educational practice is increasingly being recognised. For example, Minister Ruairi Quinn notes in his preface to the Forum report, 'This report outlines the history and evolution of patronage in Irish society. It also shows the need for the primary school system to now adapt to the needs of a more diverse society.'[15] We have seen above that while the primary school system remains dominated by a certain kind of denominational ethos, that matters are even more acute at the level of ITE for primary school teachers, where denominationalism is all-encompassing. There are issues here of both theory and practice. I will first explore some of the intra-theoretical issues, especially as they bear on some of the Forum's recommendations.

Within the theoretical literature, the first point worth noting is that the mode of denominationalism in Ireland seems rather anachronistic, even from within an intra-religious ethos. This argument is made forcefully from an intra-Catholic perspective by James Norman in his book, *Ethos and Education in Ireland*.[16] Norman contrasts the post-Vatican II perspective on school ethos which he represents philosophically as 'democratic' with the Irish Bishops' viewpoint which he represents as 'paternalistic'. This interpretation of a certain theoretical presumption seems to apply equally to the levels of ITE education *and* to primary schools, when both are understood as being grounded in a particular version of traditionalist religious denominationalism. This reactionary theological position can be contrasted sharply with a more open-minded and pluralistic philosophy from a denominational perspective, notable in Ireland in the works of Joseph Dunne, Padraig Hogan, Andrew Burke and Dermot Lane amongst others, or internationally in the work of thinkers such as Richard Pring or Terence McLaughlin.[17] McLaughlin most especially has addressed the issue of educational ethos throughout his work. He has consistently argued for a form of denominationalism (what he calls 'the separate school')[18] which remains, on his terms, wholly compatible with democratic values and the values of reason and autonomy.

Whether understood from the perspective of ITE or from within the primary school context, Pring and McLaughlin's arguments explicate some of the complexities at the heart of this debate. What values should education espouse? From a denominational viewpoint, the need for a 'deep moral and spiritual formation' of the young in a 'distinctive tradition of values and beliefs'[19] remains the paradigmatic cornerstone. Nonetheless, this version of denominational ethos is opposed to the kind of 'paternalism' which Norman has described as characteristic of the Irish Catholic system.[20] Instead, there is the need, for Pring, to balance the immersion in a distinctive tradition with a 'liberal commitment to openness, to diversity of view'[21] while also seeking the maintenance of 'common values that ensure social cohesion and citizenship'.[22] We might refer to this as a *liberal* form of denominationalism, which itself sees the concept of liberal values as 'rather more slippery than acknowledged'.[23] This is a similar point to the one made by Charles Taylor in his seminal essay, 'The Politics of Recognition', where he argues for what he terms a more 'substantive' liberalism, not necessarily incompatible with religious world views or educational philosophies.[24] From a philosophical point of view, then, we can recognise a significant intra-Catholic (or intra-denominational) diversity in educational philosophy. *There is no one, completely homogeneous denominationalism.*

McLaughlin's work stresses the internal problems faced by all kinds of ethoi in education, as they seek to transpose their philosophical values to school and college practice. In his essay 'The Burdens and Dilemmas of Common Schooling,'[25] for example, he emphasises the challenges which a multi-denominational or non-denominational ethos faces in practice. Both of the latter ethoi tend to stress what he calls a 'common school' approach to education, but McLaughlin asks how is such a commonality grounded from a philosophical perspective?[26] Citing the work of the moral philosopher Alasdair MacIntyre, McLaughlin points out that there is no consensus amongst modern and postmodern thinkers regarding values. How can such 'common' educational institutions thus found their ethical education? Similarly, he expresses concern that students will be deprived of the strength of the immersion in a distinctive tradition of values, if all ethical education begins from a more detached or supposedly objective viewpoint: 'Is it possible to truly understand the meaning of a religious and spiritual tradition from the outside, independent of religious and spiritual forms of practice and life?'[27] These are important questions for the multi-denominational or non-denominational educator, of how to educate children and students 'about' values but also how to facilitate their understanding of these values and ethics from 'within', in a more embedded and organic mode. Without doubt, simply emphasising the former at the expense of the latter runs the risk of superficiality and lack of genuine ethical engagement.

By the same token, however, McLaughlin in a different essay, 'The Ethics of Separate Schools', expresses reservations about denominational approaches which stress the embeddedness in a tradition but fail to develop 'critical contestation' in their students.[28] These kinds of school are fundamentally *illiberal* whereas what McLaughlin seems to defend is a liberal notion of the denominational ethos or school. For McLaughlin, ultimately, both kinds of education and ethos, whether denominational or multi-denominational, are necessary in a democratic society which respects diversity. What he is thus pointing to is the necessity (an urgent necessity for McLaughlin) for the varying philosophies of education to develop coherent approaches to their practice, a practice which he sees as irreducibly complex: 'a school is engaged in a practical enterprise of great complexity which calls for many forms of practical knowledge'.[29]

With theorists such as McLaughlin and Pring, we see the richness of thought which has been brought to bear on some of the educational questions which we have foregrounded in this essay. One might ask how such a theoretical diversity has been represented in the practice of Irish education, at ITE and primary school levels. Here, as one source of insight, we can look to, the Forum report and its recommendations for denominational schools and ITE colleges. While we can speak of a theoretical richness in the literature, both internationally and in Ireland, the practice in schools and in the ITE sector has remained more closely tied to the reactionary denominationalism represented by the Irish Bishops' educational philosophy[30] than to the more liberal version of theological pedagogy.[31] This is especially noticeable in the criticisms made of Catholic primary education and of denominational ITE in the Forum report. For example, the report states the following: 'The Advisory Group has a particular concern for those children who do not participate in religious programmes in denominational schools.'[32] This highlights the complete lack of official provision for children who do not subscribe to the particular school's religious ethos, who in such contexts are often simply left in a corner working on something else. It is difficult to see how this alienation of the child is consistent with the emphasis on the individual child in the 1999 Revised Curriculum, never mind being consistent with any even minimal conception of children's rights or human rights legislation. This situation is exacerbated by the integral nature of religion as a subject in schools ('the most important subject in the curriculum'), which extends far beyond the subject of religion per se. Additionally, integrated and all-pervasive symbolism in denominational schools as well as sacramental preparation within school time, increase the alienation effect on the child or children from different traditions or belief systems.[33] An analogous situation confronts the teacher in a denominational primary school. This is especially problematical for teachers who would not subscribe to the religious ethos of the school. As the Forum notes, 'Nontheist teachers may have to engage in dissimulation practices if they are to ensure a teaching appointment.'[34] The Forum report goes on to indicate a long standing vulnerability which teachers and teacher students face under Irish law. What is referred to as 'the deed of variation' in denominational schools, in effect their mission statement (which has legal binding), states that all denominational schools are allowed to do 'what is reasonably necessary to protect their ethos and to prevent an employee or a prospective employee from undermining the religious ethos'. Key here is the interpretative ambiguity around the concept of 'undermining the religious ethos' but in effect, this is at the root of the climate of 'compliance' which Norman describes in Irish (Catholic) denominational schools.[35]

Of course, the Colleges of Education, currently all denominational, share this legal right to enforce the particularity of their institutional ethos amongst staff and students alike (which is reinforced by the Employment Equality Act which gives denominational institutions an exemption to discriminate so as to protect their religious ethos). From an ITE perspective, then, the more liberal versions of denominational philosophy would seem to have remained at the purely theoretical level. At the practical level, it could be argued that denominational ITE in Ireland remains reactionary and conservative. On Pring or McLaughlin's terms, we might argue that while ITE has been immensely strong on the importance of 'a distinctive tradition of values and beliefs', it has been relatively blind to the simultaneous values of 'the liberal commitment to openness and diversity' or the 'maintenance of common values that ensure social cohesion and citizenship'.[36] This failure to balance paradigmatic values and to offer a more liberal interpretation of denominational and theological education seems especially acute in the context of an Irish society and culture, which is experiencing radical change and heterogeneity, with increasing immigration and significant shifts in the attitudes of indigenous Irish people toward religion and the Church.

Conclusion – Toward Change in Primary Education

In such a stark context, it is reassuring that The Forum report focuses clearly (if briefly) on the need for significant change at the ITE and primary school levels in Irish education. Here, in conclusion, I will focus predominantly on the recommended changes in primary school ITE which will have a very considerable impact on the nature of primary schooling and teaching, if implemented.

On one level, the report acknowledges that in principle, apart from Protestant ITE which gives priority to student teachers of Protestant faiths, 'all colleges accept students of any faith or none'.[37] It also marks the change in the Colleges of Education culture which has seen a newly understood aspiration emerge to 'prepare the students to teach religious education in a variety of school settings', while noting that students still feel compelled to undertake the Certificate in Religious Education.[38] Finally, the report acknowledges the evolution of an 'alternative programme to the religious methodology programme', which is described in the report as now taking place at two Colleges of Education.[39] While thus acknowledging the progress that has been genuinely made (if hard-won) at ITE level in Ireland, the report also focuses on some of the developments yet to take place. Significantly, from the point of view of an overall coherent approach to ITE, it places these recommendations in the context of the contemporary more generalised 'restructuring' of ITE in Ireland. This restructuring follows on from both the significant changes in the content of ITE programmes developed in the Teaching Council's *Policy on the Continuum of Teacher Education* (Teaching Council, 2011), as well as the decision to extend the three year BEd programme for primary school teachers in Ireland from three to four years, which began in September 2012.[40] In the context of such far-reaching re-evaluation of ITE programmes, the Forum report states that 'the time is apposite for incorporating a dual approach to the religious education methodology programme'.[41]

The report further clarifies what this would mean in practice. A 'course focused on ethics, morality and world religions should be compulsory for all students' as well as the provision for a 'broadly based religious methodology programme'.[42] This is a notable recommendation for a number of reasons. In the first instance, it advises to the Colleges of Education that students in ITE at primary level should be required to do *both* the denominational and multi-denominational approaches to teacher education, and specifically both these approaches to the teaching of ethics and religion in schools. This differs significantly, first, from the overarching situation in ITE up until 2010, where student teachers were compelled to only approach these issues of ethics and religion from a denominational viewpoint. Second, it differs from the situation which has developed in St Patrick's College, where students were compelled to choose between ('either/or') denominational and multi-denominational approaches. From a professional perspective, this both/and approach would seem far preferable to the other two options in that pre-service teachers would be equipped to teach in all schools of the State. From a philosophical perspective, this both/and approach might be more problematical in the measure to which the denominational faith formation methodology would seem to conflict with the comparative multi-denominational approach. This could lead to confusion but, imagining this change in a more positive light, we might see the possibility of pre-service teachers actually being allowed to think through and reflect upon these ideological and moral dilemmas, employing their own critical reason and autonomy.[43]

The reason given by the report for the need for this dual approach to become compulsory is itself instructive in terms of our overall issue. Students would need to be 'prepared for the introduction of the proposed ERB and Ethics programmes'.[44] ERB, in the first case, refers to 'Education in Religion and Beliefs', a comparative and liberal approach to ethics and religion, but this new approach to religion and ethics is recommended by the Forum to become compulsory *in all denominational schools*. There is some ambiguity around this issue in the report but the implication is similar to the recommendation for ITE denominational colleges. Faith formation will still take place in denominational schools, just as denominational religious education will still take place in denominational Colleges of Education. However, this will have to be supplemented with a significant degree of ERB or comparative religious and ethical education. This recommendation radicalises the interpretation of the overall impact of the Forum report, if, of course, these changes are implemented. For what it suggests is that State schools and State ITE can no longer tolerate educational philosophies and practices which eschew what Pring refers to as a 'liberal commitment to openness, to diversity of view' or which neglect the maintenance of 'common values that ensure social cohesion and citizenship'.[45] While the need for 'a distinctive tradition of values and beliefs'[46] may well remain a democratic right within the educational system, it can no longer be reinforced by a reactionary paternalism which continues to alienate a significant group of children, parents, teachers and teacher-educators in our national schools and colleges. It is precisely this latter denominationalist approach which has stultified the pedagogical efforts in an Irish context toward the 'the creation of multiculturality'.[47] With Freire, we call for a refreshingly new educational practice, both at ITE and primary school level, which is authentically (rather than merely rhetorically) founded on a 'respect for differences'.

NOTES

1. P. Freire, *Pedagogy of Hope* (London: Continuum, 1992), p. 137.

2. J. Norman, *Ethos and Education in Ireland* (New York: Peter Lang, 2003).

3. P. Rowe, 'Educate Together Schools: Core Values and Ethos', in *School Culture and Ethos: Cracking the Code*, ed. by C. Furlong and L. Monahan (Dublin: Marino, 2000).

4. J. Irwin, 'Interculturalism, Ethos and Ideology: Barriers to Freedom and Democracy in Irish Primary Education', *REA: A Journal of Religion, Education and the Arts*, Feb. 2010.

5. Maurice Craft, ed. *Teacher Education in Plural Societies* (London: Falmer, 1996).

6. Ethos in schools is a multilayered concept and reality and extends well beyond the issue of religion and ethics. Some school ethoi define themselves, for example, in relation to language and culture (for example, the Gaelscoileanna in Ireland which teach through the Irish language) while other schools may be defined in terms of their theory of learning or epistemology (for example, Steiner schools). This essay focuses, however, on the specific connections between ethos and the teaching of religion and ethics, as this problematic extends from ITE to schools. In this context, two other school types which may have an increasing relevance in Ireland are important to mention. In the first instance, there are now several 'Community National Schools', which combine denominational and multi-denominational approaches, employing faith formation alongside comparative approaches. Second, there is the non-denominational school ethos, which either minimises religious discussion and expression in the school or may actually prohibit any of the latter. There are presently no non-denominational state schools in Ireland.

7. Irwin, 2010; P. Donnelly, 'Governance in the Irish Colleges of Education', paper delivered to ITE conference St Patrick's College, Drumcondra, June 2011.

8. The Forum on Patronage and Pluralism in the Primary Sector, *Report of the Forum's Advisory Group* (Dublin: 2012).

9. Teaching Council, *Policy on the Continuum of Teacher Education* (Dublin: June 2011).

10. Á. Hyland, 'A Review of the Structure of Initial Teacher Education Provision in Ireland', *Background Paper for the International Review Team*, May 2012.

11. Norman, 2003, p. 15.

12. K. Williams, 'Foreword', in Norman, *Ethos and Education in Ireland*.

13. Forum, 2012, p. 98.

14. E. Callan, 'The Politics of Difference and Common Education' in *The RoutledgeFalmer Reader in Philosophy of Education*, ed. by W. Carr (London: RoutledgeFalmer, 2005), pp. 124–134.

15. Forum, 2012, p. 4.

16. Norman, 2003.

17. See, amongst others, J. Dunne, 'The Catholic School and Civil Society: Exploring the Tensions', in *The Catholic School in Contemporary Society*, ed. by Nano Brennan et al (Dublin: CMRS, 1991); P. Hogan (1997), 'Foreword', in *The Future of Religion in Irish Education*, ed. by P. Hogan and K. Williams (Dublin: Veritas, 1997); A. Burke, 'The B.Ed. Degree: Still Under Review', *Oideas*, Sept. 2009, pp. 1-43: D. Lane (1997), 'Afterword: The Expanding Horizons of Catholic Education' in *The Future of Religion in Irish Education*, Hogan and Williams, 1997; or internationally in the work of thinkers such as Richard Pring, 'Introduction' in *Liberalism, Education and Schooling: Essays by T.H. McLaughlin*, ed. by D. Carr, M. Halstead and R. Pring (Exeter: Imprint, 2008), pp. 95–98; T.H. McLaughlin, 'The Burdens and Dilemmas of Common Schooling' in *Liberalism, Education and Schooling, Essays by T.H. McLaughlin* ed. by D. Carr, M. Halstead and R. Pring, pp. 137–174; T.H. McLaughlin, 'The Ethics of Separate Schools' in *Liberalism, Education and Schooling: Essays by T.H. McLaughlin* ed. by D. Carr, M. Halstead and R. Pring (Exeter: Imprint, 2008), pp. 175–198.

18.   McLaughlin, 'The Ethics of Separate Schools'.

19.   Pring, 2008, p. 95.

20.   Norman, 2003.

21.   Pring, 2008, p. 96.

22.   Pring, 2008, p. 95.

23.   Pring, 2008, p. 96.

24.   C. Taylor, 'The Politics of Recognition' in *Multiculturalism: Examining the Politics of Recognition*, ed. by Amy Gutmann (New Jersey: Princeton University Press, 1994).

25.   McLaughlin, 'The Burdens and Dilemmas of Common Schooling'.

26.   McLaughlin, 'The Burdens and Dilemmas of Common Schooling', p. 142.

27.   McLaughlin, 'The Burdens and Dilemmas of Common Schooling', p. 166.

28.   McLaughlin, 'The Ethics of Separate Schools', p. 188.

29.   McLaughlin, 'The Ethics of Separate Schools', p. 204.

30.   Norman, 2003.

31.   McLaughlin, 'The Burdens and Dilemmas of Common Schooling'; McLaughlin, 'The Ethics of Separate Schools'; Pring, 2008.

32.   Forum, 2012, p. 102.

33.   Forum, 2012, p. 103

34.   Forum, 2012, p. 109.

35.   Norman, 2003.

36.   Pring, 2008, p. 96.

37.   Forum, 2012, p. 98.

38.   Forum, 2012, p. 98.

39.   Forum, 2012, p. 98.

40.   Hyland, 2012.

41.   Forum, 2012, p. 98.

42.   Forum, 2012, p. 99.

43.   McLaughlin, 'The Burdens and Dilemmas of Common Schooling'; McLaughlin, 'The Ethics of Separate Schools'.

44.   Forum, 2012, p. 99.

45.   Pring, 2008, pp. 96, 98.

46.   Pring, 2008, p. 98.

47.   Freire, 1992, p. 137.

CHAPTER THIRTEEN

ONLY SECULAR SCHOOLS RESPECT EVERY PERSON'S HUMAN RIGHTS EQUALLY

Michael Nugent and Jane Donnelly

There is one fundamental question that informs all debate about patronage and pluralism in education. That question is posed here as an option: A. Do you wish to bring about an education system that satisfies the desires of a majority of parents and children (perhaps to satisfy the desires of those who happen to share your own personal religious beliefs), regardless of the wishes of minority groups? B. Alternatively do you wish to bring about an education system that respects equally the human rights of all parents and all children, without sacrificing the human rights of a minority in order to satisfy the desires of a majority? The manner in which a person answers these foundational questions determines what conclusions they arrive at.

It is understandable that many parents, and representatives of particular religions, have as their priority an education system that satisfies their own desires, and the desires of those who think like them. However the role of the state should be to counteract this self-centred approach, and to ensure that the education system respects equally the human rights of all parents and all children. In practice, the only way to ensure this is for the state to establish a secular education system. A secular education system would be neutral on the question of religion and non-religion, and it would allow further educational options to develop as a supplement and not a replacement to that secular system. Religious schools or atheist schools should be an added extra for parents who want to avail of them, if they can afford them. However having religious schools as the foundation of the educational system creates only the illusion of choice.

Secular Schools

This chapter argues that society should be pluralist and not the state. Indeed, the only way to protect the rights of everybody in a pluralist society is for the state to be secular. The state has a positive obligation to ensure fairness for everybody. The State should not be a partisan player that focuses on the desires of the majority ahead of everybody's rights. Furthermore, contrary to the belief of many people in Ireland, there is no human right to have the state fund a religious education for every family in the country.

In advance of outlining why secular schools must be the foundation of an equality-based education system, it is important to explain that a secular school is not identical to an atheist school. If a religious school would teach that a god exists and an atheist school would teach that no gods exist, then a secular school would be neutral on the question of religion. Secular schools do not teach that gods either do or do not exist. Instead, a secular school teaches children in a critical, objective and pluralistic way about the different beliefs that different people have about gods, and leaves it up to parents and churches to teach specific religious beliefs outside of school hours.

There are good philosophical reasons for establishing secular schools that are neutral on the question of religion. It is good for society that all children can be educated together. The recent history of Northern Ireland illustrates how segregated schooling contributed to the difficulty children experienced in understanding and respecting each other across religious divides. Secular schools bring children together. They teach children subjects that have a basis in scientific fact, such as mathematics and languages and history and critical thinking. Secular schools teach children common ethical values such as fairness, tolerance, compassion, justice and civic cooperation. They teach them about different religious beliefs and help them to understand other beliefs and respect other people. Therefore, outside of school hours, the children's parents and churches can teach them more about their own specific beliefs about the nature of reality and personal morality.

Secular Education and Human Rights
In practical terms, the establishment of secular schools is the only way to ensure that everybody has their human rights respected with regard to education. The education policy of Atheist Ireland is based on the human right to be educated without being indoctrinated with religion and to be free from proselytism. Atheist Ireland is equally opposed to children being indoctrinated with atheism. This policy is based on international human rights legislation. In considering the demand for diversity, the human right to respect the religious and philosophical convictions of all parents, and not just those of a majority, should not only be considered but guaranteed without discrimination in the Irish educational system. By ratifying the European Convention on Human Rights and various other United Nations Conventions, the Irish State has already agreed to guarantee to respect all parents' religious and philosophical convictions in the Irish education system, and not just those of a majority.

In theory, it could be possible to respect everybody's rights by having different schools for parents and pupils of every religion, in addition to schools for parents and pupils of no religion, and to have enough of each of these schools built and operating in every part of Ireland to make it possible to vindicate every parent's rights in practice. However, in reality, this is financially and logistically impossible. In a pluralist society, the only way for an education system to vindicate everybody's rights to freedom of conscience, religion and belief, and to respect the convictions of all parents as opposed to the majority, is to establish a state secular education system that is neutral on the question of religion. For it is simply not feasible for the State to financially support the funding of various types of secular or religious schools in every area. Delivering the education system through private bodies where the state funds education on the basis of a particular majority in a given area instead of protecting the human rights of individuals, only results in segregation, discrimination and the denial of basic human rights.

Plurality of patronage will never achieve pluralism in education as no state can guarantee provision of education in accordance with the religious or non-religious affiliation of every child's parents. Therefore the patronage system cannot safeguard the preservation of the 'democratic society' as conceived by the European Convention. The European Court of Human Rights has stated that the '*travaux prèparatoires*' of Article II of Protocol 1 (the Right to Education) of the European Convention aims at safeguarding the possibility of pluralism in education which possibility is essential for the preservation of a 'democratic society' as conceived by the Convention.[1] It must also be stressed that the patronage system cannot achieve respect for the religious and philosophical convictions of all parents, because human rights are guaranteed to individuals and not to the religious majority in a given area. The current Irish situation of education represents an abuse of a dominant position. The patronage system in Ireland reinforces the identification of members of society on religious grounds and the provision of services according to religious affiliation. This patronage system coerces parents into identifying with various religious groups in society, with whom they have no real affinity (especially in situations where their children might be refused access to the local school in the event of a shortage of places) simply to access the educational system. In effect parents are being forced to uphold a school's religious ethos through the act of procuring an education for their children. In a report to the Irish Government on this issue, the Irish Human Rights Commission states:

> The overarching recommendation of the IHRC, in order to achieve human rights compliance, is that the State should ensure that there is a diversity of provision of school type within educational catchment areas throughout the State which reflects the diversity of religious and non-religious convictions now represented in the State. Diversity of provision will ensure the needs of faith (including

minority faith) or non-faith children in schools can be met. While the State has a choice of models in education, if it chooses to retain the current patronage mode, with a majority of patrons being religious denominations, significant modifications will be required in order to meet human rights standards.

The United Nations and Ireland's Educational System

As noted previously the funding of different types of secular and religious schools throughout the state cannot be financially achieved. So the state either 'provides education' in order to protect the human rights of all parents and children, or provides significant modifications to the present patronage system in order to protect the fundamental human rights of non-religious parents and children. The United Nations Human Rights Committee has raised serious concerns about Ireland's educational system. In 2008 in its concluding observations it stated:

> The Committee notes with concern that the vast majority of Ireland's primary schools are privately run denominational schools that have adopted a religious integrated curriculum thus depriving many parents and children who so wish to have access to secular primary education (arts 2, 18, 24, 26). The State party should increase its efforts to ensure that non-denominational primary education is widely available in all regions of the State party, in view of the increasingly diverse and multi-ethnic composition of the population of the State party.[2]

A religious ethos means integrating religion into the state curriculum and the general milieu of the school day. It is part of Catholic teaching that religion must be integrated into other subjects.[3] It is also part of Catholic Church teaching that Religious Education cannot be delivered in a neutral and objective manner. As a consequence of this teaching, which is protected by legislation,[4] non–religious parents cannot exempt their child from the elements of religion that are integrated into the various subjects in the school curriculum. In effect, the integrated curriculum which is operative in Irish schools means that there are potential areas within each of the curricular subject areas in the 1999 Curriculum where parents could legitimately consider it most likely that their children will experience a conflict of allegiance between the school's religious ethos and their own personal and familial values. Therefore non-religious parents cannot guarantee that their children's education is in conformity with their own convictions. Despite the Irish Constitution's guarantees on parental rights, non-religious parents are denied basic human rights in the Irish Education System.

The Primary School Curriculum leaves it to each individual Patronal body to design and deliver its own religious education curriculum and this subjects non-religious parents to a heavy burden. They must identify the areas of each particular subject and lesson that is not delivered in an objective, critical and pluralistic manner and then try to seek exemptions for their children. This can only result in the necessity of disclosing details of their philosophical convictions in order to try to opt their children out of the elements of religion that are integrated into all secular subjects. Not only does this breach their human right to respect for their private life under Article 8 of the European Convention but it simply cannot be achieved in practice.

Article 14 of the European Convention forbids discrimination and obliges the state to secure the rights and freedoms set forth in the Convention without discrimination on any ground such as sex, race, colour, language, religion, political or other opinion, national or social origin, association with a national minority, property, birth or other status. Any opt-out system should be non-discriminatory and satisfy the wishes of parents. The inordinate time currently given over to sacramental preparation in Irish primary schools denies minorities the right to an effective education. There should be no prayers during school hours or indoctrinating religious songs. Some schools have a religious symbol as part of their school uniform. Religious minorities and the children of non-religious parents are then obliged to wear a specific religious symbol since the wearing of the school uniform is compulsory. This cannot be regarded as respect. In this regard Atheist Ireland supports the recommendation of the IHRC which states:

> Section 15 of the Education Act should be amended to provide for modifications to the integrated curriculum to ensure that the rights of minority faith or non-faith children are also recognised therein. In this regard, the State must take sufficient care that information and knowledge included in the curriculum is conveyed in an objective, critical and pluralistic manner with the aim of enabling pupils to develop a critical mind with regard to religion in a calm atmosphere which is free of any misplaced proselytism.

Rule 68 of the *Rules for National Schools* which states that a religious spirit should vivify the whole school day, allied to the integration of religious education into the curriculum cannot be described as the Irish State taking a neutral stance on religion. In this regard Atheist Ireland supports the IHRC's report when it says:

> The Minister for Education and Skills should codify and review the Rules for National Schools, to ensure that the human rights standards set out in this paper are upheld. This can further be reviewed in the future in the context of increased diversity in school provision.

The Irish Education System and Non-religious Parents
There are no appropriate provisions in the Irish education system to ensure that non-religious parents' philosophical convictions are respected. The internal complaints system in place under the Education Act 1998 does not, and cannot, protect the human rights of non-religious parents. Nothing obliges Patrons and Boards of Management to interpret 'respect' in a manner consistent with the European Convention on Human Rights and the various United Nation

Conventions that Ireland has ratified. The State does not even recognise that a religious integrated curriculum violates the conscience of non-religious parents and children. Non-religious parents have no access to an effective remedy to vindicate their human rights.

The patronage system is not a balanced system that ensures the fair and proper treatment of minorities. Non-religious parents do not enjoy the liberty to ensure that their children enjoy their basic fundamental human rights as they are coerced by force of circumstances to send their children to schools where their basic human rights are disregarded. It is simply not an option for the majority of parents to educate their children at home. Despite the European Convention on Human Rights and the various UN Conventions that Ireland has ratified, the Irish State has failed to guarantee and protect these human rights. Despite Article 42.3.1 of the Irish Constitution which states 'The State shall not oblige parents in violation of their conscience and lawful preference to send their children to schools established by the State, or to any particular type of school designated by the State.' Parents seeking human rights based education for their children are obliged to send their children to schools in violation of their conscience and lawful preference as they simply have nowhere else to go. The Constitutional Review Group Report in 1995 stated that:

> ... if Article 44.2.4 did not provide these safeguards, the State might well be in breach of its international obligations, inasmuch as it might mean that a significant number of children of minority religions (or those with no religion) might be coerced by force of circumstances to attend a school which did not cater for their particular religious views or their conscientious objections. If this were to occur, it would also mean that the State would be in breach of its obligations under Article 42.3.1.

The Irish State is in breach of its international obligations and consequently is failing in its obligation under the article cited above. Any future policies and legislation must take into account the fact that non-religious parents and children are denied basic human rights in the Irish Education system and that the Constitution has failed to protect these rights in schools. The Report from the Irish Human Rights Commission says that 'Ultimately the State bears responsibility to provide for the education of children, and therefore also bears an obligation to respect the human rights of those receiving such education and those of their parents, be they of religious or non-religious beliefs.' Recently Minister Quinn said that he did not want a secular education system but a pluralist system that provides parents with choice in relation to the education of their children. It is clear that by choice he envisages choice between one private religious school and another private religious school, or if a parent is lucky, a private multi-denominational school such as Educate Together. However there will be no choice for parents who seek a secular, non-religious, human rights based education for their children.

The Irish Constitution obliges the state to ensure that all children receive a basic moral education, but the state only funds moral education based on religious values. In other words it funds a religious moral education or no moral education at all. Furthermore the Equal Status Act provides exemptions for schools that operate a religious ethos. The European Convention on Human Rights Act only applies to 'organs of the state' and schools in Ireland are not considered 'organs of the state'. It is no wonder then that the United Nations and Council of Europe are concerned about the human rights of minorities in the Irish education system. The European court and the United Nations consistently emphasise that human rights are not a theoretical illusion. Human rights are meaningless if they do not have a practical application on the ground. It is not possible to promote human rights such as freedom of conscience, religion and belief while at the same time ignoring the rights of some parents and children in our education system.

Conclusion

Going back to the fundamental question at the start of this essay, none of the contents of this chapter will pose a problem to the reader if their aim is option A: to bring about an education system that satisfies the desires of a majority of parents and children, or perhaps to satisfy the desires of those families who happen to share the reader's personal religious beliefs. These issues only become a problem if the reader has selected as their aim option B: to bring about an education system that respects equally the human rights of all parents and all children, without sacrificing the human rights of a minority in order to satisfy the desires of a majority. How the reader answers this fundamental question will determine what conclusions they come to, and what conclusions are unavailable to them.

NOTES

1.   Kjeldsen, Busk Madsen and Pedersen v Denmark 1976.
2.   United Nations, Human Rights Committee, *Concluding Observations: Ireland*, 2008, CCPR/ C/IRL/CO/3 22.
3.   Congregation for Catholic Education, *Circular Letter to the Presidents of Bishops' Conferences on Religious Education in Schools*, 5 May 2009.
4.   Government of Ireland, *Education Act 1998*, 15 (2) (b).

CHAPTER FOURTEEN

IS THERE ANY MUTUAL GROUND?
SOME CRITICAL REMARKS ON PLURALISM AND NON-DENOMINATIONALISM

Rik Van Nieuwenhove

There appears to be almost unanimity amongst policy and opinion makers that contemporary Ireland is a multi-cultural and pluralist society, and that our school system sadly fails to reflect this new reality. However, if the figures of the latest census (2011) have any validity, claims about a pluralist and more secular Ireland need to be seriously questioned. Ninety per cent of the population describe themselves as belonging to one of the three major Christian denominations (Catholic, Church of Ireland, Orthodox), while the number of people who describe themselves as non-religious, although growing, is still relatively small by international standards.[1] While immigration has undoubtedly been an important feature of Irish life in the last twenty years, most immigrants hail from countries (Poland, Baltic States, Russia, parts of Nigeria) where traditional Christian values are still held in regard, and the high number of immigrants in Ireland, especially Polish, may have further reinforced the traditional 'Catholic' outlook of the country. This chapter will reflect critically upon some intellectual arguments relating to espousing or resisting non-Christian approaches to religious education, such as the pluralist and the non-denominational ones.

Catholic Education is not Pluralist or Multi-Denominational
In stating that Catholic education is not pluralist it is not implied that it is intolerant and unwilling to engage with non-Christian views. It is a given that all world views should be tolerant of other world views in a democratic society.[2] However, those who defend multi-denominational or pluralist approaches claim that (a) no single perspective has a full grasp of reality, which is (b) why diversity needs to be encouraged. In other words such a perspective claims that different world views (both religious and non-religious) together offer more insight into the ultimate questions of meaning than any single one by itself. This is why advocates of multi-denominationalism and pluralism invite us to 'celebrate' diversity and difference.

In my view this position is philosophically incoherent since the pluralist presupposes what she sets out to deny, i.e. the possibility of making totalising claims. Making the value-judgement that there is more truth in all perspectives put together presupposes a meta-perspective which clashes with a key presupposition of the pluralist outlook itself.

If, however, the pluralist were to acknowledge that there is no meta-perspective, no over-arching standpoint which surveys, from a bird's eye perspective the different world views, and accepts that the pluralist perspective is just one amongst others, it is in danger of effectively adopting either a radical relativist stance, or implicitly slipping into a non-denominational one.

In the case of the former, it is, as with any other radical relativist stance, in danger of becoming incoherent. Indeed the statement: 'There is no truth' is, of course, intellectually self-subversive. The same applies to the statement: 'The view that all world views are equally valid, is a non-negotiable truth.' Moreover, one may wonder what the pluralist paradigm actually contributes to the dialogue amongst the different world views. After all, insofar as it merely celebrates and promotes the coexistence of different world views without explicitly aligning itself to any of them, the pluralist paradigm is a purely formal one since it does not have any content, and is actually parasitic upon the other world views (which make specific and content-driven claims about the world). As a consequence of this formal nature it is always in danger of lapsing (implicitly) into a non-denominational perspective.

In educational terms the pluralist or multi-denominational position is represented at primary level in Ireland by the Educate Together Schools.[3] Now, while it may appear attractive to expose children to all world views without inviting them to participate in any of them 'from within', the multi-denominational perspective actually fails to do justice to the richness and complexity of any of the religious world views. One can certainly teach children about religion from a detached perspective, outlining their main beliefs and practices yet religions are much more than that. They invite us to look at the world from their perspective. Religions involve deeply held convictions, values, and dispositions which cannot be captured in a mere description. Given their complexity it is not feasible to initiate children into all major world views (religious and non-religious). One could further argue that this contributes to multi-denominational perspectives lapsing into non-denominational approaches, where religion is banned from the public sphere.

Moreover, the multi-denominational or pluralist approach operates with a flawed understanding of inclusivity. Genuine inclusivity does not mean standing for everything (and thus, ultimately nothing). Rather, true inclusivity means that, from the perspective of being steeped into your own tradition, you engage in respectful and tolerant dialogue with people of different traditions. This obviously presupposes that you first have a good knowledge of your *own* tradition. Here an analogy with languages may prove helpful. While it is important to learn other languages, you will never learn any languages unless you master your own mother tongue first. The same applies to world views. Children can only be meaningfully exposed to other world views if they first have a clear understanding of their own. Thus, while the multi-denominational approach may appear, at first sight, to be inclusive and attractive by celebrating the *differences* of an allegedly more diverse Ireland, this kind of celebration of difference makes all religions, in the end, a matter of *indifference*. The multi-denominational approach is therefore bound to fail. This chapter contends that the multi-denominational or pluralist perspective often implicitly adopts a non-denominational approach. Insofar as it resists religious formation and relegates genuine religious instruction to the private sphere, it implicitly adopts a key secularist position. This non-denominational perspective will now be discussed.

Catholic Education Differs From Non-Denominational Perspectives

Secularism is the ideology which promotes a secular society. It finds its roots in one specific intellectual stream within the wider Western philosophical tradition, namely eighteenth-century Enlightenment thought. The essence of the secularist paradigm is its attempt to ban religion from the public sphere, and at most (if at all) to allocate it to the purely private realm.[4] As Bishop Murray writes:

> The suggestion that religious belief is not relevant to large areas of life is the essence of secularism. It may sound like a recipe for tolerance and harmony – 'let religion keep to its place and we will avoid a lot of divisive issues'. The reality is that this amounts to a denial or at least a profound misrepresentation of God. A god who is irrelevant to some spheres or aspects of the creation is not God at all.[5]

Thus, what sounds like a recipe for tolerance and neutrality is actually deeply intolerant of religious views and ethos. The hostility of some 'pluralists' toward Christianity reveals an implicit secularist tendency. Here the language of inclusivity and neutrality is adopted in order to effectively erase references to Christianity from the public sphere. It is this approach that leads to abolishing talk of 'St Patrick's Day' and replace it with 'O'Green Day' in a primary school in Massachusetts,[6] or the removal of Christian statues from a Community Hospital in Killarney, Co. Kerry.[7] Clearly, this is incoherent as it effectively does away with diversity (which it claims to celebrate) and enforces a secularist paradigm on all (for which religion is a merely private affair).

In intellectual terms the non-denominational or pluralist position is a kind of agnosticism. Here one is committed to the view that reserving one's judgement on questions of ultimate meaning is the most rational or sensible point of view. In purely theoretical terms, the agnostic position is, of course, a point of view as well. It is, if you like, a kind of commitment to non-commitment. While it may be an intellectually valid position one wonders whether it is existentially viable. In purely intellectual terms one can perhaps suspend judgement on whether or not God exists. However in real, existential terms the world and its urgencies do not usually give us this kind of freedom. In reality I will act in accordance with my belief or my unbelief. When it comes to existential decisions of ultimate meaning (e.g. 'Will I allow my 15-year-old daughter to terminate her pregnancy?'), we cannot suspend our choices indefinitely. In short, an allegedly neutral position is a standpoint in its own right. You cannot be truly detached or 'neutral' when it comes to the most fundamental questions in life. To draw another analogy: when you respond to a moving, heartfelt, passionate love letter by saying that you will 'reserve your judgement and consider the matter in a critical, objective and detached way' you are not giving a neutral response. It is effectively a rejection, and a fairly offensive one at that.

Catholicism, like any other monotheistic faith, deals with issues of ultimate meaning, and therefore involves more than subscribing to a set of beliefs and doctrines. More generally it involves a specific perspective on the world and human beings. It has its own ethos and values. It requires participation in its liturgical practices and prayer while cultivating a disposition of receptivity which allows the believer to discern the mystery of God at the heart of our world. Merely being taught *about* religions is not entirely without its value; but it is 'a paltry thing' compared to being formed into the Catholic religion as a living reality. It would be an absurdity to assume that one can teach somebody to play the piano by merely allowing the student to listen to recordings of piano-recitals, without any practice and real playing by either the teacher or the student. Just so, the notion that one can do justice to religious formation of children by merely teaching them about religion (as is proposed for the course Education about Religions and Beliefs which uncritically adopts a meta-perspective, secularist in outlook), and without allowing them to practice it (for example as a school community in the liturgy) is equally absurd. It displays a truncated understanding of what proper religious education is about, for it reduces it to nothing more than simply knowing a collection of facts and figures, and fails to grasp the riches of religious formation. In general any education is never just about imparting information from a detached standpoint. Education is about formation of the whole person, and is therefore always integrated.

Proponents of a non-denominational approach may perhaps argue that religious formation should not take place at all in schools but only in the family sphere and community. In this context one often hears the argument that the separation of Church and State demands a ban on religious formation in State-funded schools. This view is wrong on a number of counts. First, it appears to conveniently overlook the fact that Catholics – the vast majority of people according to the latest Census – pay taxes too, and are therefore entitled to an education that caters for their needs. More importantly, the principle of the separation of Church and State was never meant to promote a secularist agenda and create a religion-free zone in the public sphere. It was actually the opposite. The principle aims to safeguard religion from undue interference from the State. Like the American Constitution the Irish Constitution prohibits the State from favouring an 'official' religion (cf. art. 44.2.2°, 3° and 4°). However that does not mean that the State cannot support schools that have a religious denomination (as art. 44.2.4° with its reference to a school 'receiving public money' makes clear). The separation of Church and State (not explicitly mentioned in the Constitution) does not aim at creating a religion-free zone in the public sphere.[8] Rather it aims to protect religious denominations from undesirable interference by State authorities ('Every religious denomination shall have the right to manage its own affairs ...').[9]

Leaving aside the constitutional argument for now, proponents of non-denominational education further argue that the school should be about education, not formation in any world view whatsoever. As I suggested earlier, one wonders, however, whether one can truly educate (in the full sense) without formation. At any rate, if the argument assumes that no socialisation takes place in non-religious schools it starts from an inaccurate premise. Non-denominational schools also impart values to children. Indeed, international experience reveals that those who promote a non-denominational perspective are usually not shy about using the school as a medium of socialisation, in which children are being exposed to 'politically correct' progressive policies (toward minorities, other religions, ecology ...). Frank Furedi has argued that the school is increasingly seen as a medium of socialisation at the expense of its main role – education and the transmission of knowledge to the next generation so as to allow them to make sense of their world.[10] There is, however, an important difference between the new politically correct 'values' and those of religion. While the former are being artificially imposed on children at the behest of policymakers who consider the school the best place to tackle society's problems and its dysfunctionality (often implicitly at the expense of under-mining parental authority), religious values have organically grown within society and originate from within it.[11]

In summary, just as each language has its own distinctive character and there is no meta-language which all people speak, so too there is no such thing as a 'neutral stance' when it comes to world views. Every perspective is biased – be it Catholic, Anglican, Chinese, Muslim, Humanist or non-denominational. The non-denominational perspective is therefore not a neutral meta-perspective; it is just as biased as any of the denominational perspectives. As a matter of fact, the non-denominational perspective is the offspring of one specific tradition within the West: the Enlightenment tradition, which rejects appeals to tradition and reduces human understanding to 'autonomous reason', thereby completely ignoring the fiduciary nature of all human rationality.[12] Any multi-denominational perspective which opposes religious formation by the school and assigns its expression to the private sphere, shares some of the key assumptions of the non-denominational approach.

The Christian View, As One World view amongst Others, Can Lead to Insights of Universal Value; It Is Therefore Not Relativist

I have argued that all world views, including the secular one, offer different perspectives and that none of them occupies a position which allows it to 'objectively' survey all other world views. None of them is 'neutral'. They all come with presuppositions. This is not to say that different world views cannot, at times, share certain ethical positions. Most world views (religious and atheist) are in agreement on, for instance, the significance of the dignity of the human person. However, we must have the intellectual honesty to acknowledge that on a great number of issues there is no 'mutual ground' amongst the different world views, religious or otherwise. While there may be general agreement on the dignity of the human person, for instance, a religious justification of the intrinsic value of personhood (or even: what constitutes 'a person') will be radically different from an atheist one (which will resist the notion that human dignity cannot be fully grasped without reference to God in whose image we have been made). Again, the Buddhist understanding of self and desire is radically different from the Christian one; or the Muslim understanding of God and Jesus of Nazareth is utterly different from the Christian understanding of God as Trinity.

The acknowledgement of irreducible differences does not, however, have to result in the espousal of relativism (in which all views are considered to be equally valid, and ultimately there is no truth). On the contrary, by being wedded to our own particular perspective (be it Christian, Buddhist, Muslim, Atheist …) we can ultimately gain a meaningful perspective on reality, that is, the pursuit of each particular perspective may at times yield universal insights. A musical analogy may illustrate this. Any lover of classical music will know that Beethoven has a very distinctive style, highly dynamic and driven. It is almost a rhetorical, gesticulating kind of music, as Nietzsche memorably put it. Anton Bruckner, too, has his own musical idiom. Bruckner's music is very different to Beethoven's. It is multi-layered, contemplative and almost static. The point being made here is that in their very particularity both composers reveal something about what it means to be human. Their *particular* perspective opens up *universal* horizons. The same applies to world views. At their best world views may capture insights and open up horizons that have universal value. This is not to say that we will somehow find ourselves in agreement on the fundamental issues in life. Hopefully each perspective, at its best, will provide its adherents with a meaningful and enriching perspective which promotes the fulfilment of humans as individuals and members of society in every aspect of their life (intellectual, affective, moral, aesthetic …).

Conclusion: Problems with Recent Proposals by the Forum on Patronage and Pluralism
From the preceeding content of this chapter it will be clear why I consider the recent report of the *Forum on Patronage and Pluralism in the Primary Sector* (2012) to be deeply problematic.[13] Many of its proposals are founded on the implicit secularist presupposition that there is no scope for genuine religious formation in the school (sacramental preparation should not occur during normal school time); an obligatory pluralist course, called Education about Religion and Beliefs (ERB) and Ethics is to be introduced, which this chapter has argued, fails to do justice to religious formation in the proper sense, and therefore is at least implicitly secularist in nature. The Report of the Forum's Advisory Group also recommends the abolition of Rule 68 which allows for the religious spirit to 'inform and vivify the whole work of the school'. The Forum's pluralist leanings are evident in its recommendations that emblems of various religions are to be displayed in the school, and festivals of different religions are to be celebrated, without any allowance made for a religious patron's responsibility to uphold and foster its own specific ethos. Finally the Forum's recommendations also suggest that prayers are to be inclusive of the religious beliefs (and none?) of all children.[14]

It is not surprising that the Forum's recommendations display evidence of both the non-denominational and the multi-denominational approaches. After all, as this chapter suggests, the latter often lapses into the former paradigm. Both are deeply hostile to a genuine Catholic education, in which children are truly formed by being exposed to the challenging witness of the gospel, its ensuing reflection on it throughout the tradition, its embodiment in a life of Christian service, and its liturgical expression; by learning to discern the ever-elusive mystery of God in our world and other people; by being nurtured to develop a receptivity and sensitivity for all that is beautiful, good and true through encounters with humankind's most splendid achievements in science, religious and non-religious world views, great literature and art.[15]

NOTES

1. See <http://www.cso.ie> for details: 3.8 million people called themselves Catholic (out of a total population of c.4.5m); almost 130,000 Church of Ireland; 45,000 Orthodox; less than 270,000 selected 'No Religion', while around 49,000 call themselves Islamic. There are a mere 3,900 self-professed atheists in Ireland.
2. Plurality refers to the sociological reality (or fiction?) of a socio-demographical and cultural more diverse Ireland. Pluralism refers to the ideology which celebrates and promotes this

plurality. For the purpose of this paper, multi-denominationalism refers specifically to pluralism in relation to religion and ethos in educational institutes (e.g. schools, universities, etc.).

3.   On the website <http://www.educatetogether.ie/wordpress/wp-content/uploads/2010/ 02/LETS-Ethos-Guide.pdf> [accessed 12 Sept. 2012] 'Our school community is multi-denominational and multicultural. We uphold, respect and accept equality of beliefs, whether religious or non-religious, and we celebrate diverse lifestyles held by children, parents, staff and members of the wider community.'

4.   'Secularism' is different from 'secularity'. A secular society is one in which religion has no place in the public sphere (State-funded schools, courts, public hospitals, legal texts, political discourse …), and is only allowed to flourish (if at all) in the private sphere.

5. .   See Donal Murray, 'The Catholic Church's Current Thinking on Educational Provision' in *Catholic Primary Education: Facing New Challenges*, ed. by Eugene Duffy (Dublin: Columba, 2012), p. 59.

6.   One website reports; 'At the Soule Road School in Wilbraham, St Patrick's Day has been replaced as the name for the school's celebration surrounding the popular holiday. It's been replaced with the generic 'O'Green Day'. MassLive.com's Patrick Johnson calls the move 'a heavy-handed attempt to instil political correctness among the impressionable 4th and 5th graders'. The school's principal, Lisa Curtin, is apparently looking to become more inclusive. So, rather than tout St Patrick's Day, she has purportedly come up with a way to circumvent the faith-related nature of the holiday. The school apparently did something similar for St Valentine's Day, which, in some classrooms, was referred to as 'Caring and Kind Day.' See <http://www.river973.com/cc-common/news/sections/newsarticle.html? feed=104668&article=9904190> [accessed 4 Sept. 2012].

7.   See: 'HSE Forced to Review Removal of Statue from Kerry Hospital': 'The statue, which has been at the entrance to hospital for over 70 years, was removed last year by the HSE on what they said was, "safety grounds". However the HSE claimed at the time that its removal was also to accommodate other religious beliefs amid a changing culture in Killarney.' From: http://www.cinews.ie/article.php?artid=8575 [accessed 8 Sept. 2012].

8.   As the many references to 'God' in oaths of public-office holders make clear, as well as the extraordinary Art. 44.1: 'The State acknowledges that the homage of public worship is due to Almighty God. It shall hold His Name in reverence, and shall respect and honour religion.'

9.   See Art. 44.2.5°. In light of this one wonders whether the proposals of the *Forum on Patronage and Pluralism*, if implemented, are actually constitutional. For surely the demand to display religious symbols of all denominations, conduct 'inclusive' prayer, etc. constitutes a major interference in the affairs of religion?

10.   Frank Furedi, *Wasted: Why Education Does Not Educate Anymore* (London: Continuum, 2009).

11.   See Furedi's wide-ranging critique of education, in Furedi 2009.

12.   The fiduciary nature of human rationality means that human reason always operates with a set of beliefs, and that 'autonomous' reason is therefore an impossibility. Even the most 'rational' of all disciplines, classical logic, operates with key axioms (such as the principle of non-contradiction) which it simply assumes but cannot prove. I am indebted to the writings by Michael Polanyi, Alasdair McIntyre, and Hans-Georg Gadamer who, each in their own way, have developed arguments that led to the demise of the notion that reason and science are 'perspectiveless' and 'neutral'.

13.   See: http://www.education.ie/servlet/blobservlet/fpp_report_advisory_group.pdf?language =EN&igstat=true [accessed Sept. 5, 2012], for the text of the Report.

14.   See *Report from The Forum on Patronage and Pluralism in the Primary Sector*, chapter VII, esp. pp. 88–93.

15.   I have developed some of the arguments outlined in this paper in 'The End of Catholic Education in Ireland?', *The Furrow*, 63/6 (2012), pp. 278–285.

CONCLUDING REFLECTION

CHAPTER FIFTEEN

ENCOUNTERING AND ENGAGING WITH RELIGION AND BELIEF:
THE CONTEMPORARY CONTRIBUTION OF RELIGIOUS EDUCATION IN SCHOOLS

Gareth Byrne

This concluding chapter seeks to set out a number of principles that represent core mutual ground values emerging from the research and dialogue around religious education in schools presented in this volume. The argument offered here does not try to unify the disparate views of the various contributors to this debate, nor does it claim to be the final word. Rather it seeks to establish criteria upon which those engaged in religious education at a variety of levels, together with various stakeholders and interest groups, can build a secure perception of the indispensable place of religious education in schools, its contribution to the well-being of individuals, to society, and to faith communities and other organisations of conviction that colour our world.

1. Acknowledge and honour plurality in the world today
Respect for diversity is built on and demands respect for the individual and for groups of individuals in society. We cannot hide difference or pretend it does not exist. Nor can any of us claim, on the other hand, that even our most passionately held views are the only way of looking at things. This does not mean, however, that we should not strive for truth, and for the best possible understanding between peoples.

The authors writing in this volume speak about plurality and pluralism from a variety of perspectives. In reflecting on their contributions it is clear, as has been stated elsewhere, that 'the view that different individuals take in defining and interpreting that plurality represents their own particular views in the debate on pluralism'.[1] Acknowledging plurality and accepting diversity is not the same thing as embracing secularism. A distinction needs to be made continuously between pluralism, understood as recognising and honouring plurality (while seeking to eschew relativism, the proposition that all views are to be equally valued), and secularism which argues for excluding religion in its plurality from culture, from civic conversation and from public life. Most of our contributors have argued that it is essential within a truly pluralist modern liberal democracy that religious education plays its meaningful part in helping young people understand the possibilities associated with full human development. This entails encouraging them to become more aware of their own particular perspectives and to recognise the place of tolerance and dialogue in inspiring true respect and care for the other.

2. Respect and support the place of religion and belief in contemporary society
If we honour plurality then we can and must honour religion in its variety within our society. We must honour, too, the rights of those who hold a variety of diverse philosophical positions, secular convictions and other world views. Research conducted by sociologists Christian Smith and Melinda Lundquist Denton, in the United States, has shown the necessity, as well as the significance, of paying attention to the religious and spiritual interests and engagement of adolescents. Their results indicate the importance of better informed conversations in this regard among those who care about young people with all their concerns and complexities.[2] Asking teenagers what religion means for them, it becomes clear that the influence of religion and religious communities can be continuing and powerful. These researchers conclude that religious affiliation provides significant grounding in, for example, spiritual experiences, community life skills and leadership skills, self-control and personal virtue, beliefs and practices which help in coping with stress, and opportunities for engagement beyond family, school and media. Partaking in religious communities and their activities also facilitates creative cross-generational ties for young peoples as well as helping them develop dense networks of adults who pay attention to their lives. Religious affiliation, with its invitation to participation and experience of care and commitment, holds within itself the possibility of encouraging positive learning for life through its defining engagement with deepest meaning, with all of life, with love and with community.[3]

Religious education, in reflecting on such experience, and on the challenge often associated with belief in God, in self and in each other, helps the young person develop and come to a mature view of what is essential in life. The suggestion that religion has sometimes reinforced negative learning does not undermine the argument for good religious education. In fact it confirms the need for robust engagement, for dialogue as to what religious education should be at its best, and for a deeper understanding of what can help young people most in reflecting on religion, spirituality and ethics. Good religious education which respects all peoples is an undertaking to be celebrated. It contributes to building up the fabric of society, preparing young people to play their part, respectfully, in the dialogue that is humanity.

3. Recognise religious education as a valid and necessary contributor to the public space
In the past, many would have understood the study of religion, or religious instruction as it was often described, as the concern of churches rather than of the state. Religious education in Ireland has developed, over the past thirty years, from being an exclusively ecclesial area of concern to having a place in the public space and become, it has been claimed, crucial 'for the formation of global citizens, at home with diversity, at ease in a range of cultural spaces'.[4] The Irish Centre for Religious Education in its submission to the Forum on Patronage and Pluralism in the Primary Sector argued for clarity about the place of religious education in the public sphere and in all schools, a conviction supported by many of the contributors to this volume:

> Religion then must play a role in education, and religious education is a valid and indeed necessary enterprise in the public space for the good of individuals and of society. Otherwise a whole reality, and way of dealing with that reality, is lost to the community, locally and nationally.[5]

Indeed, the Irish Constitution upholds the inalienable right and duty of parents, in conjunction with schools, to provide for the religious and moral, intellectual, physical and social education of their children. This has been reinforced by the Education Act, 1998, which restates the right of the child to a moral and spiritual education in school.[6] The Department of Education's definition of the general aim of education expresses this powerfully:

> The general aim of education is to contribute towards the development of all aspects of the individual, including aesthetic, creative, critical, cultural, emotional, intellectual, moral, physical, political, social and spiritual develop-ment, for personal and home life, for working life, for living in the community and for leisure.[7]

Religious education makes a particularly focused contribution to the spiritual and moral development of the young person, but in fact engages with all the above named aspects of human development for the benefit of the individual, for the benefit of the community to which they belong and for the development of society itself.

4. Prioritise the study of religion and belief for all young people
Various contributions to this book seek to clarify language and set out from a variety of differing, though often complementary, perspectives, a basic framework for religious education as a school subject in Ireland to which people can then be invited to bring their commitments, interests and responsibilities. There is a growing consensus, in Europe and beyond, that religious education cannot only be education 'about' religion(s).[8] This was never what was understood by religious education, generally, in Ireland, and continues to be an important proposition here today, for two additional reasons, clarified in this publication. Firstly, as Robert Jackson and Andrew McGrady argue in

Chapters One and Four of this volume, there is a need, with the growing influence of diverse cultures in society, to reach out now not only to people from various, and sometimes new, religious traditions but also to those from a variety of other world views and belief systems. Secondly, Jackson, building on developing European perspectives, contends that religious education supported by the state needs to go beyond simply offering information about different religions and help young people examine their own as well as peer assumptions concerning religion and belief, assisting them to gradually formulate and clarify their own views.[9] Religious education should, generally, be education 'from' as well as 'about' religion and belief. As Suzanne Dillon indicates in her chapter, the state-certified religious education programme approved for use in all second-level schools in the Republic goes beyond simply learning 'about' religions. It seeks to develop all pupils' knowledge, understanding, skills, and attitudes in dialogue with the religious, spiritual and ethical heritage of humanity and with their own experience.[10] It is learning 'about' religion(s) and 'from' religion(s), 'about' belief(s) and 'from' belief(s), in a manner appropriate to the age and stage of development of the young people concerned.

Michael Nugent and Jane Donnelly express a view in their chapter contrary to the argument here. In maintaining that only information 'about' religions and beliefs be discussed in state sponsored schools (and they welcome this in non-denominational schools when such emerge), they contend that it is essential not to seek to draw the young person of secular conviction, or whose parents are of secular conviction, into any meaningful engagement concerning people's own experience of religion and belief. The right to freedom of religion and belief, and therefore not to be proselytised, is of the highest importance. It might be useful to consider if a right to be free from the need for dialogue with others in their beliefs could actually undermine freedom and mitigate against the search for tolerance, respect and mutual care.

5. Facilitate young people in bringing their religion and beliefs with them appropriately into the religious education classroom

It has been argued up to this point that religious education, reflected upon deeply and engaging with experience as well as information, can contribute to the development of young people, and can do so in a manner that is open, respectful and generous. Significant discussion about religious education at second-level during the 1990s saw the emergence of a form of religious education tailored to the needs of that particular age-group. The Junior Certificate Religious Education Syllabus and the Leaving Certificate Religious Education Syllabus set out a structure for religious education open to all at second level in the Irish Republic. As well as fostering an awareness of the human search for meaning and its continued expression in religion, these syllabuses and the associated curriculum framework for non-examination religious education at senior cycle, identify understandings of God, engagement with religious traditions, and in particular the Christian tradition, and how religion, and non-religious interpretations of life, have contributed to personal development and to the culture in which we live.

These syllabuses seek 'to contribute to the spiritual and moral development of the student'.[11] Thus religious education, as defined here, is intended to invite the second-level pupil to 'encounter and engage' with religious traditions, reflect on his or her own religious experiences and explore his or her individual commitment to a particular religious tradition and/or continuing search for meaning.[12] The young people involved are asked to bring their religious and/or philosophical understanding with them into school. Learners are encouraged to be responsible too for what happens in the classroom. All are to be respected and all are called to speak from their emerging self-understanding and beliefs. This programme does not suggest that young people leave their religious or other convictions in a private realm, outside the classroom, beyond the school, separate from their encounter with society. Its purpose is not fulfilled by a comfortable, abstract study of religion(s) and belief(s), separate from the real experience and search for meaning of the young person. Discussing real-life religious, spiritual and ethical experience, and the doubts and questions posed for young people, today, is a far more stimulating project, awakening and positively engaging young people, whether they are religiously committed or otherwise. It recommends for them and for their parents, teachers, neighbours and friends, the building up of a society that is plural but integrated, diverse but responsible, truth-seeking but respectful and compassionate.

6. Cultivate approaches to religious education that respond to young people's age and stage of development

This conversation having taken place at second level, the debate about religious education at primary school level is the focus of current debate. First, we need to consider the age of younger children and the kind of religious education appropriate for them as they develop their capacity for learning. Taking into account all that has been said above, religious education, including engagement with people embracing a variety of beliefs, should be considered an important element in the holistic education of children. The United Nations Convention on the Rights of the Child (1989) highlights the right of the child to freedom of thought, conscience and religion. It notes the rights and duties of parents/ guardians, to provide direction to the child in the exercise of his or her right in a manner consistent with the evolving capacities of the child. It confirms that freedom to manifest one's religion or beliefs may be subject only to such limitations as are prescribed by law and are necessary to protect public safety, order, health or morals, or the fundamental rights and freedoms of others.[13]

The evolving capacity of the young person is a significant concept within this discussion. Adolescents have generally reached a stage of development where philosophical questioning, critical reflection, problem solving, self-reliance,[14] the search for their own identity and for meaning, provide an appropriate focus, particularly at senior cycle level. Primary school pupils are at a particular stage on their journey. They are not adolescents but they are curious about the big questions.[15] Belonging and being cherished are significant requirements for the well-being of the younger child.[16] School, along with home and parish or other community, plays a significant part as the natural environment 'within which primary-level children find support, not only for their everyday physical, emotional and social requirements but also for their everyday religious, moral and spiritual needs'.[17]

The Primary School Curriculum (1999) confirms the position of religious education within a holistic vision of what education can be:

> In seeking to develop the full potential of the individual, the curriculum takes into account the child's affective, aesthetic, spiritual, moral and religious needs.[18]

Often adults with the best of intentions quickly reduce religious education to the intellectual comprehension of abstract religious and spiritual concepts, something quite alien to children of primary school age. What is helpful for adults and even for adolescents is not necessarily appropriate for children. As set out elsewhere,[19] James Fowler, following in the tradition of Piaget, Erikson and Kohlberg, has helped those involved in religious education to capture an understanding of the stages through which faith/belief may develop from childhood through adolescence to adulthood. In early childhood (aged 3–7 approximately), Fowler argues, faith is fantasy-filled and the child is responsive to imaginative interaction with the adults in their lives. In later childhood (aged 8–12) a more linear, narrative construction of coherence and meaning is experienced. A sense is developed of where and with whom the child is at home. This is 'the stage in which the person begins to take on for him or herself the stories, beliefs and observances that symbolise belonging to his or her community'.[20] The religious education of primary school children should therefore focus on helping the child become aware of and grow into the religious or other community to which they and their parents/guardians belong, while promoting openness and mutual respect for others from a different cultural, ethnic, national or religious background. Children at primary level learn through the local and particular.

7. Define the contribution that denominational, multi-denominational, interdenominational and non-denominational schools can make to dialogue in society
There is an urgent need in Irish society, today, to clarify the role of denominational, multi-denominational, interdenominational and non-denominational schooling. This language, too, emerges from Ireland's Christian

heritage. Traditionally, primary education in Ireland was supported by a variety of Christian denominations. Children learned in their family and parish community and in the school established by that community.[21] Although it might in fact be better today to speak of faith schools, multifaith schools and nonfaith schools, this seems a little awkward for now, being unrelated to the language generally employed in Ireland. In denominational schools, as well as learning 'about' and 'from' religion(s) and belief(s), pupils of the particular faith tradition learn 'for' or 'in' or even better, I would suggest, 'within', their own faith community. The denominational school facilitates the religious education and formation of pupils within a particular Christian faith. As well as learning about and from religion, these schools encourage their Christian young people to draw close to God in Jesus Christ, and experiencing his love, go out in his Spirit to live love, peace, joy and justice in the world for the good of all.[22] Other faith schools will form pupils of their religion within their faith tradition. This represents the added value that these schools provide for the parents of that religion. Responsible citizenship is well served by educated people of faith holding their own beliefs and convictions in a way that contributes to the common good. Where appropriate an inter-religious approach to education may be helpful.[23] Anne Hession, in her chapter, has spelt out foundational principles in support of such engagement within Catholic primary schools.

Denominational schools respect and cherish the freedom and beliefs of all their young people. Despite sometimes, what has been referred to in the United Kingdom as, an 'openly militant attack upon faith-based schools',[24] these schools have sought over the years, in Ireland as well as in Great Britain, to develop a keen sensitivity against any form of indoctrination or proselytism.[25] The continuing reference to the need for denominational schools to avoid such in the recent document from the Irish Human Rights Commission, *Religion and Education: A Human Rights Perspective* (2011) does not do justice to the reality of respect shown to the beliefs of all students within denominational schools in Ireland.[26] These schools are alert to such a danger and confirm wholeheartedly that young people should never be compelled to participate in any actions contrary to their own religious and other convictions or those of their family. The recent ESRI Report (November 2012) states that Catholic schools in Ireland are inclusive schools.[27] The Irish Catholic Bishops are very clear on this:

> The Catholic school promotes tolerance, respect and inclusivity. Its educational perspective is Catholic and ecumenical by nature and open to inter-religious and inter-cultural dialogues ... It promotes 'the formation of young people in the construction of a world based on dialogue and the search for community ... on the mutual acceptance of differences rather than on their opposition'. All students should be encouraged to have a good knowledge of the Catholic faith and its traditions, and also of other faith communities. On the other hand, no pupil need receive, or be present at, any religious education of which her or his parents or guardians disapprove.[28]

Multi-denominational schools, properly so-called, support a number of Christian denominations, and nowadays people of other religions and convictions. They positively encourage open discussion of religion and other world views. These schools set about creating an atmosphere where young people are happy to acknowledge, appreciate and respect the reality of difference. Multi-denominational schools, by definition, will facilitate a variety of religious opinions, rituals, and prayer options, as well as exhibiting a variety of religious symbols relevant to members of the school community.

Some suggest that a growing number of primary schools in Ireland, calling themselves multi-denominational, have in fact developed an ethos that, as Rik Van Nieuwenhove argues in this volume, would more truly be defined as non-denominational or secular. It is unclear why schools are shy of announcing their non-denominational credentials. The timely and challenging *Report of the Advisory Group of the Forum on Patronage and Pluralism in Primary Schools* suggests that while there may have been resistance to such in the past, the Department of Education and Skills declared to the Forum in June 2011 that there were 'no longer objections to the establishing of such schools, if sought by sufficiently large groups of parents, who otherwise fulfilled the requirements for patronage'.[29] Such non-denominational schools would provide a form of religious, spiritual and ethical education, described by the Forum Report as Education about Religion and Beliefs (ERB) and Ethics. A non-denominational school would not be dispensed from this responsibility but could support discussion of religious, spiritual and moral development, without promoting any particular religious or other world view. Given the argument being set out here, it is somewhat unsatisfactory that the Forum Report sets up a distinction between ERB and Ethics as 'learning *about* religions' and what it calls Denomin-ational Religious Education, also a new designation in Ireland, 'which focuses on faith formation'.[30] Religious education in these non-denominational schools, this author argues, should best focus on education not only 'about' but also 'from' religion(s) and belief(s) as described above. The child's natural openness to dialogue in the world should be encouraged by teachers who themselves have been educated in the dynamics of open and inclusive teaching methodologies. Any sense that 'we do not talk about those questions here' should be avoided as likely to undermine the child's confidence that all of life is significant, exciting, inspiring and can lead to open, respectful discussion. Clearly education 'within' a religion or belief system would not be envisaged in the non-denominational school setting, except by arrangement with a group of parents outside the normal school day.

8. Recognise the validity of faith schools and value good religious education taking place within them

It is not necessary to undermine one type of school ethos in order to value another. All schools have an ethos (whether denominational, multi-denominational, interdenominational or non-denominational), and often a particular characteristic spirit, that both informs and is reflected in every aspect of the life of the school. It is not helpful, or possible, to seek to 'restrict' the ethos of any school to one aspect of its curriculum or of its timetable. It is not clear, therefore, what is envisaged when the *Report of the Forum on Patronage and Pluralism in the Primary Sector*, speaking also about denominational schools, seeks 'to ensure that while the general curriculum remains integrated, provision be made for denominational religious education/faith formation to be taught as a discreet subject'.[31] Religious and spiritual development can no more be artificially separated from the rest of life, than can, for instance, historical, national or gender issues. What must be upheld is the need for respect for all people when addressing all such questions.

Denominational schools must, by definition, be free, working with parents/guardians, families and parishes, to provide faith formation activities for the pupils of the faith tradition of the patron or trustee board. They should do so in a manner that is respectful and positively reinforces the rights and well-being of all. The Forum Report is clear that any new ERB and Ethics programmes that may be introduced by the state 'are in no sense intended to supplant faith formation education in denominational schools'.[32] Such schools should work attentively, too, with parents and families, to support the variety of other religious faiths and secular convictions present in the school:

> Faith settings will have a positive advantage and interest in promoting understanding of religious diversity and dialogue since it is the teaching of most faiths to respect those who believe differently …[33]

The Catholic Church in Ireland, as we have seen, expects its schools to be characterised by respect, generosity, justice, critical reflection, and be open to and enriched by pupils from all cultural and religious backgrounds. Jones Irwin, in Chapter Twelve, relying on Norman (2003) comments on what he calls 'the reactionary denominationalism of the Irish Bishops' educational philosophy'. He seems to overlook the efforts made in the past decade by the Bishops' Conference, working with the Conference of Religious of Ireland (CORI) and other Catholic education partners, and since 2010 under the banner 'Catholic Schools Partnership', in responding to the growing diversity experienced in Irish society at that time. The recent documents of the Bishops' Conference, in fact, locate Catholic schools and colleges, not only within their own distinctive tradition of values and beliefs but, committed, also, to openness and awareness of the needs of a diverse population, to assisting social cohesion, to promoting positive and active citizenship and to encouraging the growth of a vibrant civil society.[34] The Catholic community is transparent in naming the service it offers in Catholic schools to Catholic parents. At the same time it welcomes others who embrace what it seeks to ensure is a hospitable education project:

> The Catholic primary school, as an outreach of the local parish, will seek to nourish the faith of its Catholic students and assist in their Christian initiation. It will respect the religious tradition of other students and facilitate them in every way.[35]

Parents of other religious traditions and world views are often happy to enrol their children in a Catholic or other faith school, because they appreciate having an atmosphere that acknowledges God and religion in the school their child attends. They, and parents of secular conviction, should be able to discuss fully with the school principal and teachers how their child can best participate in the school day and what is and is not expected of them. The ethos of such a school and the religious education that takes place there can be upheld in a way that promotes the religious freedom of pupils, staff and parents who do not share the religious faith of that school. Every faith school will and should express its ethos, using prayer, symbols, music, and ritual. This does not presuppose that all members of the school community will participate in all activities or on the other hand that a variety of symbols cannot be displayed. The Forum Report recommends 'that communal prayers, reflections, hymns, or school assemblies, where these take place, should be respectful of the beliefs and culture of all children'.[36] A Christian prayer can be a prayer for the well-being of Muslims but Muslims, or Humanists to take a further example, cannot be asked to pray 'through Christ our Lord'. The Catholic or Protestant school must, however, engage in religious celebrations, prayers, rituals and events for members of its own community, and always with a tone that is ecumenical and open to inter-religious and intercultural dialogue. The Catholic sector has confirmed that its schools will also support parents of children from other traditions in making provision for faith education for their children:

> Where parents/guardians of children, other than Catholic children, attending the school, wish to provide suitable faith education for their children, the school principal will be happy to encourage them in this regard.[37]

In everything here, clarity, respect and transparency are key. In fact, denominational schools in Ireland have opened their doors to newcomers and have become a great symbol of what is possible when diversity of culture, race and religion are recognised and embraced. People should be able to live and celebrate within their own beliefs and traditions, providing they are not undermining the rights of others. They should be able to appreciate the religious or other convictions of their neighbour, even if they are not a believer themselves. For people with religious faith, such faith needs to be educated and integrated with their general knowledge, understanding, skills and attitudes, and facilitated in a manner that helps them as citizens to embrace the common good, contribute confidently to society and help in overcoming unnecessary conflict.

9. Encourage good practice, assessment and ongoing evaluation of religious education in all contexts, overseen by faith communities as well as by the state

Language is understood in how it is used.[38] As well as seeking to clarify the language we use we must also forge ahead, and live life, building up good practice out of which new language can arise, adequate for new situations. Marie Parker-Jenkins notes in Chapter Five that policy can become separated from experience and needs to be informed by practice as it emerges and is developed. Anne Looney confirms this argument in her chapter, convinced that practice 'at the chalkface' can contribute equally or perhaps more strongly to educational reform than the writing of policies. This also allows for taking into account children's voices when designing curricula and learning activities.[39] The need for well-founded policies is not being denied here. What is being suggested, however, is that coming to an agreed understanding of the space available for religious education (among other issues) depends on respectful approaches taking hold in practice and being further reflected upon and formalised. This can then be acknowledged in language that will ring true for all – or at least for those who do not define themselves in opposition to the project.

The state, as we have seen, has through its syllabuses for religious education set out a clear rationale and support system for the inclusion of religious education for all in every post-primary school in the Republic. The state syllabuses are assessed and accredited by the State Examinations Commission, and supported by the Subject Association, the Religion Teachers Association of Ireland (RTAI) and the Professional Development Service for Teachers (PDST).[40] Assurance mechanisms are provided through the Subject Inspection Reports as well as the Chief Examiner's Report.[41]

Occasionally a larger curriculum review will be undertaken by the National Council for Curriculum and Assessment (NCCA). The recent review, and resulting *Framework for Junior Cycle* for example,[42] will impact considerably on how subjects are envisaged, learned and examined at Junior Certificate level. Many of the new learning outcomes set out for the Junior Cycle fit very well with expectations of what religious education can be and what it can contribute, including to literacy and numeracy. When these outcomes are addressed in schools, it will be recognised that religious education can respond positively and imaginatively to the current needs of young people, whether they take the state-certified religious education examination or not.

Religious education should be a core subject in schools for all the reasons highlighted in this chapter. The fact that 28,605 pupils took religious education in the Junior Certificate in 2012 (close to half the number of pupils participating) reveals it to be one of the most popular examination subjects among pupils. A schedule for reviewing each subject has recently been set out but Junior Certificate religious education will only be reviewed as one of the final subjects and not until 2017–2020. In arguing for the importance of religious education, such a review of good practice is to be welcomed and might suggest, for example, that:

- there is too much material to be covered and too wide-ranging an examination in Junior Certificate religious education
- this contributes to a feeling in schools that space for engagement, discussion, and dialogue is being curtailed in the religious education classroom
- the journal (the coursework element), a welcome and important innovation, focuses too heavily on process rather than on what has been learned, and is in urgent need of renewal.

While religious education continues to be an essential two-hour-a-week subject at senior cycle level, the fact that only about 1,000 students each year progress to take the Leaving Certificate religious education examination is a disappointing trend. A revision of learning outcomes ideal for senior cycle will presumably follow the Junior Cycle Review. In regard to Leaving Certificate religious education an evaluation of the subject might well suggest that:

- there is an urgent need to renew this worthy but intimidating course
- along with intellectual engagement, it is essential to imagine creative ways of encouraging pupils to become involved in dialogue together and with others, including the use of online material such as *FaithConnect*[43]
- continuing in-service for religious education teachers is essential if the requirements of the Leaving Certificate religious education course are to be fulfilled.

Paralleling state certification evaluation processes, and the review of religious education at Junior Cycle, patrons and trustee boards associated with denominational schooling at second level could usefully review how they assess whether the religious education that takes place in their name lives up to their best intentions.[44] Trustee boards which oversee denominational schools, keeping in mind especially schools not providing for state-certified religious education, should make a review process available for their schools, facilitating informed decision-making with regard to religious diversity, religious education, religious nurture, prayer, liturgical celebrations, chaplaincy services and so on. Themes to be considered might include:

- respect for the religion and belief of all present in the school[45]
- identification of religious education as a core subject for all

- renewed exploration of the state-certified religious education examinations syllabuses, particularly at senior cycle level, and the faith development initiatives which may be associated with them[46]
- the manner in which the characteristic spirit of a particular school is to be emphasised within the school year and liturgical year
- connection with parent/guardians, parish and other communities of conviction
- adequate resourcing and continuing in-service of religious educators and school chaplains in helping young people access their own religious, spiritual and moral development.

The model of what has been developing in religious education at second level has the potential to influence primary school religious education too. The state can and should require that all primary schools have a clear understanding of the significant role of religious education, defined appropriately in differing school systems, and that this is supported by school policies and assessment to ensure good practice. The patron body, working with the variety of partners associated with their schools, should seek to ensure that schools develop and review their mission statement, ethos statement, religious education policy, religious diversity policy and other supporting documentation regularly. These should promote:

- the valued place of religious education in each school
- reflective engagement with symbols, songs, prayer and liturgy
- Curriculum review and development
- Religious education in-service opportunities for teachers and school principals
- Participation in further study and research into religious education at primary school level.

The patron body, in discussion with stakeholders, and supported by the state, should provide quality assurance mechanisms and creative methodologies for local supervision of good practice in all these associated areas.

10. Educate teachers to help young people encounter and engage with religion and belief within a variety of religious education contexts, and to make professional decisions about the appropriate approach in given situations
Teachers and principal teachers as committed professionals concerned for the care of their young people have to conjure with religious, spiritual and moral issues every day. They should address religion and belief positively, and encourage committed reflection. Teachers cannot leave the search for meaning, truth and beauty outside and beyond the natural interaction they seek to establish about all of life with their pupils. School cannot be just about preparation for exams, for points, for a job. Education, it has been argued here, is about the whole person, their well-being personally, and their place within

family, community and society. This means that teachers must be educated and trained to support young people in reflecting on all of life and, therefore, to be able to create an atmosphere where religion, spirituality and ethics are considered fully part of the conversation.

At second level, religious education teachers should be professionally trained religious educators[47] who have learned to enable young people to encounter and engage with religion and belief, their own and that of others. They should have the ability to work with a variety of religious and associated themes and materials, encouraging dialogue and leading discussion toward authenticity and mutual respect. Such professional religious educators should, during their initial teacher education programme, have had ample opportunity to reflect, practice and reflect again on religious education, its contemporary contexts and manifestations and the various associated issues, highlighted in this chapter.

The study of religious education is also a significant element in the preparation of primary school teachers. Religious education, as one of the recognised curriculum areas in primary schools,[48] must be addressed adequately in any primary initial teacher education degree that seeks to prepare teachers for the Irish primary school system. Pre-service teachers at primary level must learn, like their second-level religious education colleagues, to help children encounter and engage with religion and belief, their own in the first place, and then to dialogue with the world and all its peoples. Such conversation in the classroom, listening too and connecting with pupils, can also be a significant stimulus for teacher enquiry and research. This does not undermine the right to freedom of thought, conscience or religion of student teachers.[49] Religious education, no matter in which setting should be respectful of all, including the teacher. The coming generation of teachers will need to be able to engage adequately with the variety of religions and belief systems they will meet in the school, whatever its ethos. They will need to learn specific methodologies suitable for engaging children in discussing religion and belief. They will have to be aware that the identity, ethos and characteristic spirit of the particular school and the make-up of the student body will shape the process in which they will participate. The board of management of a school has the right to expect its staff to uphold the ethos of the school even as that ethos continues to deepen and evolve. This does not require that a staff member be of the particular denomination, tradition or belief system of the school but that they are happy to engage, appropriately, within the life of the school. In Catholic schools this is clear: 'The school will respect the freedom of conscience of teachers in matters of personal religious belief and practice.'[50]

All of this indicates the need to strengthen rather than reduce the religious education component of initial primary teacher education degrees, allowing also as the Forum Report suggests for the variety of approaches which will be undertaken within different types of schools.[51] Student teachers should not be asked to opt for one model ahead of qualification but should be helped by professional religious educationalists to understand the plurality of models available and the reasonable expectations of patrons and trustee boards. Those in initial teacher education at primary level into the future will need to feel secure in their knowledge and understanding of religion, spirituality and morality, including in-depth study of, and reflection on, philosophy, theology and practical issues related to faith-filled and secular conviction. This means that as well as the practical religious education component of their initial teacher education degree, Colleges of Education, generally, will need to continue to provide an add-on Certificate in Theology or Religious Studies, and facilitate study of world religions and of secular world views.

Conclusion

What we have been seeking to establish here is the possibility of a mutually embraced space that acknowledges the need for good religious education and some key principles associated with that mutual ground.

There is a need at this moment in our history for open, well-founded and generous understanding and appreciation of the value of good religious education among relevant stakeholders. The range of issues is complex and requires that the multifaceted interests, rights and responsibilities of children, parents/guardians, teachers and patrons alike are taken into account. A balanced response for the good of all is what is required, within the legitimate expectations of the state, and according to the thought through and developing ethos of the school facilitated by the patron or trustee board under which it operates. A key need emerging from this discussion is for a review of religious education practice in schools, and in Colleges of Education, such that any discontent felt may in fact contribute to a renewed understanding of the subject and the valuable contribution it can make. The introduction of ERB and Ethics into the debate by the Forum Report should be seen in the context of reviewing and contributing to the development of religious education rather than as something in opposition to it. In suggesting that the NCCA develop ERB and Ethics syllabuses, the Forum Advisory Group confirms that 'where programmes, already in existence, provide for some ERB and Ethics, the NCCA programmes can be supplementary.'[55] ERB and Ethics may well become established as the minimum requirement in nondenominational schools. Denominational schools, and multidenominational schools, properly defined, will presumably argue that what is envisaged in ERB and Ethics is already being or can be provided for as an element within or alongside their present religious education programme.

There are great possibilities for dialogue in the modern world, conversations that many may have thought impossible in previous generations.

Misinformation and mistrust, fear and anxiety have often ruled, as Niall Coll reminds us in his chapter on religious education in Northern Ireland. It would be naïve to suggest that all is wholesome and light in our day, but a real discussion is taking place that acknowledges the variety of perspectives among pupils, parents, teachers, school management boards, patrons and trustee bodies. This awareness and dialogue represents the mutual ground upon which we can build. If we acknowledge a plurality of understandings and approaches to life, then we should be able to envisage, welcome and support, not a single so-called pluralist model of religious education, but, a plurality of approaches to religious education, depending on the context and people involved, but always authentically imagined and respectful of difference, supported by a state-sponsored education system hospitable to all.

NOTES

1. Robert Jackson, 'Religious and Cultural Diversity: Some Key Concepts' in *Religious Diversity and Intercultural Education: A Reference Book for Schools*, ed. by John Keast (Strasbourg: Council of Europe Publishing, 2007), p. 32.

2. Christian Smith with Melinda Lundquist Denton, *Soul Searching: The Religious and Spiritual Lives of American Teenagers* (Oxford / New York: Oxford University Press, 2005), p. 8.

3. Smith with Denton, pp. 240–251.

4. Anne Looney, 'Religious Education in the Public Space: Challenges and Contestations', in *International Handbook on the Religious, Moral and Spiritual Dimensions of Education*, ed. by M. de Souza et al. (Dordrecht: Springer, 2006), p. 964.

5. Irish Centre for Religious Education, *Submission to the Forum on Patronage and Pluralism in the Primary Sector* (2011) <http://www.materdei.ie/icre> [accessed 1 Dec. 2012].

6. Government of Ireland, *Education Act, 1998*, 9 (d).

7. Department of Education and Science, *Junior Certificate Religious Education Syllabus* (Dublin: The Stationery Office, 2000), inside cover.

8. A number of contributors have discussed a possible differentiation between teaching 'about', 'from' and 'for' (or 'in') religion. See Michael Grimmitt, ed., *Pedagogies of Religious Education* (Great Wakering, England: McCrimmons, 2000); John Hull, 'The Contribution of Religious Education to Religious Freedom: A Global Perspective', International Association for Religious Freedom <www.iarf.net/REBooklet/Hull.htm> [accessed 23 Nov. 2012].

9. Robert Jackson, *Religious Education: An Interpretative Approach* (London: Hodder and Stoughton, 1997); Robert Jackson, *Rethinking Religious Education and Plurality* (London / New York: Routledge, 2004).

10. *Junior Certificate Religious Education Syllabus*, p. 4.

11. *Junior Certificate Religious Education Syllabus*, p. 5.

12. *Junior Certificate Religious Education Syllabus*, p. 4.

13. United Nations, *Convention on the Rights of the Child* (1989), 14.

14. Department of Education and Science, *Leaving Certificate Religious Education Syllabus* (Dublin: The Stationery Office, 2003), p. 4.

15. Carmel Ní Shúilleabháin, 'Creating Space for Children's Existential Concerns' in *Nurturing Children's Religious Imagination: The Challenge of Primary Religious Education Today*, ed. by Raymond Topley and Gareth Byrne (Dublin: Veritas, 2004), pp. 27–36.

16. J.W. Berryman, 'Faith Development and the Language of Faith', in *Handbook of Children's Religious Education*, ed. by D.E. Radcliff (Birmingham, Alabama: Religious Education Press, 1992), p. 41.

17. Gareth Byrne, 'Children's Religious Education: Challenge and Gift', in *Nurturing Children's Religious Imagination*, p. 238.

18. Department of Education and Science, *The Primary School Curriculum: Introduction* (Dublin: The Stationery Office, 1999), p. 58.

19. For further development of this argument, see Gareth Byrne, 'Children's Religious Education: Challenge and Gift', pp. 237–251.

20. J.W. Fowler, *Stages of Faith: The Psychology of Human Development and the Quest for Meaning* (San Francisco: Harper & Row, 1981), pp. 133–149.

21. Irish Episcopal Conference, *Share the Good News: National Directory for Catechesis in Ireland* (Dublin: Veritas, 2010), 101.

22. *Share the Good News*, 101, 147–148.

23. Dermot A. Lane, *Challenges Facing Religious Education in Ireland Today* (Dublin: Veritas, 2008).

24. Robert A. Davies, 'Futures of Faith Schools' in Faith Schools in the Twenty-First Century, ed. by Stephen McKinney (Edinburgh: Dunedin Academic Press, 2008), p. 59.

25. See Kevin Williams, *Faith and the Nation* (Dublin: Dominican Publications, 2005), pp. 100–125.

26. Irish Human Rights Commission, *Religion and Education: A Human Rights Perspective* (May 2011).

27. Merike Darmody, Emer Smyth and Selina McCoy, *School Sector Variation Among Primary Schools in Ireland*, ESRI Report (Nov. 2012).

28. *Share the Good News*, 101.

29. John Coolahan, Caroline Hussey and Fionnuala Kilfeather, *The Forum on Patronage and Pluralism in the Primary Sector: Report of the Forum's Advisory Group* (Dublin: Department of Education and Science, 2012), p. 51.

30. Forum Report, p. 88.

31. Forum Report, p. 81.

32. Forum Report, p. 92.

33. John Keast and Heid Leganger-Krogstad, 'Religious Dimension of Intercultural Education: A Whole School Approach' in *Religious Diversity and Intercultural Education*, p. 119.

34. As well as *Share the Good News* and other documents of the Irish Catholic Bishops' Conference referred to here, see, Irish Catholic Bishops' Conference, *Catholic Primary Schools: A Policy for Provision into the Future* (Dublin: Veritas, 2007); Irish Catholic Bishops' Conference, *Vision 08: A Vision for Catholic Education in Ireland* (Dublin: Veritas, 2008); Catholic Schools Partnership, *Catholic Primary Schools: Looking to the Future* (Apr. 2011); Catholic Schools Partnership, *Catholic Primary Schools in the Republic of Ireland: A Qualitative Study* (Oct. 2011).

35. *Share the Good News*, 147.

36. Forum Report, p. 94.

37. *Share the Good News*, 101.

38. Hans-Georg Gadamer, *Truth and Method*, English edn (London: Sheed and Ward, 1975, 1985).

39. Vivienne Baumfield and Denise Cush, 'A Gift From the Child: Curriculum Development in Religious Education', *British Journal of Religious Education*, 34/3 (2012), p. 227, and this entire issue of the journal.

40. Religion Teachers Association of Ireland <http://www.rtai.ie> [accessed 25 Nov. 2012]; Professional Development Service for Teachers <http://www.pdst.ie> [accessed 25 Nov. 2012].

41. State Examinations Commission, *Leaving Certificate Examination, 2008, Religious Education: Chief Examiner's Report* <http://www.examinations.ie/archive/examiners_reports/cer_2008/LC_Religion_2008.pdf> [accessed 23 Nov. 2012].

42. Department of Education and Skills, *A Framework for Junior Cycle* (Oct. 2012) <http://www.education.ie> [accessed 1 Dec. 2012].

43. *FaithConnect* (Dublin: Veritas) <http://www.faithconnect.ie> [accessed 27 Nov. 2012].

44. Irish Catholic Bishops' Conference, *Towards a Policy on RE in Post-Primary Schools* (Dublin: Veritas, 2003).

45. Aiveen Mullally, *Guidelines for the Inclusion of Students of Other Faiths in Catholic Secondary Schools* (Dublin: Joint Managerial Body/Association of Catholic Secondary Schools, 2010).

46. Irish Catholic Bishops' Conference, *Guidelines for the Faith Formation and Development of Catholic Students: Junior Certificate Religious Education Syllabus* (Dublin: Veritas, 1999); Irish Catholic Bishops' Conference, *Guidelines for the Faith Formation and Development of Catholic Students: Leaving Certificate Religious Education Syllabus/Curriculum Framework for Senior Cycle* (Dublin: Veritas, 2006).

47. The Teaching Council are at the time of writing reviewing subject criteria for teaching individual subject at second level <http://www.teachingcouncil.ie/teacher-education/1123.html> [accessed 27 Nov. 2012].

48. Department of Education and Science, *Primary School Curriculum: Introduction* (Dublin: The Stationery Office, 1999), p. 40.

49. The suggestion that such might be the case seems overstated. See Irish Human Rights Commission, *Religion and Education: A Human Rights Perspective*, p. 106.

50. *Share the Good News*, 151.

51. Forum Report, p. 99.

52. Forum Report, p. 92.

ENDWORD

Michael A. Hayes

The emergence of a pluralist society in Ireland poses many challenges to contemporary Irish culture. The role of education and in particular religious education in such a pluralist context is especially challenging. In addressing some of these challenges *Toward Mutual Ground: Pluralism, Religious Education and Diversity in Irish Schools*, itself the fruit of a particular conversation, offers to a wider audience an opportunity to engage in the dialogue.

It would certainly be a pity to view the emergence of a pluralist society as a chronological development in terms of 'new is good' and 'old is bad' or vice versa. While Ireland no longer has, and it is questionable if it ever had, a mono-religious world view, it certainly had and still has a dominant religious patronage in terms of education – an issue itself the subject of much discussion. With the emergence of a pluralist society it is also true that Ireland is now both a post-Christian society and a post-Secularist society. This does not mean that there is no role for a Christian world view or for a Secularist world view but none can be given dominance. This plurality does offer, however, an opportunity for dialogue with and between world views. The dialogue is not about world views in competition but about engaging with world views and their contribution to a diverse society. Such dialogue might take place in the first instance around a dialogue for life and for creation, and that which different traditions hold in common specifically about the dignity of the human person. While theological differences are extremely important and in time need to be addressed, it is not helpful if the dialogue begins here. The intent of such dialogue will then be for the building up of the common good in society, to create conditions and structures that benefit all its citizens.

As indicated in the introduction the words 'toward', 'mutual', and 'ground' in title of this book have been carefully chosen by the Irish Centre for Religious Education. These texts offer a direction of exploration rather than assume an arrival point, hence the use of the word *Toward* in the title. Honest dialogue requires as a minimum mutual respect for all voices, and therefore *Mutual* is central to this current discussion. The *Ground* refers to the terrain covered. For the religious educator that terrain is always sacred as he or she leads others into the mystery and exploration of belief, faith, and traditions. It is always holy ground.

Michael A. Hayes   March 2013

SELECT BIBLIOGRAPHY

Abercrombie, Nicholas et al., eds, *Dictionary of Sociology* (London: Penguin, 2000)

Albright, Madeleine, *The Mighty and the Almighty: Reflections on America, God, and World Affairs* (New York: HarperCollins, 2006)

Alexander, Robin, ed., *Children, Their World, and Their Education: Final Report and Recommendations of the Cambridge Primary Review* (Routledge, 2009)

Archambault, R.D., ed., *Philosophical Analysis and Education* (London: Routledge and Kegan Paul, 1965)

Archer, L. and B. Francis, *Understanding Minority Ethnic Achievement: Race, Gender, Class and 'Success'* (Abingdon: Routledge, 2007)

A Shared Future: Policy and Strategic Framework for Good Relations in Northern Ireland (2005) <http://www.ofmdfmni.gov.uk/asharedfuturepolicy2005.pdf> [accessed 25 Nov. 2012]

Barnes, L. Philip, ed., *Debates in Religious Education Teaching* (London: Routledge, 2011)

Barnes, L. Philip, 'Impact N. 17: Religious Education: Taking Religious Difference Seriously' (Philosophy of Education Society of Great Britain, 2008) <https://www.philosophy-of-education.org/Pdfs/17_barnes_ impact_text.pdf> [accessed 25 Nov. 2012]

Barnes, L. Philip, 'Religion, Education and Conflict in Northern Ireland', *Journal of Beliefs and Values*, 26 (2005), pp. 123–138

Barnes, L.P. and W.K. Kay, *Religious Education in England and Wales: Innovations and Reflections* (Leicester: RTSF, 2002)

Baumeister, R.F. and M.R. Leary, 'The Need to Belong: Desire for Interpersonal Attachments as a Fundamental Human Motivation', *Psychological Bulletin*, 117 (1995), pp. 497–529

Baumfield, Vivienne and Denise Cush, 'A Gift From the Child: Curriculum Development in Religious Education', *British Journal of Religious Education*, 34/3 (2012), pp. 227–230

Bea, Augustin, *The Church and the Jewish People* (London: Geoffrey Chapman, 1966)

Benedict XVI, *Address of His Holiness Benedict XVI*, Westminster Hall, 17 Sept. 2010 <http://www.vatican.va> [accessed 12 Sept. 2012]

Berger, David, 'Dominus Iesus: a Jewish Response' <http://www.bc.edu/dam/files/research_sites/cjl/texts/cjrelations/resources/articles/berger.htm> [accessed 29 Jan. 2011]

Berling, Judith A., *Understanding Other Religious Worlds* (New York: Maryknoll, 2004)

Berryman, J.W., 'Faith Development and the Language of Faith', in *Handbook of Children's Religious Education*, ed. by D.E. Radcliff (Birmingham, Alabama: Religious Education Press, 1992)

Bhopal, K., 'Gypsy Travellers and Education: Changing needs and changing perceptions', *British Journal of Educational Studies*, 52 (2004), pp. 47–64

Bhreathnach, N. 'Realities for Schools in 2000 AD: 1' in *Pluralism in Education: Conference Proceedings 1996*, pp. 15–18

Braaten, Oddrun M.H., 'A Comparative Study of Religious Education in State Schools in England and Norway' (unpublished PhD Thesis, University of Warwick, 2010)

Brennan, Nano et al., eds, *The Catholic School in Contemporary Society* (Dublin: CMRS, 1991)

Brewer, John D., and Gareth I. Higgins, *Anti-Catholicism in Northern Ireland, 1600–1998: The Mote and the Beam* (Houndmills, Basingstoke: Macmillan Press, 1998)

Bryan, A., 'Corporate Multiculturalism, Diversity Management and Positive Interculturalism in Irish Schools and Society', *Irish Educational Studies*, 29 (2010), pp. 253–269

Burke, A., 'The B.Ed. Degree: Still Under Review', *Oideas*, 54 (2009), pp. 1–43

Burrows, William R., ed., *Redemption and Dialogue: Reading 'Redemptoris Missio' and 'Dialogue and Proclamation'* (Maryknoll, NY: Orbis, 1993)

Byrne, D. et al., 'Immigration and School Composition in Ireland', *Irish Educational Studies*, 29 (2010), pp. 271–288

Byrne, Gareth, 'Communicating Faith in Ireland: From Commitment, through Questioning to New Beginnings', in *Communicating Faith*, ed. by John Sullivan (Washington DC: Catholic University of America Press, 2011), pp. 261–276

Byrne, Gareth, 'Children's Religious Education: Challenge and Gift', in *Nurturing Children's Religious Imagination: The Challenge of Primary Religious Education Today*, ed. by Raymond Topley and Gareth Byrne (Dublin: Veritas, 2004), p. 237–251

Byrnes, T.A. and P.J. Katzenstein, eds, *Religion in an Expanding Europe* (Cambridge: Cambridge University Press, 2006)

Cantwell Smith, W., *Towards a World Theology: Faith and the Comparative History of Religions* (Maryknoll, NY: Orbis Books, 1989)

Carr, D. et al., eds, *Liberalism, Education and Schooling: Essays by T.H. McLaughlin* (Exeter: Imprint, 2008)

Carr, W., ed., *The RoutledgeFalmer Reader in Philosophy of Education* (London: RoutledgeFalmer, 2005)

Casanova, José, *Public Religions in the Modern World* (Chicago: University of Chicago Press, 1994)

Catechism of the Catholic Church (London: Geoffrey Chapman, 1994) <http://www.vatican.va> [accessed 12 May 2012]

Catholic Bishops of Northern Ireland, *Building Peace Shaping the Future* (Armagh: 2001)

Catholic Schools Partnership, *Catholic Primary Schools in the Republic of Ireland: A Qualitative Study* (Oct. 2011) <http://www.catholicbishops.ie> [accessed 27 Nov. 2012]

Catholic Schools Partnership, *Catholic Primary Schools: Looking to the Future* (Apr. 2011) <http://www.catholicbishops.ie> [accessed 27 Nov. 2012]

Central Statistics Office, *This is Ireland: Highlights from the Census 2011, Part 1* (Dublin: Stationary Office, 2012)

Cole, W. Owen, *Religion in the Multifaith School*, first edn (Yorkshire: Yorkshire Committee for Community Relations, 1972)

Congregation for Catholic Education, *Circular Letter to the Presidents of Bishops' Conferences on Religious Education in Schools* <http://www.vatican.va> [accessed 11 June 2012]

Congregation for Catholic Education, *The Catholic School* (1977) <http://www.vatican.va> [accessed 12 Sept. 2012]

Connolly, P., 'Racist Harassment in the White Hinterlands: Minority Ethnic Children and Parents' Experiences of Schooling in Northern Ireland', *British Journal of Sociology of Education*, 23 (2002), pp. 341–355

Connolly, P., *'Race' and Racism in Northern Ireland: A Review of the Research Evidence* (Belfast: Office of the First Minister and Deputy First Minister, 2002)

Connolly, P. and R. Khaoury, 'Whiteness, Racism and Exclusion in Northern Ireland: A Critical Race Perspective', in *Northern Ireland after the Troubles? A Society in Transition*, ed. by C. Coulter and M. Murray (Manchester: Manchester University Press, 2008), pp. 54–76.

Coolahan, J., C. Hussey, and F. Kilfeather, *The Forum on Patronage and Pluralism in the Primary Sector: Report of the Forum's Advisory Group* (Dublin: Department of Education and Science, 2012)

Council for Catholic Maintained Schools, *Life to the Full: A Vision for Catholic Education* (Hollywood, Co. Down: 1996)

Council of Europe, *White Paper on Intercultural Dialogue: 'Living Together as Equals with Dignity'* (Strasbourg: Council of Europe Publishing, 2008)

Council of Europe, *The Religious Dimension of Intercultural Education* (Strasbourg: Council of Europe Publishing, 2004)

Cox, E., *Changing Aims in Religious Education* (London: RoutledgeFalmer, 1966)

Cox, E., 'Understanding Religion and Religious Understanding', *British Journal of Religious Education*, 6 (1983), pp. 3–13

Craft, Maurice, ed., *Teacher Education in Plural Societies* (London: RoutledgeFalmer, 1996)

Dadosky, John D., 'Towards a Fundamental Re-interpretation of Vatican II', *Heythrop Journal*, 49/Sept. (2008), pp. 742–763.

D'Arcy, M.C., ed., *Saint Augustine* (New York: Meridian, 1957)

Darmody, M., D. Byrne and F. McGinnity, 'Cumulative Disadvantage? Educational Careers of Migrant Students in *Irish Secondary Schools*', *Race, Ethnicity and Education* (London: Taylor and Francis, 2012), published online <http://dx.doi.org/10.1080/13613324.2012.674021> [accessed 11 Nov. 2012]

Darmody, M. and E. Smyth, 'Religious Diversity and Schooling in Ireland' in *The Changing Faces of Ireland: Exploring the Lives of Immigrant and Ethnic Minority Children*, ed. by M. Darmody, N. Tyrell and S. Song (Rotterdam: Sense, 2011).

Davie, Grace, *Religion in Modern Europe: A Memory Mutates* (Oxford: Oxford University Press, 2000)

Day, C. *A Passion for Teaching* (New York: RoutledgeFalmer, 2004)

D'Costa, Gavin, *Christianity and the World Religions* (Oxford: Blackwell, 2010)

D'Costa, Gavin, *The Catholic Church and the World Religions* (London: Continuum, 2010)

D'Costa, Gavin, *The Meeting of Religions and the Trinity* (Edinburgh: T&T Clark, 2000)

Debray, Régis, *L'enseignment du fait religieux dans L'École laïque: Rapport au Ministre de l'Éducation nationale* (Paris: Odile Jacob, 2002)

Department for Children, Schools and Families, *Guidance on the Duty to Promote Community Cohesion* (London: Department of Children, Schools and Families, 2007)

Department of Education and Science, *Leaving Certificate Religious Education Syllabus* (Dublin: The Stationery Office, 2003)

Department of Education and Science, *Junior Certificate Religious Education Syllabus* (Dublin: The Stationery Office, 2000)

Department of Education and Science, *The Primary School Curriculum: Introduction* (Dublin: The Stationery Office, 1999)

Derrington, C. and S. Kendall, 'Challenges and Barriers to Secondary Education: The Experiences of Young Gypsy Traveller Students in English Secondary Schools', *Social Policy and Society*, 7 (2008), pp. 119–128

de Saussure, Ferdinand, *The Course on General Linguistics* (Peru, Illinois: Open Court Publishing, 1983)

de Souza, M. et al., eds, *International Handbook of the Religious, Moral and Spiritual Dimensions of Education* (Dordrecht: Springer, 2006)

Dessain, C.S., ed., *The Letters and Diaries of John Henry Newman*, vol. 11 (Oxford: Clarendon Press, 1961)

Devine, D., *Immigration and Schooling in the Republic of Ireland: Making a Difference?* (Manchester: Manchester University Press, 2011)

Devine, D. and M. Kelly, 'I Just Don't Want To Be Picked On by Anybody: Dynamics of Inclusion and Exclusion in a Newly Multi-ethnic Primary School', *Children and Society*, 20 (2006), pp. 128–139

De Vries, H., ed, *Religion: Beyond a Concept* (New York: Fordham University Press, 2008)

Donnelly, P., 'Governance in the Irish Colleges of Education', paper delivered to ITE conference, St Patrick's College, Drumcondra, June 2011

Donovan, Peter, 'The Intolerance of Religious Pluralism', *Religious Studies*, 29 (1993), 218–221

Duffy, Eugene, ed., *Catholic Primary Education: Facing New Challenges* (Dublin: Columba, 2012)

Engebretson, K. et al., eds, *International Handbook of Inter-religious Education* (Dordrecht: Springer, 2010)

FaithConnect (Dublin: Veritas) <http://www.faithconnect.ie> [accessed 27 Nov. 2012]

Faith in the System: The Role of Schools with a Religious Character in English Education and Society (London: Department of Children Schools and Families, 2007)

Felderhof, Marius et al., eds, *Inspiring Faith in Schools* (Aldershot, Hampshire: Ashgate, 2007)

Fowler, J.W., *Stages of Faith: The Psychology of Human Development and the Quest for Meaning* (San Francisco: Harper & Row, 1981)

Freire, P., *Pedagogy of Hope* (London: Continuum, 1992)

Furedi, Frank, *Wasted: Why Education Does Not Educate Anymore* (London: Continuum, 2009)

Furlong, C., and Monahan, L., eds, *School Culture and Ethos: Cracking the Code* (Dublin: Marino, 2000)

Gadamer, Hans-Georg, *Truth and Method*, English edn (London: Sheed and Ward, 1975, 1985)

Gallagher, Eric, and Stanley Worrall, *Christianity in Ulster, 1968–1980* (Oxford: Oxford University Press, 1982)

Gallagher, Tony, 'Faith Schools in Northern Ireland: A Review of Research' in *Faith Schools: Consensus or Conflict*, ed. by Roy Gardner, Jo Cairns and Denis Lawton (London: Routledge, 2005), pp. 156–165

Gatt, S., H. Lombaerts, E. Osewska and A. Scerri, *Catholic Education, European and Maltese Perspectives: Church School's Response to Future Challenges* (Floriana: Secretariat for Catholic Education, 2004)

Geertz, Clifford, *The Interpretation of Cultures: Selected Essays* (New York: Basic Books, 1973)

Gill, Robin, ed., *Theology and Sociology: A Reader* (London: Cassell, 1996)

Gillborn, H. and S. Mirza, *Educational Inequality: Mapping Race, Class and Gender: A Synthesis of Research Evidence*, Her Majesties Inspectorate 232 (London: OFSTED, 2000)

Government of Ireland, *Education Act 1998*

Grace, Gerald R., and Joseph O'Keefe, eds, *International Handbook of Catholic Education: Challenges for School Systems in the 21st Century* (Dordrecht: Springer 2007)

Griffiths, Paul, *Problems of Religious Diversity* (Malden, MS: Blackwell, 2001)

Grimmitt, Michael, ed., *Pedagogies of Religious Education* (Great Wakering, England: McCrimmons, 2000)

Gutmann, Amy, ed., *Multiculturalism: Examining the Politics of Recognition* (Princeton NJ: Princeton University Press, 1992)

Habermas, Jürgen et al., *An Awareness of What is Missing: Faith and Reason in a Post-secular Age*, trans. Ciaran Cronin (Cambridge/Malden, MA: Polity Press, 2010).

Hargreaves, A., *Teaching in the Knowledge Society: Education in the Age of Insecurity* (New York: Teachers College Press, 2003)

Hayes, Michael A., and Liam Gearon, eds, *Contemporary Catholic Education* (Herefordshire: Gracewing, 2002)

Heim, S. Mark, *The Depth of the Riches: A Trinitarian Theology of Religious Ends* (Grand Rapids, MI: Eerdmans, 2001)

Hession, Anne and Patricia Kieran, eds, *Exploring Theology: Making Sense of the Catholic Tradition* (Dublin: Veritas, 2007)

Hobson, Peter R., and John S. Edwards, *Religious Education in a Pluralist Society* (London: Woburn Press, 1999)

Hogan, P. and K. Williams, eds, *The Future of Religion in Irish Education* (Dublin: Veritas, 1997)

Holder, D., *30 Years Seen But Not Heard: A Listening Session with the Bangladeshi (Sylheti) Community in Northern Ireland* (Belfast: Multicultural Resource Centre, 2001)

Howard, Thomas A., *God and the Atlantic: America, Europe and the Religious Divide* (Oxford: Oxford University Press, 2011)

Hull, John, 'The Contribution of Religious Education to Religious Freedom: A Global Perspective', International Association for Religious Freedom <www.iarf.net/REBooklet/Hull.htm> [accessed 23 Nov. 2012]

Hulme, E., *Education & Cultural Diversity* (Harlow: Longman, 1989)

Hurley, Michael, 'Northern Ireland and the Post-Vatican II Ecumenical Journey', in *Christianity in Ireland; Revisiting the Story*, ed. by Dáire Keogh and Brendan Bradshaw (Dublin: The Columba Press, 2002), pp. 259–70

Hyland, Áine, *A Review of the Structure of Initial Teacher Education Provision in Ireland: Background Paper for the International Review Team* (HEA, May 2012)

Ipgrave, J., R. Jackson, and K. O'Grady, eds, *Religious Education Research through a Community of Practice: Action Research and the Interpretive Approach* (Münster: Waxmann, 2009)

Irish Catholic Bishops' Conference, *Vision '08: A Vision for Catholic Education in Ireland* (Dublin: Veritas, 2008) <http://www.catholicbishops. ie> [accessed 1 Dec. 2012]

Irish Catholic Bishops' Conference, *Catholic Primary Schools: A Policy for Provision into the Future* (Dublin: Veritas, 2007)

Irish Catholic Bishops' Conference, *Guidelines for the Faith Formation and Development of Catholic Students: Leaving Certificate Religious Education Syllabus/Curriculum Framework for Senior Cycle* (Dublin: Veritas, 2006)

Irish Catholic Bishops' Conference, *Towards a Policy on RE in Post-Primary Schools* (Dublin: Veritas, 2003)

Irish Catholic Bishops' Conference, *Guidelines for the Faith Formation and Development of Catholic Students* (Dublin: Veritas, 1999)

Irish Centre for Religious Education, *Submission to the Forum on Patronage and Pluralism in the Primary Sector* (2011) <http://www.materdei.ie/icre> [accessed 1 Dec. 2012]

Irish Episcopal Conference, *Share the Good News: National Directory for Catechesis in Ireland* (Dublin: Veritas, 2010)

Irish Human Rights Commission, *Religion and Education: A Human Rights Perspective* (May 2011)

Irwin, J., 'A Perspective on Ethos and Philosophy in an Irish Educational Context', *REA: A Journal of Religion, Education and the Arts*, 5 (2005), pp. 39–49

Irwin, J., 'Interculturalism, Ethos and Ideology: Barriers to Freedom and Democracy in Irish Primary Education, *REA: A Journal of Religion, Education and the Arts*, 6 (2009), pp. 1–26

Jackson, Alvin, *Ireland 1798–1998* (Oxford: Wiley-Blackwell, 1999)

Jackson, R., ed., *Religion, Education, Dialogue and Conflict: Perspectives on Religious Education Research* (London: Routledge, 2012)

Jackson, R., 'The Interpretive Approach as a Research Tool: Inside the REDCo Project', *British Journal of Religious Education*, 33 (2011), pp. 189-208

Jackson, R. et al., eds, *The Toledo Guiding Principles; Materials Used to Teach about World Religions in Schools in England* (London: Department for Children, Schools and Families, 2010) <http://www2.warwick.ac.uk/fac/soc/wie/research/wreru/research/completed/dcsf> [accessed 9 Feb. 2012]

Jackson R., *Religion and Education in Europe: Developments, Contexts and Debates* (Münster: Waxmann, 2007)

Jackson, R., *Rethinking Religious Education and Plurality: Issues in Diversity and Pedagogy* (London: RoutledgeFalmer, 2004)

Jackson, R., ed., *International Perspectives on Citizenship, Education and Religious Diversity* (London: RoutledgeFalmer, 2003)

Jackson, R., *Religious Education: An Interpretive Approach* (London: Hodder and Stoughton, 1997)

Jackson, R., and E. Nesbitt, *Hindu Children in Britain* (Stoke-on-Trent: Trentham, 1993)

Jarman, N., and R. Monaghan, *Racist Harassment in Northern Ireland* (Belfast: Institute for Conflict Research, 2004)

Jarman, N. and R. Monaghan, *Analysis of Incidents of Racist Harassment Recorded by the Police in Northern Ireland* (Belfast: Institute of Conflict Research, 2003)

Kay, William K. and D. Linnett Smith, 'Religious Terms and Attitudes in the Classroom (Part 1)', *British Journal of Religious Education*, 22 (2000), pp. 81–90

Keast, J., ed., *Religious Diversity and Intercultural Education: A Reference Book for Schools* (Strasbourg: Council of Europe Publishing, 2007)

Kieran, Patricia and Anne Hession, eds, *Exploring Religious Education: Catholic Religious Education in an Intercultural Europe* (Dublin: Veritas, 2008)

Knauth, T. et al., eds, *Encountering Religious Pluralism in School and Society: A Qualitative Study of Teenage Perspectives in Europe* (Münster: Waxmann, 2008)

Kuyk, E. et al., eds, *Religious Education in Europe: Situation and Current Trends in Schools* (Oslo: Iko & ICCS, 2007)

Lane, Dermot A., *Stepping Stones to Other Religions: A Christian Theology of Inter-Religious Dialogue* (Dublin: Veritas, 2011)

Lane, Dermot A., *Challenges Facing Religious Education in Ireland Today* (Dublin: Veritas, 2008)

Leaman, O., 'Taking Religion Seriously,' *The Times*, 6 Feb. 1989, p. 18

Learning: the Treasure Within (the Delors Report), The Report to UNESCO of the International Commission on Education for the Twenty-first Century (Paris: UNESCO, 1996)

Lindbeck, George, *The Nature of Doctrine: Religion and Theology in a Postliberal Age* (Philadelphia: Westminster, 1984)

Lovat, Terence J., 'Educating about Islam and Learning about Self: An Approach for Our Times', *Religious Education*, 100/1 (2005), pp. 38–51

MacLure, M., *Discourse in Educational and Social Research* (Maidenhead: Open University Press, 2003).

MacMullen, Ian, 'Education for Autonomy: The Role of Religious Elementary Schools', *Journal of Philosophy of Education*, 38/4 (2004)

McGill, P. and Q. Oliver, *A Wake-Up Call on Race: Implications of the Macpherson Report for Institutional Racism in Northern Ireland* (Belfast: Equality Commission, 2002)

McGrath, Michael, *The Catholic Church and Catholic Schools in Northern Ireland: The Price of Faith* (Dublin: Irish Academic Press, 2000)

McKenna, U., J. Ipgrave, and R. Jackson, *Inter Faith Dialogue by Email in Primary Schools: An Evaluation of the Building E-Bridges Project* (Münster: Waxmann, 2008)

McKinney, Stephen, J., *Faith Schools in the Twenty-first Century*, Policy and Practice in Education 23 (Edinburgh: Dunedin, 2008)

McLaughlin, T.H., 'Parental Rights and the Upbringing of Children', *Journal of Philosophy of Education*, 18/1 (1984), pp. 79–81

Merrigan T., and Ian T. Ker, eds, *Newman and the Word*, Louvain Theological and Pastoral Monographs (Grand Rapids, MI: Eerdmans, 2000)

Moran, Gabriel, *Reshaping Religious Education* (Louisville: Westminster John Knox Press, 1998)

Morris, Ronald W., 'Cultivating Reflection and Understanding: Foundations and Orientations of Québec's Ethics and Religious Culture Program', *Religion & Education*, 38 (2011), pp. 188-211

Mullally, Aiveen, *Guidelines for the Inclusion of Students of Other Faiths in Catholic Secondary Schools* (Dublin: Joint Managerial Body / Association of Catholic Secondary Schools, 2010)

Murray, Donal, 'Teaching the Faith and Sharing the Gospel', *The Furrow*, 63/5 (2012), pp. 259-273

Norman, J., *Ethos and Education in Ireland* (New York: Peter Lang, 2003)

Nuusbaum, Martha, *The New Religious Intolerance* (Harvard University Press, 2012).

Osewska, E., and J. Stala, eds, *Religious Education/Catechesis in the Family: A European Perspective* (Warszawa: UKSW, 2010)

O'Sullivan, D., *Politics and Irish Education since the 1950s: Policy, Paradigms and Power* (Dublin: IPA, 2005)

Pajer, F., ed., *Europa, scuola, religioni: Monoteismi e confessioni cristiane per una nuova cittadinanza europea* (Torino: SEI, 2005)

Parker-Jenkins, M. et al., *Aiming High: Raising the Attainment of Pupils from Culturally Diverse Backgrounds* (London: SAGE, 2007)

Parker-Jenkins, M. et al., *In Good Faith: Schools, Religion and Public Funding* (Aldershot: Ashgate, 2005)

Parker-Jenkins, M., *Children of Islam* (Stoke-on-Trent: Trentham Books, 1995)

Paul VI, *Evangelii nuntiandi* (1975) <http://www.vatican.va> [accessed 12 Sept. 2012]

Phenix, P.H., *Realms of Meaning* (New York: McGraw-Hill, 1964)

Pollefeyt, D., ed., *Interreligious Learning* (Leuven: Peeters, 2007)

Pontifical Council for Inter-Religious Dialogue, *Dialogue and Proclamation* (1991) <http://www.vatican.va> [accessed 12 Sept. 2012]

Pontifical Council for Inter-religious Dialogue, *Letter to Presidents of Bishops' Conferences on the Spirituality of Dialogue* (1999) <http://www.vatican.va>

Rafferty, Oliver P., 'The Catholic Church and the Nationalist Community in Northern Ireland', *Éire-Ireland*, 43 (2008), pp. 99–125

Rafter, Kevin, 'Priests and Peace: The Role of Redemptorist Order in the Northern Ireland Peace Process', *Estudios Irlandeses*, 28 (2003), pp. 159–176

Religious Education in English Schools: Non-statutory Guidance 2010 (London: Department for Children, Schools and Families, 2010)

Richardson, Norman, 'Religious Education in Northern Ireland' (2011) <http://www.mmiweb.org.uk/eftre/reeurope/northern_ireland_2011.html>

Rymarz, Richard, 'Catechesis and Religious Education in Canadian Catholic Schools', *Religious Education*, 106/5 (2011), pp. 537–549

Schweitzer, Friedrich, 'Children's Right to Religion and Spirituality: Legal, Educational and Practical Perspectives,' British Journal of Religious Education, 27/2 (2005), pp. 103–113

Shain, F., The New Folk Devils: Muslim Boys and Education in England (Stoke-on-Trent: Trentam Books, 2001)

Shaw, T., 'Realities for Schools in 2000 AD: 2', in Pluralism in Education: Conference Proceedings 1996, pp. 21–25

Smart, Ninian, Secular Education and the Logic of Religion (London: Faber, 1968)

Smith, Christian with Melinda Lundquist Denton, Soul Searching: The Religious and Spiritual Lives of American Teenagers (Oxford / New York: Oxford University Press, 2005)

Smyth, G., 'Foreword', in Pluralism in Education: Conference Proceedings 1996, pp. 3–7

Sottocornola, Franco 'Some Notes Regarding Formation to Inter-religious Dialogue', Religious Education of Boys and Girls, Concilium 2002/4 (SCM Press: London), pp. 99–100

Stala, J., and E. Osewska, Anders erziehen in Polen: Der Erziehungs – und Bildungsbegriff im Kontext eines sich ständig verändernden Europas des XXI Jahrhunderts (Tarnów: Polihymnia, 2009)

State Examinations Commission, Leaving Certificate Examination, 2008, Religious Education: Chief Examiner's Report <http://www.examinations.ie/archive/examiners_reports/cer_2008/LC_Religion_2008.pdf> [accessed 23 Nov. 2012]

Strand, S., 'The Limits of Social Class in Explaining Ethnic Gaps in Educational Attainment', British Educational Research Journal, 37 (2011), pp. 197–229

Sullivan, John, ed., Communicating Faith (Washington DC: Catholic University of America Press, 2011)

Teaching Council, Policy on the Continuum of Teacher Education (Dublin: 2011)

ter Avest, I. et al., eds, Dialogue and Conflict on Religion: Studies of Classroom Interaction in European Countries (Münster: Waxmann, 2009)

Thompson, N.H., ed., Religious Pluralism and Religious Education (Birmingham: Religious Education Press, 1988)

Tillich, Paul, Ultimate Concern: Dialogues with Students, ed. by D.M. Brown (London: SCM, 1965)

Tillich, Paul, Theology of Culture (Oxford: Oxford University Press, 1959)

The Toledo Guiding Principles on Teaching about Religions and Beliefs in Public Schools (Warsaw: Organisation for Security and Co-operation in Europe, Office for Democratic Institutions and Human Rights, 2007) <http://www.osce.org/odihr/29154> [accessed 10 Feb. 2012]

Tomasi, S., 'Freedom of Religion or Belief in Education', Organisation for Security and Co-operation in Europe, Supplementary Human Dimension Meeting, Vienna, 9–10 Dec. 2010 <http://www.osce.org/odihr/75755> [accessed 9 Feb. 2012]

Topley, Raymond, and Gareth Byrne, eds, Nurturing Children's Religious Imagination: The Challenge of Primary Religious Education Today (Dublin: Veritas, 2004)

Tormey, Roland, Teaching Social Justice and Development Education Perspectives on Education's Context, Content and Methods (Dublin: Ireland Aid and CEDR, 2003)

Tracy, David, Plurality and Ambiguity: Hermeneutics, Religion and Hope (New York: Harper & Row, 1987)

United Nations, Convention on the Rights of the Child (1989)

United Nations, Human Rights Committee, Concluding Observations: Ireland, 2008, CCPR/C/IRL/CO/3 22

Valk, P. et al., eds, Teenagers' Perspectives on the Role of Religion in Their Lives, Schools and Societies: A Quantitative Study (Münster: Waxmann, 2009)

van der Want, A. et al., eds, Teachers Responding to Religious Diversity in Europe: Researching Biography and Pedagogy (Münster: Waxmann, 2009)

Van Nieuwenhove, Rik, 'The End of Catholic Education in Ireland?', *The Furrow*, 63/6 (2012), pp. 278–285

Vatican II, *Ad gentes divinitus: Decree on the Church's Missionary Activity* (7 Dec. 1965) <http://www.vatican.va> [accessed 12 May 2012]

Vatican II, *Gaudium et spes: Pastoral Constitution on the Church in the Modern World* (7 Dec. 1965) <http://www.vatican.va> [accessed 12 May 2012]

Vatican II, *Nostra aetate: Declaration on the Relation of the Church to Non-Christian Religions* (28 Oct. 1965) <http://www.vatican.va> [accessed 12 May 2012]

Vatican II, *Lumen gentium: Pastoral Constitution on the Church* (21 Nov. 1964) <http://www.vatican.va> [accessed 12 May 2012]

Vatican II, *Unitatis redintegatio: Decree on Ecumenism* (21 Nov. 1964) <http://www.vatican.va> [accessed 12 May 2012]

Wach, Joachim, *Essays in the History of Religions*, ed. by J.M. Kitagawa and G.D. Alles (London: Macmillan, 1988)

Wach, Joachim, *The Comparative Study of Religions*, ed. by Joseph M. Kitagawa (New York: Columbia University Press, 1958)

Wach, Joachim, *Types of Religious Experience: Christian and Non-Christian* (Chicago: University of Chicago Press, 1951)

Watson, Brenda, *Education and Belief* (Oxford: Blackwell, 1987)

Wedemeyer C.K., and W. Doniger, eds, *Hermeneutics, Politics, and the History of Religions: The Contested Legacies of Joachim Wach & Mircea Eliade* (Oxford: Oxford University Press, 2010)

Williams, Kevin, *Faith and the Nation* (Dublin: Dominican Publications, 2005)

Woodhead, L. and R. Catto, eds, *Religion and Change in Modern Britain* (London: Routledge, 2012)

Woods, Thomas E.J., *How the Catholic Church Built Western Civilization* (Washington DC: Regnery Publishing, 2005)

Wright, A., 'Contextual Religious Education and the Actuality of Religions', *British Journal of Religious Education*, 30 (2008)

Wright, A., *Critical Religious Education, Multiculturalism and the Pursuit of Truth* (Cardiff: University of Wales Press, 2007)

Wright, A., *Spirituality and Education* (London: RoutledgeFalmer, 2000)

Wright, A., 'Language and Experience in the Hermeneutics of Religious Understanding', *British Journal of Religious Education*, 18 (1996), pp. 166–180

INDEX